*Instructor's Manual and Test Questions
to accompany
Elliot Aronson's*

The Social Animal

Seventh Edition

Ruth Thibodeau
University of California, Santa Cruz

Wendy Dunn
Coe College, Cedar Rapids, Iowa

Elliot Aronson
University of California, Santa Cruz

W. H. Freeman and Company

New York

ISBN 0-7167-2704-8

Copyright© 1995 by W. H. Freeman and Company

No part of this book may be reproduced by any mechanical, photographic, or electronic process, or in the form of a phonographic recording, nor may it be stored in a retrieval system, transmitted, or otherwise copied for public or private use, without written permission from the publisher.

Printed in the United States of America

1 2 3 4 5 6 7 8 9 0   9 9 8 7 6 5 4

Contents

	Introduction v
1	What is Social Psychology? 1
2	Conformity 15
3	Mass Communication, Propaganda, and Persuasion 43
4	Social Cognition 73
5	Self-Justification 109
6	Human Aggression 149
7	Prejudice 179
8	Liking, Loving, and Interpersonal Sensitivity 211
9	Social Psychology as a Science 245
	Readings About the Social Animal 271
	Suggested Videos and Films 335

Introduction

The purpose of this manual is to provide assistance to instructors of social psychology who are using Elliot Aronson's *The Social Animal* for their courses. It is intended to help make the task of teaching more enjoyable for instructors by enhancing their efforts to convey material in an exciting and accessible manner.

In the first portion of the manual, a separate chapter is devoted to each corresponding chapter of *The Social Animal*. The basic content of the chapter is presented in outline and summary form, and key terms and concepts are listed. The manual also provides ideas for teaching material from *The Social Animal*, as well as suggestions and resources for lectures that complement the chapter's offerings. In addition, ideas for student projects and discussion topics are offered, along with a list of supplementary readings. Books and articles in the readings section may be used as a reference for students who are interested in more information about a given topic, or as an additional source of lecture material. Each chapter ends with a selection of multiple-choice and essay questions.

The second part of the manual provides a bank of multiple choice questions based on the research articles presented in *Readings About the Social Animal*, edited by Elliot Aronson. In composing their exams, instructors who use the *Readings* volume may wish to include these questions, which tend to probe for more detailed information about experimental findings and procedures. In a few instances, questions from the *Readings* cover material that is also covered in questions based on *The Social Animal*.

Finally, the manual concludes with a list of films relevant to each chapter, along with the addresses of film distributors. Films have been listed separately to assist the instructor in ordering in a timely fashion, and many may be available from local university libraries. Although the films on the list come well recommended, it is a good idea to preview a film before using it in the classroom.

We hope this manual provides useful ideas to enliven theory and research in social psychology for your students and helps to make your life as an instructor a little easier as well. Your comments and suggestions regarding this manual are most welcome and may be addressed to: Jonathan Cobb, Senior Editor, W.H. Freeman and Company, 41 Madison Avenue, New York, New York 10010.

Ruth Thibodeau, Wendy Dunn, and Elliot Aronson

1

What Is Social Psychology?

I. Introduction

   Some examples of how we are "social animals"

II. Social Psychology: A Definition

   Social psychology and common sense
   The "hindsight effect"
   Professional vs. amateur social psychologists

III. People Who Do Crazy Things Are Not Necessarily Crazy

   Aronson's "first law"
   Situations vs. dispositions (Stanford "prison" study)

Terms & Concepts

social influence
hindsight effect
amateur social psychologists
professional social psychologists
Aronson's first law
dispositional view

Chapter Overview

Chapter 1 offers a working definition of social psychology as the study of the influences that people have upon the beliefs or behavior of others. A general orientation to the field and its methods is provided, including several illustrations of the broad range of questions and real-world phenomena that are of central interest to social psychologists. Key issues and questions include:

How are people influenced by one another? Why do they accept social influence—that is, what's in it for them? What are the variables that increase or decrease the effectiveness of social influence?

How does one person come to like another person? How does a person develop prejudices against an ethnic or racial group? Is prejudice akin to liking—but in reverse—or does it involve an entirely different set of psychological processes?

Most people are "amateur" social psychologists. Because we spend so much of our time interacting with other people, it is not surprising that most of us develop our own intuitive theories about human behavior. However, our everyday understanding of social behavior lacks the rigor and impartiality of careful scientific investigation. Systematic research is important because, in many instances, "common sense" hypotheses about human behavior turn out to be false when carefully investigated.

Aronson's first law is that "People who do crazy things are not necessarily crazy." When situational pressures are strong, people are often led to behave in ways that are unpleasant, destructive, or bizarre. Although some of this behavior may be due to individual psychopathology, social psychologists find it more useful to try to understand the situational variables that move otherwise "normal" people to engage in unappetizing or seemingly "crazy" behavior. This point is illustrated dramatically in a classic study conducted by Zimbardo and his colleagues, in which psychologically healthy young men were randomly assigned to play the roles of guard and prisoner in a "simulated prison" set up at Stanford University. Within a few days, the majority of subjects had taken their roles to heart: "prisoners" became dehumanized and servile, while "guards" took pleasure in their cruel treatment of prisoners.

Lecture Ideas & Teaching Suggestions

Common Sense and Science. One way to help students appreciate the limitations of common sense in explaining social behavior is to present several examples of research findings that either contradict most people's intuitions, or that offer a more complex picture of behavior than common sense would suggest. One method of doing this is to ask the class to respond as "amateur social psychologists" to a series of true-false statements regarding various social-psychological phenomena. After hearing students' responses, you can proceed to discuss some of the research that is relevant to each statement. Here are some examples, taken from later chapters in the book.

1. When it comes to liking other people, we are attracted to people who are similar to us. (True—but not always. See Jones, Bell & Aronson on the conditions under which we tend to prefer dissimilar others, and Winch's research on need complementarity in long-term relationships. Chapter 8.)

2. If you were alone in a big city and hurt yourself, you would be more likely to get help if there were ten people standing nearby, rather than one or two. (False. Research by Latane & Darley and others shows that the greater the number of bystanders, the lower the chances that someone will help. Chapter 2.)

3. Doing a favor for someone will increase the possibility that they will like you. (True—but not always. Jones' research indicates that doing favors may backfire if the recipient feels manipulated or that "strings" are attached to the favor. Also, sometimes getting someone to do *you* a favor will make them like you more, according to work by Jecker & Landy. Chapter 8.)

4. If someone rewards you for performing an interesting activity (e.g., by paying you money), you'll probably like that activity even more. (False. Deci's research on the effects of rewards on intrinsic motivation indicates just the opposite. Chapter 5.)

5. If you're feeling angry, the best thing to do is "blow off a little steam" by venting some of your hostility. This reduces the chances that you

will behave in a far more hostile or aggressive manner in the future. (False. Several studies testing the "catharsis hypothesis" have demonstrated that rather than reducing aggression, violent behavior increases the likelihood of even greater violence in the future. Chapter 6.)

This exercise serves two purposes: It underscores the need to use scientific methods in studying social behavior, and it provides students with a brief introduction to some of the topics and phenomena that will be covered later in the course.

Power of the Situation. A demonstration of the "power of the situation" can be achieved by describing the experimental setting and procedure of one of the classic studies in social psychology—such as Asch's conformity experiment or Milgram's study of obedience, both from Chapter 2. (This exercise should be done before students have read these studies.) After giving a detailed description of the study, ask students to imagine how they think they would have acted in the same situation. Typically, students will greatly underestimate the extent to which they themselves, and other people, would conform under such circumstances. Next, explain the actual results of the study and the reasons why the situational pressures had such a powerful impact on subjects. You may then want to invite students to comment on these findings and to reconsider whether they still think they would have been able to resist the pressure to conform. Finally, this demonstration can be used as a point of entry into a methodological discussion of why simply asking people how they would behave in a given situation is likely to lead to invalid conclusions.

Applying Social Psychology. Discussing some of the applied uses of social-psychological findings is an effective way to introduce students to the importance of the field and its relevance to real-world issues. Research in the areas of law and health offer some interesting examples of applied social psychology. For material, you may wish to draw upon studies presented in later chapters: For example, Haney's research on the "death qualification procedure" is covered in Chapter 2, and Loftus's work on memory distortion in eye-witness testimony is presented in Chapter 4. Health-related research includes Axsom and Cooper's study of obesity and justification of effort (Chapter 5) and McAlister et al.'s use of the "inoculation technique" to prevent teenagers from smoking (Chapter 3).

Additional sources of material may be found in: Oskamp, S. (1984). *Applied Social Psychology*, Englewood Cliffs, NJ: Prentice-Hall. Also, you may also want to refer to issues of *Applied Social Psychology Annual, The Journal of Social Issues*, and *The Journal of Applied Social Psychology*.

Projects and Discussion Topics

1. PROJECT: For a few days, carefully observe events and behavior (your own and others') in everyday life that strike you as the kinds of phenomena that would interest a social psychologist. (A good strategy is to pretend you are an anthropologist studying a completely foreign culture, or an alien visiting from another planet.) Keep a journal of these observations, including your own hypotheses, explanations, and questions regarding the behavior and events you have observed. Share your observations and interpretations with your classmates.

2. PROJECT: Examine several copies of newspapers and magazines, looking for examples of behavior and events that would interest a social psychologist. Does the report contain any explicit or implicit explanations of the behavior being described? If so, do these explanations reflect a "situational" or "dispositional" view of the world? What kind of evidence, if any, is presented to support these interpretations? Bring a few examples to class and be prepared to describe your findings.

3. DISCUSSION: Consider one or two of the following sets of questions. a) What makes a person prejudiced? How can prejudice be reduced? b) Why are two people attracted to each other? What makes two people dislike each other? c) Why do people engage in violent behavior? Why do people cooperate or help each other? d) Why do people conform to the behavior and opinions of others? When do they tend to think and act independently? For each set of questions, list as many possible answers as you can think of, based on common sense and your intuitions about social behavior. Share your ideas with other students in your discussion group, noting the similarity and differences in your explanations. On what basis could you decide the relative merits of these different "hypotheses" about human behavior? Is common sense and evidence gained from personal experience a sufficient basis for

deciding the relative merits of these different "hypotheses"? Why or why not?

4. DISCUSSION: What does Aronson mean by the statement: "People who do crazy things are not necessarily crazy?" Do you agree or disagree? What are the broader implications of explaining unpleasant or bizarre behavior as primarily the result of individual "craziness" or "badness"? Why, in your opinion, is this kind of interpretation of behavior so common in our society? On the other hand, what issues regarding individual responsibility would be raised if we were to explain all problematic behavior as the result of situational pressures and influences?

Additional Readings

Aron, A. & Aron, E.N. (1989). *The heart of social psychology: a backstage view of a passionate science.* Lexington, MA: Lexington Books.

Campbell, D. & Tavris, C. (1975, December). The experimenting society: To find programs that work, government must measure its failures. *Psychology Today*, pp. 46–56. (Advocates using scientific method to assess social programs.)

Festinger, L. (1980) *Retrospections on social psychology.* New York: Oxford University Press.

Kipnis, D. (1994). Accounting for the use of behavioral technologies in social psychology. *American Psychologist, 49*, (3), 165–172.

Loftus, E.F. (1991). Resolving legal questions with psychological data. *American Psychologist, 46*, 1046–1060.

Tetlock, P.E. (1994). The psychology of futurology and the future of psychology. *Psychological Science, 5*, (1), 1.

West, S.G. & Wicklund, R.A. (1980). *A primer of social psychological theories.* Monterey, CA: Brooks/Cole.

Wiggins, J.G., Jr. (1994). Would you want your child to be a psychologist? *American Psychologist, 49,* (6), 485–492.

Multiple-Choice Questions

Answer: b
Page: 6

1. Aronson defines social psychology as:
   a. how people learn to behave in accordance with society's rules.
   b. the influences that people have upon the beliefs or the behavior of others.
   c. how societies and social groups work.
   d. the study of roles and social norms.

Answer: c
Page: 6

2. In his first chapter, Aronson defines social psychology as the study of:
   a. human behavior and mental processes.
   b. people and events.
   c. social influence.
   d. actions that appear to be crazy but are not.

Answer: d
Page: 6

3. "The influences that people have upon the beliefs and behavior of others" is the text's definition of:
   a. dispositions.
   b. the self-fulfilling prophecy.
   c. the hindsight effect.
   d. social psychology.

Answer: a
Page: 7

4. Once we know the outcome of an event, we have the sense that we knew all along that things would turn out as they did. The term for this phenomenon is:
   a. the hindsight effect.
   b. common-sense social psychology.
   c. the self-fulfilling prophecy.
   d. the "deja vu" effect.

Answer: b
Page: 7

5. According to the "hindsight effect" you would predict which of the following results:
   a. People would be more likely to blame a prisoner than a guard for a prison uprising.
   b. If after a race were over, people were asked how confident they were that a particular horse would win, they would remember being more confident if he did win than if he did not.
   c. We tend to behave the way that people expect us to.
   d. We are more likely to make situational judgments when explaining our future behavior and make dispositional explanations when explaining our past behavior.

Answer: d
Page: 6–8

6. It is important that "common-sense" truisms be tested in a rigorous scientific manner because:
   a. common sense is nothing but superstition.
   b. social psychology will allow us to make precise quantitative predictions about human behavior.
   c. until tested, common sense is of little value in human life.
   d. these truisms are often false or overly simplistic.

Answer: b
Page: 6

7. According to Aronson's text, the statement that we are all "amateur" social psychologists means that:
   a. we all give advice to our close friends and relatives.
   b. we all try to figure out why people act as they do, and we develop explanations for their behavior.
   c. we don't have as much training as professional social psychologists.
   d. our theories about human behavior are too complex.

Answer: d
Page: 6–8

8. In his or her attempts to understand human social behavior, the professional social psychologist has the advantage of being able to:
   a. study at the same time all of the factors that influence people in a situation.
   b. know how to control every individual's behavior.
   c. create and study exact duplicates of actual situations and events.
   d. control the influence of irrelevant factors when studying a problem.

Answer: a
Page: 6–8

9. Which of the following is *not* an advantage that professional social psychologists have over amateur social psychologists?
   a. Professionals use observation of social phenomena in their thinking about social phenomena, whereas amateurs cannot.
   b. Professionals can make things happen.
   c. Professionals can hold everything constant except what they are interested in studying.
   d. Professionals' conclusions are based on more precise data.

Answer: c
Page: 8

10. According to "Aronson's first law," people who do crazy things:
    a. are, by definition, crazy.
    b. may not be crazy, but are different from normal people.
    c. may be crazy, but may also be normal people trying to adjust to extraordinary social influences.
    d. are perceived as crazy by people with rigid standards for behavior.

Answer: d 11. Explaining unpleasant behavior by labelling people
Page: 8–9   "crazy" or "sadistic":
    a. is useful because it allows us to develop tests to help classify people.
    b. is dangerous because it makes these people angry and violent.
    c. is useful because it warns the general public to watch out for certain people.
    d. is dangerous because it gives the general public a false sense of security and invulnerability.

Answer: a 12. Aronson states, "People who do crazy things are
Page: 8–9   not necessarily crazy." By this he means that:
    a. situations can cause most normal people to behave in abnormal ways.
    b. psychosis, at least from a social psychological point of view, does not exist.
    c. people generally think of others in very much the same way they think of themselves.
    d. human behavior can be explained by using the scientific method.

Answer: d 13. Which of the following best reflects a dispositional
Page: 9–10   view of human behavior?
    a. "That test was so difficult no one could do well."
    b. "Mandy is so attractive that the men just flock around her."
    c. "When I don't eat breakfast, I feel rotten all day."
    d. "Bob is so self-centered that he has trouble getting along with other people."

Answer: d   14. Tomoko explains that her teacher is a kind, gentle person and that is why Tomoko does well in school. Tomoko's appraisal of her teacher is best thought of as an example of:
Page: 9–10
a. Aronson's first law.
b. the hindsight effect.
c. the situational view.
d. the dispositional view.

Answer: a   15. People tend to explain the causes of other people's behavior as being the result of their personalities. Thus, if Luke gets a bad grade on a test, it must be because he is stupid. This tendency is called:
Page: 9–10
a. the dispositional view.
b. the self-fulfilling prophecy.
c. Aronson's first law.
d. the hindsight effect.

Answer: b   16. In Zimbardo's "Stanford Prison Experiment," young, psychologically normal men were randomly assigned to the role of playing a guard or a prisoner. After five days, the "prisoners" grew withdrawn and unsympathetic, while "guards" became sadistic and brutal. In general, the results of this study probably indicate that:
Page: 10
a. the veneer of civilization is very thin, and the true nature of humans is to be callous and unfeeling.
b. the situation is often primarily responsible for behavior, not the personalities of subjects.
c. prisoners are basically antisocial and, thus, are unable to cope with the prison environment.
d. guards probably choose their profession because they enjoy power and being brutal.

Answer: d   17. You and a friend are watching the news and hear
Page: 9–10   a report regarding a murder in New York City,
                      witnessed by dozens of bystanders—none of whom
                      attempted to help the victim or even telephone the
                      police. Your friend expresses utter disgust at this
                      incident, remarking "People who live in big cities
                      have no compassion for others. They lack
                      fundamental decency—all they care about is
                      themselves." Your friend's remark best reflects:
                      a. astute insight into the effects of living in large
                          cities.
                      b. the primacy effect.
                      c. a situational view of the world.
                      d. a dispositional view of the world.

Answer: d   18. In Zimbardo's "prison" study, how were subjects
Page: 10   assigned the role of prisoner or guard?
                      a. Younger men were made prisoners so as to
                          better replicate the actual prison situation.
                      b. More intelligent subjects were assigned to be
                          guards.
                      c. Based on the results of a psychological test,
                          those with more stable personalities were
                          assigned to be guards.
                      d. By flipping a coin, that is, randomly.

Answer: d   19. The subjects in Zimbardo's prison study were:
Page: 10   a. prison guards.
                      b. prisoners.
                      c. both prison guards and prisoners.
                      d. normal, stable young men.

Answer: c   20. Why did Zimbardo discontinue his prison
Page: 10   experiment?
                   a. The public judged it to be unethical.
                   b. All of his subjects quit.
                   c. The subjects became too involved with their
                      "prisoner" or "guard" role.
                   d. The procedure was completed and the data
                      were so clear and impressive that it did not
                      need to be continued.

Essay Questions

1. In your own words, what is Aronson's definition of social psychology? Give an example of behavior that social psychologists would be interested in studying.

2. Is social psychology simply common sense? Why or why not? Why is it important to conduct scientific investigations of hypotheses about social behavior?

3. Describe three advantages that professional social psychologists have over amateurs.

4. "People who do crazy things are not necessarily crazy." Explain the meaning of this statement and how it is relevant to a social-psychological perspective on understanding social behavior. What are some of the drawbacks of explaining unpleasant behavior by labeling it as sadistic or crazy?

5. Define and give an example of a "dispositional" view of the world.

2
Conformity

I. Introduction

    "Johnny Rocco" deviance study (Schachter)
    "Groupthink" (Janis)

II. What is Conformity?

    Asch experiment

III. Variables That Increase or Decrease Conformity

    Why do people conform, group pressure or to be correct?
    Variations on Asch's basic experiment
    The effects of: unanimity, prior commitment, self-esteem, task ability, composition group
    Physical reality versus "social reality"

IV. Rewards and Punishments Versus Information

    Social influence and emotion (Schachter & Singer)
    Social influence: Life and death (Haney)

V. Responses to Social Influence

    Compliance, identification, internalization
    Power, attractiveness, credibility

VI. Obedience as a Form of Compliance

    Milgram's studies of obedience

VII. The "Uninvolved" Bystander as Conformist

"Lady in Distress" experiment (Latane & Rodin)
Epileptic "attack" experiment (Darley & Latane)
"Good Samaritan" study (Darley & Batson)
Costs and benefits of helping (Piliavin, Baron)

Terms & Concepts

anticonformity
groupthink
concurrence-seeking
unanimous majority
social reality
compliance
identification
internalization

power
attractiveness
credibility
secondary gain
behavior modification
bystander intervention
empathy

Chapter Overview

Chapter 2 focuses on the topic of conformity, defined as a change in a person's behavior or opinions as a result of real or imagined pressure from a person or group of people. Basic issues covered in the chapter include:

Is conformity good or bad? As a society, Americans are ambivalent about the merits of conformity—nonconformists or individualists are valued, while deviates and oddballs are scorned. On the other hand, conformists and "sheep" are devalued, while the "team player" is lauded. When the chips are down, however, we tend to value conformity over nonconformity—a fact reflected in the findings of Schachter's "Johnny Rocco" study in which the person expressing the "modal" viewpoint was most attractive to other group members. Although conformity is necessary to the smooth running of daily life, an illustration of its negative aspects can be found in the phenomenon of "groupthink," a maladaptive decision-making process that appears to have contributed to the Challenger space-shuttle tragedy.

Why do people conform to group pressure? Variations on Asch's "line judgment" study indicate that a unanimous group opinion, low self-esteem, and lack of expertise are contributing factors. In addition, greater conformity is produced when the group is composed of experts, similar others, and when the acceptance by other group members is important to the individual. Factors that decrease conformity include prior public commitment to an opposing attitude or behavior, as well as the presence of another group member who opposes the group's opinion. People may conform due to group pressure or to be correct. Research shows that the greater the privacy a subject has, the less conformity, suggesting that group pressure is a motivating factor.

When physical reality is uncertain, we tend to rely on "social reality"—the behavior and attitudes of others—as a guide to appropriate action. This form of conformity is motivated by our need for information, rather than our desire to avoid punishment (e.g., social rejection) or gain a reward (e.g., love and acceptance). This tendency is vividly demonstrated in Schachter and Singer's experiment of the effects of others' behavior on an individual's emotional experiences.

Three major forms of response to social influence are compliance, identification, and internalization. The least permanent of the three, compliance is motivated by the desire to avoid punishment or gain reward. Compliance is a response to the power held by the agent of influence. Identification is motivated by a person's desire to be similar to the person or group exercising influence. Thus, identification depends on the attractiveness of the source of influence. Internalization is motivated by the desire to be right, or correct, and represents the most permanent form of social influence. The key component underlying internalization is the credibility of the source of influence.

Acts of compliance, while often temporary, can have consequences that are far from trivial. This point is dramatically demonstrated in Milgram's classic studies of obedience to authority, in which subjects believed they were delivering lethal doses of shock to fellow subjects as part of a "learning" experiment. Variables that decrease obedience to authority include: reducing the perceived "legitimacy" of the authority figure, the subject's closer proximity to the victim, and the physical absence of the authority figure.

Why don't bystanders come to the aid of victims of injury or crime? In the notorious Kitty Genovese case, dozens of neighbors watched passively for 30 minutes as a young woman was stabbed to death outside of her New York City apartment. Not one helped or even picked up a phone to call the police. Experiments by Latane, Darley, and their colleagues indicate that conformity processes underlie the apparent apathy of onlookers at the scene of an emergency. According to their findings, the greater the number of bystanders, the least likely any single one of them is to offer assistance. Nonintervention, in this case, can be viewed as an act of conformity. For each individual bystander, the behavior of other people at the scene provides important cues regarding appropriate behavior. Thus, the failure of others to respond to the emergency serves as a potent model of nonintervention for each individual onlooker. Observers do, though, sometimes respond, especially when they believe they can provide assistance and when they find themselves in a situation in which they cannot escape or ignore the emergency situation.

Lecture Ideas & Teaching Suggestions

Dramatic Examples of Conformity. Students' interest in the topic of conformity can be readily engaged through the presentation of dramatic examples from history or current events. Examples include: the My Lai massacre, the atrocities of the Third Reich, the mass suicide at Jonestown, and the Challenger shuttle disaster. Such illustrations of conformity processes at work tend to make a profound and lasting impression on students, leaving them with an acute awareness of the relevance of social psychology to real-world events and problems. (See "readings" section for background material and analyses of these events.)

Demonstrating Conformity. The ease with which most people obey the commands of authority figures can be vividly demonstrated in the classroom. For example, at the beginning of class, ask all students to perform some sort of odd behavior—such as putting their pen or pencil behind their ear, or standing up and turning around three times. Ask students why they complied with your strange request, and use their responses as a way of introducing the topic of obedience to authority. After concluding this demonstration and discussion, you may also want to illustrate the phenomenon of reactance, which involves the tendency for people to resist conformity pressures when they feel their freedom is being threatened. Thus, after reminding students that people tend to blindly obey the dictates of authority, ask them once again to perform some kind of silly behavior. On this second occasion, the chances are very good that many students will refrain from carrying out your command. You could use their refusal to obey as a springboard for explaining the concept of reactance and our need to see ourselves as autonomous, self-governing individuals. At this point, you may wish to move on to a broader discussion of the high value placed on individual freedom in American society—as illustrated by the reactance phenomenon, as well as our national penchant for idealizing nonconformity and rugged individualism in history, fiction and films. Yet, this value is also at odds with the our tendency to reward conformity and punish deviance, to conform to fads and fashions of all kinds, as well as the practical necessity of conformity for the smooth functioning of everyday life. A more detailed discussion of American ambivalence regarding the issue of conformity and individualism can be found in the introductory section of Chapter Two.

The Good Society. One way to make the concepts of compliance, identification, and internalization come alive for students is to introduce them within the context of the conditions necessary for the creation of "the good society." After explaining these three forms of social influence—and their component factors of power, attractiveness, and credibility—ask students to consider which form of social influence they believe stands the best chance of promoting their idea of a "good society." Elaborate on students' responses and help them to articulate their notions of an ideal (or improved) society and the conditions necessary for its realization. You may wish to discuss (or assign for student reading) B.F. Skinner's *Walden Two* as an example of a utopian society built on principles of compliance, generated by the systematic use of principles of operant conditioning.

Projects and Discussion Topics

1. PROJECT: For one week, carry a pocket-sized notebook with you and record examples of conformity as it occurs in everyday life. In keeping this diary, draw upon your own experiences of conformity, as well as your observations of others' responses to social influence. (Some possibilities: interactions with dorm members or housemates; behavior

in public places such as bus stops, supermarkets or movie theaters.) Choose three examples from your diary and analyze them from a social-psychological perspective, drawing upon insights gleaned from readings and lectures on conformity.

2. PROJECT: Recall and describe any incidents in your life in which you witnessed an emergency or similar situation in which help was needed. What were your feelings and behavior in these situations? Did you offer assistance? Why or why not? Ask two friends to tell you about their experiences with emergency situations. What factors seemed to play a role in whether they either helped or did not help?

3. PROJECT: Make a list of several groups to which you belong—both informal as well as formally organized ones. (Examples might include: your immediate family; your college dormitory; your church or temple; your social psychology class; a group of casual acquaintances; a close circle of friends; political, volunteer, or campus organizations, etc.) Next, think of situations in which you might feel some pressure (however subtle) to conform to the opinion or behavior of the majority of the members of each group. In which of these groups would you be more likely to conform? Conversely, in which groups would you be likely to feel greater amounts of freedom to resist conformity pressures? Based on your knowledge of group conformity, explain the social-psychological factors and processes that could account for the different levels of conformity you might display within each of these groups.

4. PROJECT: Either alone or with a friend or classmate, engage in a mild form of non-conformist behavior in a public setting. Record the reactions of onlookers, as well as your own feelings while performing this behavior. Discuss your "experiment" in class. (If this exercise is done in pairs, one person can be the non-conformist, while the other carefully observes and takes notes on the verbal and non-verbal responses of unsuspecting others. Partners can then switch roles.) Some possibilities: 1) stand backwards while waiting in line at the grocery store or cafeteria; 2) arrive early for class, sit behind or next to a classmate, and proceed to hum loudly or sing for a minute or two; 3) when riding an elevator, face the back wall instead of the doors, or make somewhat sustained eye contact with a fellow passenger; 4) stand overly close to someone while having a conversation with him or her.

5. DISCUSSION: Research on conformity, such as Milgram's studies of obedience and Zimbardo's prison simulation, indicates that under certain conditions people who are otherwise moral and decent are capable of engaging in acts of considerable cruelty toward others. What issues do these findings raise regarding the problem of holding individuals responsible for their actions? Given our understanding of the power of situations in influencing behavior, can you think of ways to use this knowledge to reduce the likelihood of conformity-based acts of inhumanity?

6. DISCUSSION: What are the ethical problems raised by Milgram's obedience study? What justifications could be made for conducting this study? Do you think the study should have been performed? Why or why not?

7. DISCUSSION: Think of a time when you found yourself in the midst of a situation in which you behaved or reacted "out of character"—that is, in a manner very different from your accustomed mode of behavior. Describe the nature of this situation and your feelings regarding your own behavior. Try to make sense of your experience in light of your knowledge of conformity and the power of situational pressures. Share your experiences and insights with other members of your discussion group.

8. DISCUSSION: Ask class members to think of emergency situations they may have observed or been involved in, for example, a car accident, near-drowning, and so forth. Ask them to describe how they and others reacted. Try to get them to analyze the similarities and differences between their experiences and the research results of the bystander intervention studies.

Additional Readings

Allen, V.L. (1975). Social support for non-conformity. In L. Berkowitz (Ed.), *Advances in experimental social psychology* (Vol. 8). New York: Academic Press.

Colman, A.M. (1991). Crowd psychology in South African murder trials. *American Psychologist, 46,* 1071-1079.

Janis, I.L. Groupthink. (1971, November). *Psychology Today,* pp. 24–26.(A "groupthink" analysis of several high-level government decisions.)

Janis, I.L. (1982). *Groupthink: Psychological studies of policy decisions and fiascos.* (2nd ed.). Boston: Houghton Mifflin.

Kelman, H.C. & Hamilton, V.L. (1989). *Crimes of obedience: Toward a social psychology of authority and responsibility.* New Haven, CT: Yale University Press.

Kelman, H.C. & Lawrence, L.H. (1972, June). American response to the trial of Lt. Calley. *Psychology Today,* pp. 41–45, 78–81. (Discusses obedience to authority in light of Milgram's studies and the case of Lt. Calley and the My Lai massacre in Vietnam.)

Kruglanski, A.W. (1984, November). Freeze-think and the Challenger. *Psychology Today,* pp. 43–46. (A social-psychological analysis of the events and faulty decision-making strategies surrounding the space-shuttle Challenger tragedy.)

Latane, B. & Darley, J.M. (1970). *The unresponsive bystander.* New York: Appleton-Century-Crofts.

Milgram, S. (1974). *Obedience to authority.* New York: Harper & Row.

Muson, H. Blind obedience. (1978, January). *Psychology Today,* p. 112. (Panelists John Dean, Stanley Milgram, Thomas Szasz, and Herbert Speigal discuss the problem of conformity to pressure from authority figures.)

Nissani, M. (1990). A cognitive reinterpretation of Stanley Milgram's observations on obedience to authority. *American Psychologist, 45,* 1384–1385.

Osherow, N. (1992). Making sense of the nonsensical: An analysis of Jonestown. In E. Aronson (Ed.), *Readings about The Social Animal* (6th ed.). New York: Freeman.

Pines, M. (1976, January). Unlearning blind obedience in German schools. *Psychology Today*, pp. 59–65. (Describes efforts of German schools to teach students how to resist conformity pressures.)

Saks, M.J. (1992). Obedience versus disobedience to legitimate versus illegitimate authorities issuing good versus evil directives. *Psychological Science, 3*, (4), 221-223.

Skinner, B.F. (1976). *Walden Two.* New York: Macmillan. (Skinner's novel depicting a utopian society based on compliance via the systematic use of operant conditioning.)

Speer, A. (1970). *Inside the Third Reich: Memoirs* (R. Winston & Winston, Trans.). New York: Macmillan.

Multiple-Choice Questions

Answer: d
Page: 14–15

1. Generally speaking, nonconformity
   a. is usually admired by others in our culture.
   b. is highly adaptive.
   c. is highly maladaptive.
   d. may be either adaptive or maladaptive, depending on the situation.

Answer: d   2.   In an experiment by Schachter, subjects engaged in
Page: 15   a group discussion of a juvenile delinquent named
                  Johnny Rocco and were asked to suggest treatment
                  for him ranging from "very lenient" to "very
                  hard." When later asked how much they liked
                  other members of their group—some of whom
                  were confederates of the experimenter—subjects
                  gave the highest ratings to:
                  a. the "slider" confederate—who first deviated,
                     but later conformed, to the opinions of real
                     subjects on how Johnny should be treated.
                  b. the "leader" confederate—who played a major
                     role in influencing the opinions of real subjects
                     on how Johnny should be treated.
                  c. the "reluctant" confederate—who refrained
                     from voicing any opinion until all the other
                     subjects had decided on how Johnny should be
                     treated.
                  d. the "modal" confederate—who consistently
                     conformed to the opinions of real subjects on
                     how Johnny should be treated.

Answer: a   3.   Aronson describes an experiment in which groups
Page: 15   of subjects discuss the punishment appropriate for
                  "Johnny Rocco," a juvenile delinquent. In this
                  experiment, subjects best liked a confederate when
                  he played the role of a:
                  a. person who agreed with the group
                     (conformist).
                  b. person who disagreed with the group (deviate).
                  c. person who originally agreed and then came to
                     disagree with the group (lost soul).
                  d. person who disagreed and then came to agree
                     with the group (slider).

Answer: a
Page: 15–16

4. Because Joe's parents can't stand his wild friend Larry, Joe spends even more time hanging out with Larry. Joe's behavior is best thought of as an example of:
   a. anticonformist.
   b. nonconformist.
   c. individualistic behavior.
   d. antisocial behavior.

Answer: d
Page: 17–18

5. According to Aronson's analysis of the Challenger disaster, which of the following most likely did *not* contribute to the disaster?
   a. NASA had already conducted two dozen successful launches
   b. A schoolteacher who was on board, which created more publicity than normal.
   c. At NASA a lift-off was a more desirable decision than a delay.
   d. NASA engineers assured management that all safety measures had been taken.

Answer: c
Page: 18–19

6. Which of the following is *not* a characteristic of groupthink?
   a. the illusion of invulnerability
   b. the illusion of unanimity
   c. the illusion of too many good alternatives
   d. a strong leader who does not challenge the group to express doubts

Answer: c
Page: 18–19

7. According to Janis, groupthink most often leads a group to make:
   a. mostly good quality decisions.
   b. mostly average quality decisions.
   c. mostly poor quality decisions.
   d. some very good and some very bad decisions.

Answer: a   8. Which of the following would *not* be a productive
Page: 18–19   strategy to prevent groupthink from occurring?
                      a. moving quickly to consensus before too many
                         opposing views are expressed
                      b. seeking all the information you can get
                      c. having a nondirective, less powerful leader
                      d. trying to reduce the cohesiveness of the group

Answer: b   9. Disastrous decisions made by members of the
Page: 18   Third Reich, Nixon's "palace guard," and NASA
                      officials involved in the launch of the ill-fated
                      Challenger space shuttle were a consequence of a
                      maladaptive decision-making strategy Irving Janis
                      calls:
                      a. mind-guarding.
                      b. groupthink.
                      c. high-risk conformity.
                      d. collective momentum.

Answer: b   10. According to Irving Janis, the maladaptive
Page: 18   phenomenon of "groupthink" is more likely to
                      occur when:
                      a. groups are composed of diverse members who
                         seek agreement in order to overcome their
                         different points of view.
                      b. concurrence-seeking processes override
                         realistic considerations of alternative courses of
                         action.
                      c. differences among group members prevent the
                         group from reaching a well-considered,
                         realistic decision.
                      d. the desire of each group member to be well-
                         liked by other group members overrides
                         concurrence-seeking processes.

Answer: d   11. Which of the following statements about Asch's
Page: 20–21   conformity experiments is *true*?
                    a. Subjects were rewarded with money when they answered correctly.
                    b. Subjects were rewarded with money when they went along with the group.
                    c. The judging task was very difficult.
                    d. Only one of the seven group members was a naive subject.

Answer: a   12. In Asch's conformity experiments, the discomfort felt by subjects who expressed agreement with the incorrect judgments of the majority could result from the conflict between two important goals. It was suggested that the goals in conflict are:
Page: 21–22
                    a. the goal of being correct and the goal of staying in the good graces of others by living up to their expectations.
                    b. the fear of being wrong and the fear of being right.
                    c. the goal of being correct and the goal of making others appear to be conforming and wishy-washy.
                    d. the goal of being admired and the goal of expressing one's individuality.

Answer: b 13. Research indicates that when people observe a
Page: 22 conformity experiment like Asch's (in which
subjects conformed to the erroneous judgments of
others regarding the length of lines) they typically
predict that:
a. the subjects will exhibit *less* conformity than
they actually do.
b. that they, *personally*, would exhibit less
conformity than the subjects they are
observing.
c. that they, *personally*, would exhibit about the
same amount of conformity as the subjects
they are observing.
d. that they, *personally*, would exhibit more
conformity than the subjects they are
observing.

Answer: b 14. An individual is *less* likely to conform to group
Page: 24–25 pressure when:
a. everyone else in the group conforms.
b. he or she has high self-esteem.
c. he or she feels insecure about being liked by
other group members.
d. the individual is uncertain about his or her
opinion.

Answer: b 15. Which of the following variables has been found to
Page: 24–25 lead to an *increase* in the degree of conformity a
person will exhibit in a group setting?
a. high levels of subject self-esteem
b. a unanimous majority opinion
c. a dissenter from the majority opinion
d. a prior commitment from the subject to his or
her opinion

Answer: a 16. If a person makes a prior commitment to a view
Page: 24–25   that differs from the group opinion, he or she will
                 tend to be:
                 a. less susceptible to group pressure to conform.
                 b. more open to group pressure to conform.
                 c. less confident of his or her own view.
                 d. more open to conform to the group's opinion
                    on a different issue.

Answer: a 17. Joe is involved in a group discussion about the
Page: 25   U.S. political system. On one particular issue, Joe's
                 opinion is very different from the others in the
                 group. Under which of the following conditions
                 would Joe be most likely to express his
                 disagreement with the rest of the group?
                 a. If he felt liked and totally accepted by other
                    group members.
                 b. If he felt rejected by other group members.
                 c. If he felt somewhat liked and accepted by
                    other group members.
                 d. If he believed the other group members were
                    uninformed on the issue.

Answer: a 18. According to Aronson, most people believe that
Page: 22   they are motivated by a desire to _____ whereas
                 others are motivated by a desire to _____.
                 a. be correct; be respected by others
                 b. be respected by others; be correct
                 c. get rewards; avoid punishments
                 d. avoid punishments, get rewards

Answer: b 19. In studying the relationship between conformity
Page: 23–24   when making judgments in public versus private,
                 the general finding is that when subjects are given
                 more privacy:
                 a. they conform more.
                 b. they conform less.
                 c. they make better decisions.
                 d. they make poorer decisions.

Answer: c   20. Imagine you are walking down the street and passed by a driver who needed money for the parking meter. According to research on compliance, under which of the following conditions would you be most likely to give the driver some spare change?
Page: 26–27
   a. when the request for change came from a fashionably dressed person
   b. when the request for change came from a poorly dressed person
   c. when the request for change came from a uniformed parking officer
   d. when the request for change came from the driver's young child

Answer: c   21. A good rule of thumb to use in predicting conformity in an ambiguous situation is that there will be a greater dependence on _____ when physical reality is lacking as a basis for judgment.
Page: 26–27
   a. objective reality
   b. personal intuition
   c. social reality
   d. groupthink

Answer: a   22. Studies on conformity and jaywalking indicate that:
Page: 28
   a. pedestrians are less likely to jaywalk when they observe a high-status, well-dressed person who refrains from jaywalking.
   b. pedestrians are less likely to jaywalk when they observe a low-status, shabbily dressed person jaywalking.
   c. pedestrians are more likely to jaywalk in large cities than in small towns.
   d. pedestrians are more likely to jaywalk in small towns than in large cities.

Answer: b
Page: 27

23. According to Aronson, when physical reality ___, people's reliance on social reality ___.
    a. increases; increases
    b. decreases; increases
    c. increases; becomes unpredictable
    d. decreases; decreases

Answer: a
Page: 27

24. According to Festinger, conformity is more likely to occur when physical reality is _____ and social reality is _____.
    a. low; high
    b. low; low
    c. high; low
    d. high; high

Answer: d
Page: 28–29

25. Aronson and O'Leary conducted a study designed to encourage water conservation among male students showering at the university field house. They found that students were more likely to conserve water (by turning off the shower while soaping up) after:
    a. a colorful, vivid sign urging water conservation was placed in the shower room.
    b. a water-conserving "model" told them that they, too, should turn off the shower while soaping up.
    c. listening to a high-status university official explain the importance of conserving water.
    d. observing the behavior of a "model" who turned off the shower while soaping up.

Answer: b
Page: 29

26. Aronson describes a study in which male students were observed showering to determine if they complied with a request to conserve water. Subjects showered alone, with a conserving model, or with two conserving models. The percentages of subjects who conserved water in the alone, one model, two model conditions were:
a. 6%, 8%, 10%, respectively.
b. 6%, 49%, 67%, respectively.
c. 6%, 67%, 49%, respectively.
d. 67%, 49%, 6%, respectively.

Answer: b
Page: 30

27. According to research presented in the text, people are *least* likely to throw a flier on the ground if the parking lot has:
a. no other fliers littering it.
b. one other flier littering it.
c. lots of other fliers littering it.
d. lots of fliers and lots of other trash littering it.

Answer: b
Page: 32–33

28. Schachter and Singer (1962) conducted an experiment in which subjects were injected with either adrenalin or a placebo, and were either informed or misinformed as to the real symptoms produced by an adrenalin injection. Later, they were exposed to the behavior of either an angry or a euphoric cohort. Subjects in which of the following conditions were most likely to imitate the behavior of the cohort?
a. adrenalin - informed
b. adrenalin - misinformed
c. placebo - informed
d. placebo - misinformed

Answer: c
Page: 32–33

29. Schachter and Singer (1962) (in their study in which subjects were injected with adrenalin, but thought they were getting the vitamin "suproxin") demonstrated that:
   a. internal states of physiological arousal are always interpreted by internal cues.
   b. internal states of physiological arousal are interpreted by external cues only when we have a ready explanation for internal causes of the arousal.
   c. physiological arousal for which we have no ready explanation will often be interpreted in terms of various external cues.
   d. internal states are unrelated to external cues.

Answer: d
Page: 32-33

30. In the experiment by Schachter and Singer, some subjects were given a drug causing physiological arousal and were warned about the side effects of the drug (i.e., hand tremors and heart palpitations). How did subjects who were given the same drug, but who were not warned of the drug's effects, interpret their feelings of arousal?
   a. They thought that they were angry.
   b. They felt happy at first, but later felt angry.
   c. They didn't even feel the drug's effects at all, since they had no idea about what they were supposed to feel.
   d. They thought that they were happy or angry, depending on the behavior of the confederate in the experiment.

Answer: a   31. Haney has conducted research on murder trials that
Page: 33–34   use the *death qualification procedure,* in which
                   potential jury members who are opposed to the
                   death penalty are systematically excluded from jury
                   duty. Compared to subjects who did not witness a
                   film segment showing this procedure, subjects who
                   did observe the procedure were more likely to:
                   a. believe that the defendant was guilty and
                       would end up receiving the death penalty.
                   b. believe that the defendant was innocent but
                       would end up receiving the death penalty
                       anyway.
                   c. believe that the judge thought the defendant
                       was innocent.
                   d. believe that the defense attorney thought the
                       defendant was guilty.

Answer: b   32. Six–year–old Lisa finds hitting her little brother is
Page: 34–35   the quickest way to get him to stop bugging her.
                   Her mother, however, finds Lisa's behavior
                   unacceptable, and threatens to take away her
                   favorite toy for a whole week if she hits her
                   brother again. Lisa stops hitting her brother. Lisa's
                   behavior illustrates what form of response to social
                   influence?
                   a. identification
                   b. compliance
                   c. secondary gain
                   d. identification

Answer: a   33. Influencing someone by means of insisting that he
Page: 34–35   or she behave in a particular way is called:
                   a. compliance.
                   b. identification.
                   c. modeling.
                   d. determinism.

Answer: a
Page: 35

34. Suppose you saw a small child eating lima beans with obvious reluctance. When asked why she was eating them if she wasn't fond of them, she replied, "Because Big Bird eats his vegetables, and I want to be like him!" What type of conformity is she displaying?
    a. identification
    b. internalization
    c. reactance
    d. compliance

Answer: d
Page: 35

35. Even though you believe college tuition should be increased to meet rising expenses, you go along with a group of friends as they organize a protest for lower tuition. This is an example of:
    a. diffusion of responsibility.
    b. reactance.
    c. audience inhibition.
    d. identification.

Answer: a
Page: 36

36. Which of the following is *not* characteristic of internalization?
    a. It is based on the admiration or liking of another.
    b. It is the most deeply rooted and permanent response to social influence.
    c. It is based on the desire to be right.
    d. The behavior is internally or intrinsically motivated.

Answer: a
Page: 38

37. According to Aronson, power is the essential component in:
    a. compliance.
    b. internalization.
    c. identification.
    d. deindividuation.

Answer: c 38. Three responses to social influence are compliance,
Page: 38   identification, and internalization. The major
                component for each of them, respectively, is:
                a. power, liking, and loving.
                b. status, attractiveness, and reason.
                c. power, attractiveness, and credibility.
                d. power, attractiveness, and liking.

Answer: c 39. Fear of negative consequences would be the major
Page: 38   motivation in which of the following?
                a. internalization
                b. identification
                c. compliance
                d. all of the above

Answer: b 40. The essential component of internalization is:
Page: 38   a. power to reward or punish.
                b. being convinced the new attitude is correct.
                c. admiration of another person.
                d. obedience to authority.

Answer: c 41. The type of conformity which is most likely to
Page: 39   persist the longest is that which results from:
                a. social reality.
                b. compliance.
                c. internalization.
                d. identification.

Answer: b 42. Gary's parents promised him an interest-free loan
Page: 39-40   for a new car, if only he would quit smoking for 3
                months. Gary really wanted the car, so he quit.
                After not smoking for 3 months, he realized he had
                more energy, more money, and his food tasted
                better. Gary decided he would not start smoking
                again. Gary's experience is an example of:
                a. primary gain.
                b. secondary gain.
                c. primary reward.
                d. secondary reward.

Answer: c
Page: 39–40

43. Bobby's mother promises that if he will take swimming lessons for two weeks, she will buy him a toy he wants. Even though he doesn't want to swim, he complies and, in the process, learns to like swimming. This is best thought of as an example of:
a. groupthink.
b. identification.
c. secondary gain.
d. anticonformity.

Answer: a
Page: 45

44. In his studies of obedience to authority, Milgram found that:
a. the closer subjects were to the victim, the less they shocked him.
b. the more similar the victim was to the subject, the less the subject shocked him.
c. subjects shocked the confederate less when the experiment was conducted at a prestigious university than in a rundown commercial building.
d. subjects from Australia and Spain were less obedient to authority than subjects from the United States.

Answer: c
Page: 42

45. A comparison of personality characteristics of subjects in Milgram's studies of obedience to authority revealed:
a. that subjects who fully obeyed were more sadistic and cruel than those who did not.
b. that subjects who refused to obey were more intelligent than those who obeyed the most.
c. no differences between subjects who were fully obedient and those who refused to obey.
d. that subjects who took part in the experiment for free were more obedient than those who were paid for their participation.

Answer: b	46.	In Milgram's study of obedience, which of the following participants was (were) a confederate of the Experimenter?
Page: 41
a. the Teacher
b. the Learner
c. both the Teacher and the Learner
d. neither the Learner nor the Teacher

Answer: d	47.	Although a group of psychiatrists who were asked to predict the results of Milgram's experiment on obedience thought that _____ percent of the subjects would use the highest possible shock, in fact _____ percent delivered all the shocks available.
Page: 42
a. almost 100; less than 1
b. 33; 62
c. 90; 100
d. less than 1; 62

Answer: c	48.	Suppose you were told to give a painful electric shock to another person, either by a research scientist or by a volunteer paid to make this request. Furthermore, suppose you either had to watch the person receive the shock or could simply push a button and never see the person's response. Under which set of conditions would you be most likely to administer the shock?
Page: 44–45
a. scientist — viewing the subject
b. volunteer — viewing the subject
c. scientist — pushing the button
d. volunteer — pushing the button

Answer: c 49. Research conducted by Latane, Darley, and their
Page: 47–48 colleagues on bystander intervention has revealed
that:
a. people tend to help more when they're in a hurry.
b. people in big cities help more than people in small towns.
c. the more witnesses there are to an emergency, the less likely it is that an individual will decide to help.
d. the more witnesses there are to an emergency, the more likely it is that an individual will decide to help.

Answer: c 50. In the "lady in distress" study, in which subjects
Page: 48 waiting for an experiment were led to believe that a female experimenter in the next room had fallen and hurt herself, subjects were more likely to come to her assistance when:
a. they heard her moan, "Oh, my God, my foot . . . I can't move it."
b. she was silent, as if unconscious.
c. they were waiting alone in the next room.
d. they were waiting with a stranger in the next room.

Answer: d 51. According to research on bystander intervention, an
Page: 50–52 individual is more likely to be helped when potential helpers:
a. feel themselves to be very different from the person in need of help.
b. are great in number.
c. have trouble determining if the situation is a real emergency.
d. assume personal responsibility for intervening.

Answer: b 52. Studies involving the "costs and benefits" of helping indicate that:
Page: 52
   a. people help more when the costs of helping are high.
   b. people help less when the costs of helping are high.
   c. costs are unrelated to helping, but people help when benefits are high.
   d. emergencies occur so quickly that bystanders do not have time to estimate costs and benefits.

Answer: c 53. In a series of studies on bystander intervention, conducted on the New York subway system, an accomplice of the experimenters staggered and collapsed on the floor of the train. Overall, these studies found that:
Page: 51
   a. the "victim" was offered help more often when the train had relatively few passengers.
   b. the "victim" was almost never offered help, regardless of how crowded the train was.
   c. the "victim" was almost always offered help when he was made to seem obviously ill.
   d. the "victim" was almost never offered help when he was carrying a liquor bottle and was made to reek of alcohol.

Essay Questions

1. "When physical reality is unclear, other people become a major source of information." Is this statement supported by research? How might the Schachter-Singer experiment (in which subjects were injected with a stimulant or a placebo) or the Latane-Rodin bystander intervention experiment (in which subjects, alone or in pairs, heard a confederate "fall off a ladder") be used to support or disconfirm this statement?

2. *The Social Animal* describes instances of bystander nonintervention, where people failed to help victims of crimes or accidents. Suppose

you were to fall from your bicycle and break your leg. How would you arrange things (theoretically) so that people would be more likely to help you?

3. The chapter on conformity reviews several variables that serve to either increase or decrease the degree to which people will exhibit conformity. Briefly discuss FOUR of these factors and how they affect conformity.

4. Define and give examples of compliance, identification, and internalization. Which of these has the most permanent influence on an individual's behavior? What are the social-psychological processes or components underlying the effects of each of them? Under what circumstances might compliance or identification lead to internalization?

5. Define "groupthink" and the social-psychological processes that underlie it. Imagine you were a member of a group that might be subject to "groupthink" processes. Based on your understanding of group conformity, what steps might you take to minimize the problem?

6. Although conformity processes are often a mundane part of daily life, they may also be implicated in more serious matters—some involving life and death itself. Describe Haney's research on the "death qualification procedure" and explain how it illustrates this point.

3

Mass Communication, Propaganda, and Persuasion

I. Introduction

   Impact of "The Day After"
   Copycat suicides (Phillips)

II. Effectiveness of Media Appeals

   Familiarity (Zajonc)
   Political advertising (Grush)

III. Education or Propaganda?

   Education as propaganda (Zimbardo, Ebbesen, & Maslach)

IV. Two Major Routes to Persuasion

   Elaboration likelihood model (Petty & Cacioppo)

V. The Source of the Communication

   A. Credibility

      Credible source: Oppenheimer vs. *Pravda* (Hovland & Weiss)
      Race of communicator (Aronson & Golden)

   B. Increasing Trustworthiness: Joe "the Shoulder" (Aronson, Walster, & Abrahams)

      "Unintentional" persuasion (Walster & Festinger)

C. Attractiveness

  Beauty and likability (Mills & Aronson; Eagly & Chaiken)

VI. The Nature of the Communication

  A. Logical versus emotional appeals (Leventhal)

  B. Statistics versus vivid examples (Nisbett)

  C. One-sided versus two-sided arguments

  D. Order of presentation (Miller & Campbell)

  E. Discrepancy (Zimbardo; Hovland et al.; Aronson, Turner, & Carlsmith)

VII. Characteristics of the Audience

  A. Self-esteem

  B. Prior experience of the audience

  Forewarning (Freedman & Sears)
  Reactance (Bensley & Wu; Heilman)
  Distraction/heckling (Festinger & Maccoby; Sloan et al.)
  Inoculation effect (McGuire)

VIII. How Well Do the Principles Work?

  A. Audience resistance to persuasion (Canon)

  B. Impact of television (Gerbner; Haney & Manzolati)

Terms & Concepts

copy-cat suicide
education vs. propaganda
elaboration likelihood model
central route
peripheral route
credibility
one-sided argument
two-sided argument

discrepancy of communication
primacy effect
recency effect
reactance
inoculation effect
attitude
opinion

Chapter Overview

Chapter 3 covers the specific factors and social-psychological processes underlying effective persuasion, as well as the broader implications of living in an age of mass communication. Highlights of the chapter include:

Media influence is pervasive, affecting our opinions, attitudes, and behavior, regardless of whether direct attempts to persuade are involved. For example, executives in charge of news programming can exert a subtle influence on our opinions simply by determining which events are given exposure. Because these decisions are typically based on the entertainment value of events, news coverage does not present a balanced picture of what is happening in the world. Instead, it puts a heavy emphasis on catastrophic events, violence, crime, and other social ills, leaving viewers with an impression of the world as a more dangerous and troubled place than it really is. Similarly, television dramas, sitcoms, crime shows and other forms of entertainment also tend to contribute to this unrealistic view of the world.

Selective emphasis also places the media in the position of determining subsequent events—not simply reporting them. This is well documented in Phillips' research on the role of the media in the phenomenon of "copycat suicides."

Despite widespread skepticism regarding the truthfulness of media advertising, such blatant attempts of mass persuasion tend to be highly effective. In the case of many products, the public will tend to buy a specific brand for no other reason than that it was heavily advertised. Research suggests that mere familiarity tends to increase attractiveness.

The elaboration likelihood model of communication suggests that there are two major routes to persuasion, the central route that relies on relevant facts that people carefully consider and the peripheral route that uses cues to stimulate acceptance of a message without deep consideration of the issues. Both can be effectively used in advertising.

What characteristics of the communicator contribute to effective persuasion? A crucial factor is credibility, which depends on the communicator being both an expert and trustworthy source of information. One way a communicator can appear more trustworthy is to argue against his or her self-interest. Persuasion is also enhanced when the audience believes the communicator is not trying to influence them. The attractiveness and likability of the communicator also tends to increase the persuasive appeal of a given message, but only when relatively trivial issues are concerned (e.g., such as what shaving cream to buy).

What characteristics of the message serve to increase its persuasive appeal? Fear-arousing messages are likely to facilitate attitude change, but behavior change (e.g., quitting smoking) is likely to occur only when specific, preventive instructions are provided. One-sided arguments tend to be more effective with poorly informed audiences, or audiences that already agree with the communicator's point of view. Conversely, two-sided arguments are more apt to persuade audiences that are well-informed or are initially opposed to the communicator's argument. Finally, the credibility of the communicator is important in determining how discrepant a message should ideally be from the audience's initial position. When a communicator has high credibility, the greater discrepancy between his or her view and that of the audience, the more the audience will be persuaded; but, when the communicator's credibility is doubtful or slim, he or she will produce maximum opinion change at moderate discrepancies.

What characteristics of the audience are important in persuasion? As we have seen, the audience's initial position, and whether it is well-informed or poorly informed about an issue, are significant factors. In addition, individual self-esteem plays a central role: people with low self-esteem tend to be more easily persuaded than people with high self-esteem. The prior experience of an audience is also an important consideration in determining the impact of a persuasive appeal. For example, people who are forewarned of an influence attempt tend to be more resistant to persuasion. Similarly, individuals who are "inoculated" against a future attempt at persuasion—by learning to defend their beliefs against a mild attack—display greater resistance to persuasion. Resistance is also increased by the phenomenon of reactance, which occurs when the individual perceives a persuasive appeal as a threat to his or her freedom of choice. Finally, when an audience is distracted during the presentation of a message, resistance to persuasion is reduced, presumably because the distraction prevents people from coming up with counterarguments to refute the message.

Lecture Ideas & Teaching Suggestions

Who Says What to Whom? An effective strategy for helping students assimilate and remember the many factors that influence persuasion is to organize the material under the categories of: WHO says WHAT to WHOM? You might want to put this question on the board, listing briefly each set of findings under the appropriate heading as you discuss them. This is also a useful method for presenting a review of material from the chapter prior to exams. Students should also find it helpful to make their own charts of persuasion findings according to these categories.

Persuasion in Daily Life. In our daily lives, we are all subject to a tremendous number of attempts to influence our attitudes and behavior. As a result, the various persuasion tactics used by advertisers and sales personnel is an area that tends to be intrinsically fascinating for most students. Engaging material on sales pitches and other influence strategies, and the social-psychological processes underlying them, can be found in several of the books and articles listed in the suggested readings for this chapter. Of special interest are Pratkanis and Aronson's (1991) *The Age of Propaganda*, and Cialdini's (1988) *Influence: Science and Practice*, both of which explore the methods employed by those who are highly skilled in the art of persuasion. (Note: Some of these strategies are also examined in Chapter 4; thus, a lecture covering this material might provide an effective transition into theory and research on social cognition.)

Routes to Persuasion. Petty and Cacioppo's "elaboration likelihood model" of persuasion offers an information-processing theory of attitude change. In their view, people process a persuasive message in one of two basic ways: 1) via a central processing route, in which they carefully and systematically evaluate the issues and arguments presented in the message; and 2) via a peripheral route, in which little thought is devoted to the content of the message itself. In the latter case, changes in attitudes result from relatively superficial characteristics associated with the message—such as the attractiveness of the communicator. When people are highly involved in an issue, they are more likely to engage in central processing modes, whereas an issue with low personal relevance will probably evoke peripheral processing. Research and further details on the elaboration likelihood model are presented in Petty and Cacioppo (1986a, 1986b), which are referenced in the "additional readings" for this chapter.

Projects and Discussion Topics

1. PROJECT: Collect advertisements or public service messages from various magazines or newspapers—paying special attention to those that seem very persuasive or very unpersuasive. Drawing on your knowledge of persuasion tactics, identify the features of these ads that you believe would either maximize or detract from their persuasive impact. (For example, look at such factors as source credibility and attractiveness, the use of vivid information, one- vs. two-sided arguments, the use of fear, and other variables discussed in Chapter 3.) What kinds of people are the different ads directed toward? Can you find examples of ads that might succeed with one kind of audience, but could totally backfire with another kind of audience? Why do you think advertisers might risk alienating some audience members, rather than presenting a message with universal (or near-universal) appeal? Bring some examples to class and share your analyses with your classmates.

2. PROJECT: Go to the children's room of your local public library and locate books and magazines that are designed to be educational. Can you find examples of subtle—or even blatant—forms of propaganda within these books? You might want to pay particular attention to how certain groups in society—the elderly, women, racial minorities—are portrayed or NOT portrayed. In your search, make a comparison of

books published in the last 5–10 years and those published earlier. Do there appear to be any changes in the amounts or kinds of "propaganda" presented in children's books over the years?

3. PROJECT: Suppose you were hired to develop a program to persuade high school students to refrain from drinking and driving. Assume that, from the outset, these students tend to believe that drinking and driving is nothing to worry about and that they have been (or will soon be) exposed to peer pressure to do so. What kind of program would you design? What factors involving the audience, the source of communication, and the message itself would you need to consider in order to enhance the effectiveness of your program? Can you think of any ways to get around the potential problem of students simply "turning off" to your direct efforts to persuade them? Be imaginative! And, for the sake of convenience, assume that you have ample funds to carry out your program. (This project may be done in small groups or individually.)

4. PROJECT: Over the course of one day, keep a diary of all the various attempts to influence your behavior and beliefs and whether or not they were successful. In recording these attempts at social influence, look for messages coming from a broad variety of sources, including television, radio, print media, billboards, product packaging, etc. In addition, be sure to make note of persuasive appeals that come from "live" interaction with friends, family, teachers, sales clerks, strangers, and others you encounter during the day. Finally, make a special effort to look for "hidden" attempts to influence your beliefs and behavior—that is, those that do not constitute direct or obvious efforts to persuade.

5. DISCUSSION: How, and to what extent, does the mass media influence the public's attitudes and behaviors? Do television shows and newscasts, for example, simply reflect what is happening in the world or do they carry the potential to actually cause real-life events? Apart from advertising, do you believe the members of the media engage in deliberate attempts to persuade people to adopt certain opinions and attitudes?

6. DISCUSSION: To the best of your knowledge, how easily are you influenced by attempts to change your attitudes or behavior? Under what conditions are you more or less likely to be persuaded? Do you think your knowledge about strategies of persuasion, propaganda, and communication can help you to resist unwelcome attempts at persuasion? Since we live in an age of mass communication—in which we are subject to a daily onslaught of influence attempts—should children should receive some kind of formal training or education about persuasion? Why or why not?

Additional Readings

Ball-Rokeach, S.J., Rokeach, M. & Grube, J.W. (1984, November). The great American values test. *Psychology Today*, pp. 34–41. (An experimental TV show assesses the extent to which television can influence basic values and beliefs.)

Cialdini, R.B. (1988). *Influence: Science and practice.* Glenview, IL: Scott, Foresman.

Diamond, E. & Bates, S. (1984, November). The political pitch. *Psychology Today*, pp. 23–32. (Explores the uses of persuasion within the context of political advertising campaigns.)

Entman, R.M. (1993). Framing: Toward clarification of a fractured paradigm. *Journal of Communication, 43,* 51–58. (Special issue: The future of the field: Between fragmentation and cohesion.)

Kipnis, D. & Schmidt, S. (1985, April). The language of persuasion. *Psychology Today*, pp. 40–46. (Covers the conditions under which "soft" and "hard" persuasion tactics work best.)

McGuire, W.J. (1970, February). A vaccine for brainwash. *Psychology Today*, pp. 63–64. (Explores the uses of the "inoculation technique" as a strategy for resisting persuasion.)

Petty, R.E. & Cacioppo, J.T. (1981). *Attraction and persuasion: Classic and contemporary approaches.* Dubuque, Iowa: W.C. Brown.

Petty, R.E. & Cacioppo, J.T. (1986a). *Communication and persuasion: Central and peripheral routes to attitude change.* New York: Springer–Verlag.

Petty, R.E. & Cacioppo, J.T. (1986b). The elaboration likelihood model of persuasion. In L. Berkowitz (Ed.), *Advances in experimental social psychology*, (Vol. 19), (pp. 874–884). New York: Academic Press.

Poindexter, J. (1983, May) Shaping the consumer. *Psychology Today*, pp. 64–68. (A look at how big business monitors consumer habits, and then uses this information to its advantage in creating commercial messages.)

Pratkanis, A. R. & Aronson, E. (1991). *The age of propaganda.* New York: Freeman.

Roskos-Ewoldson, D.R. & Fazio, R.H. (1992). The accessibility of source likability as a determinant of persuasion. *Personality and Social Psychology Bulletin, 18*, 19–25.

Schwartz, L.L. (1991). The historical dimension of cultic techniques of persuasion and control. *Cultic Studies Journal, 8*, 37–45.

Tykocinski, O., Higgins, E.T. & Chaiken, S. (1994). Message framing, self-discrepancies, and yielding to persuasive messages: The motivational significance of psychological situations. *Personality and Social Psychology Bulletin, (20)*, 107–115.

Multiple-Choice Questions

Answer: d
Page: 58

1. According to research on the television film, *The Day After*, which graphically depicted the aftermath of a nuclear attack on the United States:
   a. viewers thought that surviving a nuclear war was very unlikely, while nonviewers thought surviving a nuclear war was very likely.
   b. viewers were more preoccupied than usual with thoughts of nuclear war, while nonviewers were less preoccupied than usual with thoughts of nuclear war.
   c. viewers went into "denial" and believed that the movie presented a highly exaggerated depiction of the horrors of nuclear war.
   d. both viewers and nonviewers said they intended to work toward preventing nuclear war by supporting a nuclear-weapons freeze and other antinuclear activities.

Answer: b
Page: 63–64

2. In his study of the effects of media coverage of teenage suicides, David Phillips found that:
   a. coverage of the confusion and grief surrounding the suicides produced a decrease in teen suicides following the coverage.
   b. there was a large increase in teen suicides following the coverage.
   c. the suicide rate following the coverage remained surprisingly unchanged—pointing to the limited effects of media coverage of news events.
   d. the suicide rate increased moderately at first, followed by a sharp decrease as mental health workers responded to the crisis.

Answer: b 3. Phillips's research on the impact of media coverage of car-crash suicides revealed that following a publicized suicide:
Page: 63–64
   a. there was a decrease in single-car, one-passenger "suicide" accidents.
   b. victims of "suicide" accidents tended to be of similar age as the victim of the publicized suicide.
   c. there was an increase in multiple-car accidents.
   d. there was an increase in pedestrian fatalities involving hit-and-run drivers.

Answer: b 4. According to the text, a phenomenon that may have contributed to Nixon's success in the presidential election of 1968 was:
Page: 65–66
   a. the intentional cover-up by the media of news related to the Watergate break in.
   b. the well-rehearsed speaking and improved physical appearance of Nixon on TV.
   c. his insistence on always speaking first in the presidential debates.
   d. a short-term but rapid rise in his trustworthiness as rated by voters.

Answer: d 5. The impact of television commercials on very young children is reflected in the fact that:
Page: 67
   a. most children express a desire to imitate the behavior of TV characters.
   b. fewer than 20 percent of preschool-aged children asked for toys or food they saw advertised on TV.
   c. very young children tend to be quite cynical about advertising claims.
   d. according to their mothers, a majority of preschoolers were able to sing commercial jingles learned from television.

Answer: a
Page: 67

6. According to the text, what percent of tenth-grade students believed that TV commercials were truthful most of the time?
   a. 4 percent
   b. 33 percent
   c. 60 percent
   d. 80 percent

Answer: a
Page: 69–70

7. Studies examining the effect of campaign expenditures for political advertising suggest that:
   a. unfamiliar candidates in primary elections may benefit from political advertising.
   b. when candidates are already familiar to the voters, advertising campaigns vastly enhance their popularity.
   c. too much political advertising makes voters feel manipulated, thus reducing a candidate's chances of winning the election.
   d. people who pay close attention to political advertisements are often the same people who don't bother to vote.

Answer: b
Page: 71–72

8. According to Zimbardo, Ebbesen, and Maslach, who analyzed the content of elementary-school arithmetic texts, examples of math problems from most textbooks:
   a. are intentional forms of propaganda designed to brainwash students.
   b. subtly endorse and legitimize the capitalist economic system that is dominant in our society—presenting it as "natural and normal."
   c. are value-free ways of teaching children the basics of mathematics.
   d. reflect alternative systems of economics that threaten our society's established economic practices.

Answer: a 9. Bobby, a second-grader, is working on a problem in his arithmetic book. The problem reads: "Mary and her sister are baking three cakes for the school bake sale. To bake one cake, they will need 2 cups of flour and 1 egg. How many cups of flour and how many eggs will they need to bake 3 cakes?" According to Aronson, Bobby's math problem might be considered by some people to be a subtle form of:
Page: 71–72
   a. propaganda.
   b. persuasion.
   c. the inoculation effect.
   d. a one-sided argument.

Answer: a 10. In Petty and Cacioppo's elaboration likelihood model, there are two routes to persuasion:
Page: 73
   a. the central and the peripheral.
   b. the primacy and the recency.
   c. the expert and the trustworthy.
   d. the fluency and the probability.

Answer: d 11. Suppose you watch a TV ad for a deodorant that tells you almost nothing about the product, but presents it being used by beautiful, popular, successful people. The elaboration likelihood model would describe this ad as one influencing:
Page: 73
   a. the primacy effect.
   b. the inoculation effect.
   c. the central route.
   d. the peripheral route.

Answer: a   12.   Suppose you see an ad for a deodorant that
Page: 73   focuses on how effective it is in comparison tests,
                         how it compares in cost to other products, and
                         that it is all-natural. The elaboration likelihood
                         model would classify this ad as one emphasizing:
                         a.   the central route.
                         b.   the peripheral route.
                         c.   the logical route.
                         d.   the inoculation effect.

Answer: b   13.   In a study by Hovland and Weiss, subjects heard
Page: 75–76   arguments regarding the feasibility of atomic
                         submarines. Subjects were more persuaded by
                         physicist J. Robert Oppenheimer, rather than the
                         Soviet newspaper *Pravda*, because:
                         a.   Oppenheimer was an attractive source and,
                              thus, subjects wished to identify with him.
                         b.   Oppenheimer was perceived as an expert and
                              trustworthy source of information, unlike
                              Pravda.
                         c.   Oppenheimer's arguments contained vivid
                              examples, whereas *Pravda* presented the
                              information in the form of statistics.
                         d.   Subjects knew that *Pravda* was arguing
                              against its own self-interest and, thus, could
                              not be trusted.

Answer: a   14.   Research in attitude change suggests that in order
Page: 76   to be a credible source, a communicator should
                         be both:
                         a.   expert and trustworthy.
                         b.   respected and feared.
                         c.   attractive and intelligent.
                         d.   trustworthy and intelligent.

Answer: d
Page: 77

15. A study by Golden revealed that sixth-graders were more persuaded of the importance of arithmetic after listening to the pro-math arguments of a prizewinning engineer, as compared to a dishwasher. However, when the engineer giving the speech was a black man:
   a. all students found his arguments less persuasive than those of the white engineer.
   b. all students found his arguments more persuasive than those of the white engineer.
   c. most students devalued engineering as a profession.
   d. only students who were highly prejudiced against blacks found his arguments less persuasive than those of the white engineer.

Answer: c
Page: 80–81

16. Suppose you are going to organize a program for high school students advocating stricter enforcement of the drug laws. All other things being equal, your most persuasive speaker would be a:
   a. police officer.
   b. concerned and well-liked parent.
   c. person serving a jail sentence for drug possession.
   d. student who has always supported this view.

58 The Social Animal

Answer: a
Page: 81

17. In an experiment by Eagly, which involved a dispute between business interests and environmental groups over a company's pollution of a river, subjects were *least* likely to be persuaded by the statements of:
   a. a business spokesman addressing a group of business owners.
   b. a business spokesman addressing a group of environmentalists.
   c. an environmentalist addressing an environmental group.
   d. an environmentalist addressing a group of business owners.
   e. a business spokesman addressing a group of neighbors whose homes were situated near the polluted river.

Answer: b
Page: 83

18. Walster and Festinger conducted an experiment in which subjects "overheard" a conversation between two graduate students, one of whom expressed an opinion on a certain issue. Subjects' opinions were influenced by the graduate student's opinion when:
   a. the graduate student had previously performed a favor for the subject.
   b. the subject believed the graduate students were unaware of his or her presence.
   c. the graduate student was an expert on the particular issue in question.
   d. the graduate student presented a two-sided argument regarding the issue in question.

Answer: d
Page: 84

19. Attractive or likable communicators tend to be more persuasive when they are obviously trying to persuade us. This statement is:
   a. true, but only when the communicator is delivering a message that the audience already agrees with.
   b. false, except when the communicator is an expert source of information regarding the issue.
   c. true, but only when the audience is composed of men.
   d. true, but only in the case of trivial issues.

Answer: c
Page: 84–85

20. In general, research on attractiveness, expertise, and attitude change supports which of the following conclusions?
   a. Attitude change is generally greater in response to an attractive communicator than an expert communicator.
   b. Attractiveness makes no difference in attitude change unless the communicator is expert to begin with.
   c. An attractive communicator is more effective when he or she expresses a desire to influence the audience with regard to the relevant issue, while the reverse is true for the expert communicator.
   d. An expert communicator is more effective when he or she expresses a desire to influence the audience with regard to the relevant issue, while the reverse is true for the attractive communicator.

Answer: d
Page: 87

21. All other things being equal, the overwhelming weight of experimental evidence on fear and persuasion suggests that, *in general*, the more frightened a person is by a communication:
   a. the more likely he or she is to come up with counterarguments that oppose the fear-arousing communication.
   b. the more likely he or she is to refuse to take positive, preventive action.
   c. the more likely he or she is to "go into denial" and refuse to listen to future communications on the same issue.
   d. the more likely he or she is to take positive, preventive action.

Answer: b
Page: 89

22. In a study by Leventhal, some students were exposed to a high-fear message regarding the importance of taking tetanus shots. Later, half of them were given specific instructions about where and when the shots were available, while the other half was not. Compared to the group that received instructions, students who did *not* receive them:
   a. displayed less favorable attitudes toward taking the shots.
   b. displayed equally favorable attitudes toward the shots, but were less likely to actually take the shots.
   c. displayed less favorable attitudes toward the shots, and were less likely to actually take the shots.
   d. were equally likely to take the shots, but only after a 2–day delay.

Answer: a
Page: 89–90

23. Generally, high-fear appeals are more effective than low-fear appeals in producing behavior change when:
    a. specific instructions are provided on how to avoid painful consequences.
    b. the issue is unimportant to the audience.
    c. the issue is moderately important to the audience.
    d. the audience is challenged to come up with their own plan for avoiding painful consequences.

Answer: b
Page: 89–90

24. The more frightened a person is by the communication, the more likely he or she is to take immediate preventive action. This statement:
    a. is true for most people.
    b. describes the way a person with high self-esteem might react to the message.
    c. describes the way a person with low self-esteem might react to the message.
    d. is false for most people.

Answer: c
Page: 89–90

25. According to research presented in the text, people with high self-esteem are most likely to be persuaded by campaigns using:
    a. low fear.
    b. moderate fear.
    c. high fear.
    d. all of the above are equally effective

Answer: c
Page: 89–90

26. Elizabeth, a high-school student who smokes cigarettes, saw a film in her health class that depicted horrible scenes of people dying from lung cancer. After class, a friend asked her whether the film had convinced her to quit smoking. Elizabeth said no. However, a few days later, she realized she did want to quit and decided to sign up for a program to help her stop smoking. Based on research on persuasion, what might you conclude?
   a. High-fear messages are based on the primacy effect.
   b. Elizabeth was distracted while watching the film.
   c. Elizabeth has low self-esteem.
   d. Elizabeth was experiencing the self-fulfilling prophecy.

Answer: c
Page: 89–90

27. In the case of people with low self-esteem, communications that arouse a great deal of fear tend to:
   a. be ineffective under all circumstances.
   b. be effective when accompanied by instructions regarding appropriate action.
   c. inhibit immediate action, but are effective after a delay.
   d. persuade the person to take immediate action.

Answer: a
Page: 89–91

28. Fear appeals seem to function best when:
   a. followed by clear recommendations for reducing arousal.
   b. the fear is extremely high.
   c. the fear cannot be reduced.
   d. recommendations offered produce an increase in arousal.

Answer: d
Page: 89–90

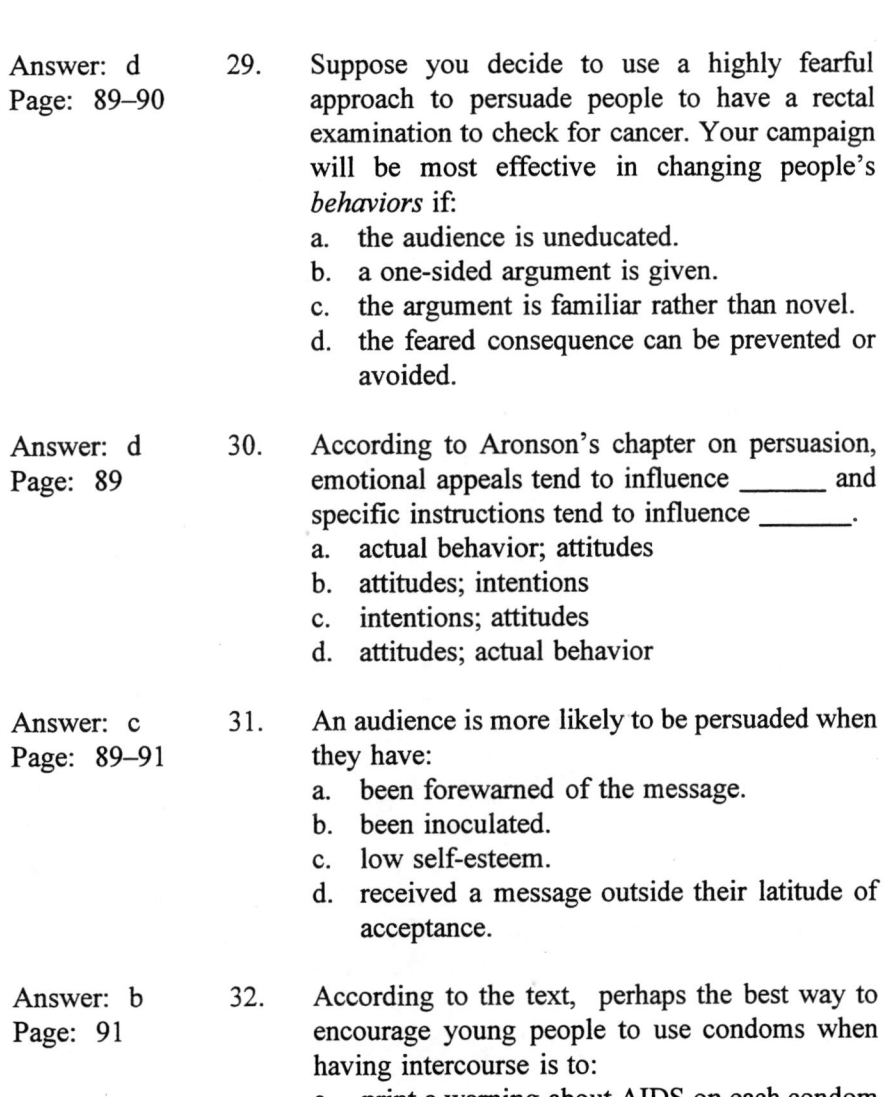

29. Suppose you decide to use a highly fearful approach to persuade people to have a rectal examination to check for cancer. Your campaign will be most effective in changing people's *behaviors* if:
    a. the audience is uneducated.
    b. a one-sided argument is given.
    c. the argument is familiar rather than novel.
    d. the feared consequence can be prevented or avoided.

Answer: d
Page: 89

30. According to Aronson's chapter on persuasion, emotional appeals tend to influence _____ and specific instructions tend to influence _____.
    a. actual behavior; attitudes
    b. attitudes; intentions
    c. intentions; attitudes
    d. attitudes; actual behavior

Answer: c
Page: 89–91

31. An audience is more likely to be persuaded when they have:
    a. been forewarned of the message.
    b. been inoculated.
    c. low self-esteem.
    d. received a message outside their latitude of acceptance.

Answer: b
Page: 91

32. According to the text, perhaps the best way to encourage young people to use condoms when having intercourse is to:
    a. print a warning about AIDS on each condom label.
    b. encourage people to think of condoms as part of erotic foreplay.
    c. present the startling statistics about how high the risk of AIDS is for young American heterosexuals.
    d. show explicit film footage of people dying from AIDS.

Answer: c
Page: 92–93

33. You are in the market for a new car and think you would like to own a Saab. According to research reported by Richard Nisbett and his associates, which of the following would be most likely to influence your decision?
   a. television commercials for Saab that are both informative and emotionally appealing
   b. print ads for Saab that are primarily informative
   c. hearing about the huge repair bills a neighbor's sister had on her Saab
   d. a high ranking made by *Consumer Reports* based on a sample of 75,000 miles of testing

Answer: c
Page: 92–93

34. Energy auditors were more successful in persuading homeowners to make improvements that would increase the energy-efficiency of their homes when:
   a. the auditors were expert and trustworthy.
   b. the auditors showed homeowners reports of how much money they would save if they made the improvements.
   c. the auditors used highly vivid language and examples when making their recommendations to homeowners.
   d. the auditors used a two-sided argument when making their recommendations.

Answer: a
Page: 93–94

35. A one-sided argument for why nuclear power should be discontinued would be more persuasive than a two-sided argument with which of the following groups?
   a. a local anti-nuke group
   b. a college physics class
   c. a group of soldiers who had been drafted into the Army
   d. the U.S. Department of Energy staff

Answer: b   36. Which of the following conditions tends to make a
Page: 93–94   one-sided argument *more* effective in persuading an
                       audience than a two-sided argument?
                       a. an intelligent and sophisticated audience
                       b. a relatively unintelligent and uninformed
                          audience
                       c. a very rational and unemotional audience
                       d. an audience which is initially opposed to the
                          speaker's argument

Answer: c   37. When is a two-sided message likely to be more
Page: 93–94   effective than a one-sided message?
                       a. when the position advocated falls within the
                          audience's latitude of acceptance
                       b. when the audience is poorly informed and in
                          general agreement with the source
                       c. when the audience is well-informed and in
                          general opposition to the position of the
                          source
                       d. when the position advocated falls in the
                          audience's latitude of rejection

Answer: a   38. Under certain conditions, a two-sided argument
Page: 93–94   may be more persuasive than a one-sided
                       argument because:
                       a. a well-informed audience is aware of both
                          sides of the issue and, thus, would tend to
                          perceive a one-sided argument as unfair or
                          biased.
                       b. all audiences appreciate hearing both sides of
                          a controversial issue.
                       c. an uninformed audience needs to hear both
                          sides of the issue before forming an opinion.
                       d. a one-sided argument would probably be
                          confusing to an uninformed audience.

Answer: b 39. Which of the following conditions tends to make
Page: 93–94 a one-sided argument *more* effective in
persuading an audience than a two-sided
argument?
a. a well-informed and sophisticated audience
b. a relatively uninformed audience
c. a very rational and unemotional audience
d. an audience which is initially opposed to the speaker's argument

Answer: c 40. Suppose you are trying to persuade an educated
Page: 95–96 audience that they should vote for you. Both you and your opponent will speak at a meeting the same day and the election will be held in two weeks. You should choose to speak _____ and give a _____ presentation.
a. first; one-sided
b. second; one-sided
c. first; two-sided
d. second; two-sided

Answer: a 41. According to Aronson, if you were to give one of
Page: 95–96 two persuasive speeches, you would choose to speak second if the time interval between the first and second speech were _____ and the time interval between the second speech and the audience's action were _____.
a. long; short
b. short; long
c. long; long
d. short; short

Answer: b　　　42.　Suppose you were running for office and were going to debate your opponent. If you both will present your arguments one right after the other and the election is still several days away, you should probably try to speak _____, in order to make use of the _____ effect.
Page: 95–96
　　　a.　second; recency
　　　b.　first; primacy
　　　c.　second; primacy
　　　d.　first; recency

Answer: d　　　43.　If you wanted to be sure that you had the opportunity to present your point of view first and hope that listeners stopped paying attention to the speakers who followed you, you would be trying to use to your advantage the influence of the:
Page: 95
　　　a.　recency effect.
　　　b.　inoculation effect.
　　　c.　foreplay effect.
　　　d.　primacy effect.

Answer: b　　　44.　In thinking about the relative importance of the primacy and recency effects, the most crucial variable is:
Page: 95
　　　a.　expertise.
　　　b.　time.
　　　c.　trustworthiness.
　　　d.　vividness.

Answer: b　　　45.　There appears to be a linear relationship between one's attitude change and the credibility of the source of the communication as long as:
Page: 100–102
　　　a.　the person has high self-esteem.
　　　b.　the message is within one's latitude of acceptance.
　　　c.　a primacy effect is operating.
　　　d.　the argument presents both sides of the issue.

Answer: a 46. According to Aronson, under which of the
Page: 102 following conditions of persuasive
communication would people's attitudes typically
change the most?
a. when an expert argues an extreme position
b. when a nonexpert argues an extreme position
c. when an expert argues a moderate position
d. when a nonexpert argues a moderate position

Answer: d 47. To change a person's attitude the most, a
Page: 101–102 communicator should present a position that is
highly distant or discrepant from the person's
initial position.
a. The statement is true.
b. The statement is false.
c. The statement is true only for low-credibility
communicators.
d. The statement is true only for high-credibility
communicators.

Answer: b 48. Assume a speaker has low credibility with the
Page: 102 audience. For maximum attitude change, how
discrepant from the audience's initial position
should the communication be?
a. not at all discrepant
b. moderately discrepant
c. highly discrepant
d. Discrepancy is not a significant factor if the
speaker has low credibility.

Answer: c 49. "Persuasive communications, if blatant or coercive, can be perceived as intruding upon one's freedom of choice, thereby activating a person's defenses to resist the messages." This statement reflects the central idea of which of the following theories or concepts?
Page: 103–104
a. reinforcement theory
b. the inoculation effect
c. reactance theory
d. the primacy effect

Answer: d 50. Martha's mother tells her that she is absolutely never to dye her hair a "funny color." Martha proceeds to dye her hair purple. Martha's behavior is best thought of as an example of:
Page: 103–104
a. the primacy effect.
b. the recency effect.
c. the inoculation effect.
d. reactance.

Answer: b 51. When a person is exposed to a watered-down attack upon his or her beliefs, this produces resistance to later persuasion because:
Page: 106
a. the person becomes bored with the topic.
b. the person gains some practice in defending his or her beliefs.
c. the person feels that he or she is not conforming to another's wishes.
d. None of the above is true, since prior exposure *decreases* resistance to later persuasion.

Answer: b 52. One way of *decreasing* the persuasibility of
Page: 106–107   members of an audience is:
    a. to feed them desirable food while someone is trying to persuade them.
    b. to forewarn them that someone is going to try to persuade them.
    c. to remind them that even though the speaker might be credible, he or she may not be trustworthy.
    d. to hide from them the fact that someone is going to try to persuade them.

Answer: b 53. McAlister's field experiment was successful in
Page: 106–107   helping seventh-graders resist peer pressure to smoke cigarettes. His strategy involved teaching students:
    a. how to be assertive and just say "no."
    b. a series of counterarguments they could use against peer pressure, such as, "I'd be a real chicken if I smoked just to impress you."
    c. how to educate their peers about the tremendous health risks involved in smoking.
    d. how to maintain high self-esteem, so they would be more resistant to peer pressure.

Answer: a 54. According to research by Gerbner and his
Page: 110–111   associates, heavy viewers of television are more likely than light viewers to:
    a. hold exaggerated views about the prevalence of violence in society.
    b. believe the police do an effective job of fighting crime and violence.
    c. hold less prejudiced attitudes toward women and racial minorities.
    d. be more easily persuaded by attractive communicators.

Answer: b   55. According to the analysis of "television
Page: 111–112   criminology" conducted by Craig Haney and
John Manzolati:
   a. television accurately portrays criminals as committing crimes because of psychopathology or insatiable greed, as happens in the real world.
   b. television tends to ignore situational pressures which lead to criminal activity.
   c. television police officers are portrayed as being about as effective as their real-world counterparts.
   d. heavy viewers of such crime shows tend to be more lenient and to believe in the presumption of innocence for the defendant.

Answer: a   56. The main way in which an attitude differs from
Page: 113–114   an opinion is that an attitude:
   a. includes an emotional component.
   b. is held for a briefer period of time.
   c. pertains to people, not just facts.
   d. is more resistant to change through persuasion.

Essay Questions

1. "The mass media exerts a powerful and pervasive impact on our attitudes and behavior—even if direct attempts at persuasion are not involved." Explain the meaning of this statement, and describe two pieces of research that support it.

2. In your own words, define and discuss the difference between education and propaganda. Why is it often true that, in real life, these two phenomena are difficult to distinguish? Provide an example of how information designed to educate might also serve as a subtle form of propaganda.

3. In accordance with the elaboration likelihood model, give an example of an advertisement using a central route strategy and one using a peripheral route strategy. What is the major feature that distinguishes between these two approaches?

4. What characteristics associated with the audience play a significant role in determining the impact of a persuasive communication? Why are they important? Support your reasoning by discussing the results of research involving audience characteristics.

5. Suppose you belonged to an antinuclear group that wanted to persuade an audience that the development of nuclear power plants should be curtailed. The audience is composed of relatively uninformed adults who are already somewhat in favor of nuclear power. Based on your readings on persuasion, what kind of message would you want to deliver? Would you give the speech yourself or, if not, what kind of speaker would you want to hire? Provide examples of relevant research to support your arguments.

6. Pretend you are a candidate for public office and you are planning to engage in a debate with your opponent. Given the choice, under what circumstances would you wish to speak first? Under what circumstances would you choose to speak last? Explain the reasoning behind your choices.

7. Compared to logical or rational appeals, how effective are persuasive communications that arouse a high level of fear? Under what conditions are fear-arousing messages most effective in influencing behavior? Under what conditions might they be less effective? Be sure to support your answer with examples of relevant research.

8. In general, how successful are obvious attempts to persuade? Under what special conditions are direct efforts to persuade more likely to succeed? Discuss one piece research that supports the notion that direct efforts to persuade are effective, and one that indicates that such efforts are relatively ineffective.

4

Social Cognition

I. How Do We Make Sense of the World?

   Are we rational thinkers? (Bentham; Kelley)
   Cognitive misers (Fiske & Taylor)

II. The Effects of Context on Social Judgment

   A. Reference points and contrast effects

      Decoys (Pratkanis)
      Attractiveness (Kenrick & Gutierres)

   B. Priming and construct accessibility

      Impression formation (Higgins, Rholes & Jones; Heath, et al.)
      Media exposure (McCombs & Shaw; Iyengar & Kinder)

   C. Framing the decision

      Gain and loss information (Kahneman & Tversky; Gonzales, Aronson, Gonzales & Costanzo; Meyerowitz & Chaiken)

   D. Ordering of information

      Primacy effect and first impressions (Asch; Jones; Aronson & Jones)

   E. The amount of information

      Dilution effect (Zukier)

III. Judgment Heuristics

    A. The representative heuristic (Tversky & Kahneman)

    B. The attitude heuristic (Pratkanis & Greenwald; Pratkanis)

    Halo effects
    False consensus effect (Ross et al.)

    C. When do we use heuristics?

IV. Categorization and Social Stereotypes

    A. Stereotypic knowledge and expectations (Darley & Gross)

    B. Illusory correlation (Hamilton & Rose)

    C. In-group/out-group effects (Park & Rothbart; Tajfel)

V. Reconstructive Memory

    Eye-witness testimony (Loftus)
    Memory and attitude change (Ross, McFarland & Fletcher)

VI. How Conservative Is Human Cognition?

    Confirmation bias (Snyder & Swann)
    Hindsight bias (Fischhoff)
    Pros and cons of cognitive conservatism

VII. How Do Attitudes and Beliefs Guide Behavior?

    A. The attitude-behavior relationship in our heads

    LaPiere's innkeepers
    Correspondent inferences (Jones; Jones & Harris)

    B. When do attitudes predict behavior?

        Attitude accessibility (Fazio; Fazio & Williams)

    C. Acting on perceptions (Herr)

VIII. Three possible biases in social explanation

    A. Fundamental attribution error (Bierbrauer; Ross, Amabile & Steinmetz)

    B. Actor-observer bias (Storms)

    C. The self-biases

        Egocentric thought (Jervis; Langer; Petty & Brock)
        Self-serving bias (Weary; Alloy & Abramson)

    D. value of self-biases (Grove, et al.; Taylor; Seligman)

Terms & Concepts

felicific calculus
naive scientist
consistency
consensus
distinctiveness
cognitive misers
contrast effects
priming
construct accessibility
decision framing
primacy effect
recency effect
attention decrement
interpretive set
dilution effect
heuristics

representative heuristic
attitude heuristic
halo effect
false consensus effect
categorization
illusory correlation
in-group/outgroup effects
minimum group paradigm
reconstructive memory
confirmation bias
hindsight bias
cognitive conservatism
attitude accessibility
fundamental attribution error
actor-observer bias
dispositional factors

situational factors
self-serving bias
illusion of control
Barnum statement
depressive realism

Chapter Overview

Social cognition refers to a broad class of processes and influences that affect how people make sense out of the social world. Under the right conditions, we are capable of behaving like scientists in our everyday thinking—seeking out and evaluating information in a systematic and rational manner. More commonly, however, our perceptions and judgments are subject to a variety of biases and other distorting influences. It is important to identify and understand these influences because, to a very large extent, our perceptions of the social world play a central role in determining our behavior. Key issues covered in the chapter are summarized below.

The "social context"—how things are presented and described—has a major impact on our perceptions and judgments of people and events. Kelley, for example, argues that people function as "naive scientists," evaluating information according to its consistency, consensus, and distinctiveness. Also, an object can strike us as better or worse, depending on the characteristics of the objects against which it is compared. This phenomenon, known as the contrast effect, is demonstrated in research showing that men were less attracted to a potential blind date after viewing a television program (*Charlie's Angels*) that featured three glamorous actresses.

One way that people cope with the enormous amount of information they encounter in everyday life is through the use of heuristics, which provide a short-cut method for processing information. Requiring very little thought, heuristics are simple—but often only approximate—strategies for solving problems. One commonly used heuristic is the halo effect, in which a favorable or unfavorable impression of a person colors our future expectations and inferences about that person. Another heuristic is the false consensus effect, which involves the tendency to overestimate the percentage of people who agree with us on a given issue.

Our perceptions, judgments, and behavior are strongly influenced by the categories we use to define and interpret events and people. Categorization has particularly important consequences when it involves the use of stereotypes. Once we have categorized a person according to a stereotype, our perceptions of that person's behavior, as well as our expectations regarding future interactions, will tend to be consistent with the stereotype. As a result, we are unlikely to process information that contradicts our stereotypes—a tendency which reinforces prejudiced beliefs and behavior.

Human memory is primarily reconstructive in nature. Our recollections do not reflect a literal translation of past events; rather, we recreate many of our memories from bits and pieces of what we can recall, as well as our beliefs and expectations about what should have been. Research on eyewitness testimony offers a compelling demonstration of the real-world implications of reconstructive memory. For example, the use of "leading questions" by interrogators can seriously distort a witness's memory of the facts regarding a crime, leading to erroneous conclusions on the part of those who must weigh the evidence in a given case.

Human cognition tends to be highly conservative. That is, people have a strong tendency to preserve their pre-existing knowledge, beliefs, attitudes, and hypotheses. One important benefit of this tendency is that it allows us to perceive the social world as a coherent and stable place. However, as many of the findings presented in the chapter demonstrate, cognitive conservatism can often cause a person to distort events or miss important information. One strategy for avoiding these negative consequences is to try to think of persons and important events as unique, rather than automatically assigning them to a salient category. Another is to remain vigilant regarding our vulnerability to cognitive biases, realizing that, in any particular situation, we may be mistaken in our perceptions and judgments of a person or event.

What is the relationship between beliefs and behavior? Research indicates that a person's attitudes often are not a good predictor of his or her behavior, even though our intuitions suggest otherwise. In part, the common perception that attitudes do correspond with behavior stems from the fundamental attribution error—the tendency to attribute the cause of an individual's behavior to his or her stable personality traits, rather than to situational influences. Certain conditions do, however, increase the probability of attitude-behavior consistency. One of these is attitude accessibility, or the relative ease with which a relevant attitude comes to mind when we encounter an opportunity to act on it.

Cognitive biases involving the self play a major role in allowing us to fulfill an important psychological goal: maintaining and enhancing our view of ourselves. These self-biases include egocentric thought, which involves perceiving the self as more central to events than it actually is. Another is the self-serving bias, which refers to our tendency to make dispositional attributions for our successes, while attributing our failures to situational factors. Although such biases reflect a distorted view of the self, they can play a vital role in psychological health and functioning. For example, the tendency to take responsibility for successes, but not failures, may protect a person from becoming discouraged while pursuing a goal requiring great effort and persistence. Conversely, research has revealed that depressed individuals are not subject to the self-serving bias; rather, their more accurate way of seeing the world leaves them "sadder but wiser."

Lecture Ideas & Teaching Suggestions

How Decisions are Framed. The importance of context in determining how information about the social world is perceived and interpreted is a major issue addressed in Chapter 4. The impact of seemingly minor changes in the way information is presented can be demonstrated in the classroom by using the decision framing example from the Kahneman and Tversky experiment (discussed on pages 129–130 in *The Social Animal*). In this procedure, subjects are asked to choose between two programs for combating an epidemic illness which could kill 600 people unless measures are taken to curb its impact. The programs are presented in two different ways: one that emphasizes the potential for the LOSS of lives, and one in which the information is framed in terms of a given program's potential to SAVE lives. Although, regardless of wording, the respective impact of each program is identical, the majority of subjects tend to reject the program that appears to entail greater loss of life.

To replicate this effect with your students, you will need to give half the class the opportunity to choose between Program A and B as they are presented in Version 1, with the remaining students choosing between the two programs presented in Version 2 (see paragraphs below). A convenient way to do this is to copy both versions on a single sheet of paper, placing one on the top half and the other on the bottom half. The sheets can then be cut in half and randomly distributed to the class, such that each student receives only one version.

VERSION 1 If Program A is adopted, two hundred people will be saved. If Program B is adopted, there is a one-third probability that six hundred people will be saved and a two-thirds probability that no people will be saved.

VERSION 2 If Program A is adopted, four hundred people will die. If Program B is adopted, there is a one-third probability that nobody will die and a two-thirds probability that six hundred people will die.

As with Kahneman and Tversky's subjects, most of the students who received Version 1 should choose Program A; while those who received Version 2 should show a strong preference for Program B. According to Kahneman and Tversky, the power of decision framing in this example stems from the fact that people are more threatened by the idea of losing something than they are by the possibility of gain. In explaining this effect to your students, you may also wish to point out its practical implications, which are demonstrated in the energy conservation study by Gonzales, Aronson, and Costanzo (discussed on pages 130–131). (NOTE: This demonstration should be conducted before students have read Chapter 4. For maximum impact, you may wish to collect students' responses a week or so prior to assigning the chapter, saving the results until you are ready to cover this topic in lecture.)

Attributions for Success and Failure. If you would like to explore the topic of attribution theory in greater depth, you may wish to discuss Weiner's work on attributions regarding success and failure. According to his model, people focus on two major dimensions in attempting to explain the reasons for another person's success or failure at a given task. The first consists of an internal/external dimension, which is similar to the distinction between dispositional and situational attributions for a behavior. The second dimension consists of the distinction between stable and temporary causes of behavior. These two independent dimensions, when combined in various ways, lead to different conclusions about a person's performance as well as different predictions regarding future behavior. For example, confronted with the fact that Ellen received an A on her social psychology exam, we might variously attribute her performance to: 1) stable/internal causes—she is highly intelligent; 2) stable/external causes—the exam was very easy; 3) temporary/internal causes—she put a great deal of effort in studying for the exam; or 4) temporary/external causes—she was very lucky. The kinds of attributions we make will have important consequences for our predictions about Ellen's future performance. Thus, if we believe Ellen succeeded because she is highly intelligent, we are likely to expect her to do well on future exams. On the other hand, if we believe Ellen succeeded primarily because she studied hard (a less stable cause), our predictions would be less certain, since other factors could prevent her from being equally diligent when preparing for exams in the future. In addition to affecting our predictions, our attributions will influence the kind of treatment we believe a person deserves as a result of his or her performance. For example, if Ellen had failed the exam because she was sick, her instructor would probably be more willing to let her take a make-up exam than if she had failed simply because she hadn't studied hard enough. Similarly, we tend to believe that people deserve greater rewards when their success is due to internal factors, such as effort and ability, rather than to luck or other external factors.

More information about Weiner's model, as well as its implications for achievement motivation, can be found in: Weiner, B., Frieze, I., Kukla, A., Reed, L., Rest, S. & Rosenbaum, R.M. (1972). Perceiving the causes of success and failure. In E.E. Jones, D.E. Kanouse, H.H. Kelley, R.E. Nisbett, S. Valins, and B. Weiner (Eds.), *Attribution: Perceiving the causes of behavior*. Morristown, NJ: General Learning Press; and Weiner, B. (1974). *Achievement motivation and attribution theory*. Morristown, NJ: General Learning Press.

Social Cognition and Depression. The interface between social cognition and the fields of clinical and health psychology offers a number of interesting possibilities for lecture material. For example, the application of findings from social-cognition research has improved understanding and treatment of the problem of depression. Work in this area indicates that depressed individuals are typically caught in a vicious cycle of negative thinking, which leads to self-defeating behavior, which leads to negative experiences, which increase negative thinking, and so forth. Cognitive therapies for breaking this cycle involve various strategies for modifying negative thought patterns. One such method is called "attributional style therapy," which involves teaching depressed persons to make attributions that are more typical of nondepressed persons—such as taking credit for success experiences, and focussing on situational factors that contribute to failure. A useful source information on this form of therapy, as well as other cognitive approaches to clinical issues, may be found in Abramson, L.Y. (1988). *Social cognition and clinical psychology: A synthesis*. New York: Guilford. In addition, Taylor (1989) discusses the value of self-biases and other "positive illusions" in maintaining psychological and physical well-being (see additional readings for this chapter).

Projects and Discussion Topics

1. PROJECT: The "contrast effect" involves the tendency for evaluations of an object to reflect the context within which the object is presented. Using friends and acquaintances as subjects, you can try to demonstrate this effect by conducting a modified replication of Kenrick and Gutierres' experiment (in which a "blind date" was seen as less attractive when young men evaluated her after, as opposed to before, viewing a TV show featuring three glamorous actresses—see page 125).

    First, you will need to find photos of THREE very attractive men, and photos of THREE unattractive men. Then, find a photo of ONE moderately attractive man to serve as the "target" photo.

    [HINT: Use photos of men whom your "subjects" are unlikely to know, and try to keep extraneous factors—such as age and style of dress—relatively constant for all photos. Good sources for photos are high school or college yearbooks (you can make photocopies), and magazine or newspaper articles that are accompanied by a "mug shot" of the person featured in the article. Also, it's a good idea to use only female subjects for your study.]

The procedure involves having the subject look at only one of the two series of photos: Group A, which contains the three unattractive photos plus the "target" photo; and Group B, which contains the "target" photo and the three highly attractive photos. In each group of photos, put the target photo last, and assign the other three photos to the first, second and third positions in the series. (Keep the order of the photos constant for all subjects.) After assigning the subject to group A or B, ask her to examine the photos from that group. Next, for each of the four photos, ask her: "How physically attractive is this person?" For each photo, have the subject indicate her rating on a 1–7 scale (1 = very unattractive, 7 = very attractive). Use this procedure on at least 10 subjects, working things out so that roughly half of your subjects view Group A, with the other half viewing Group B.

To determine your results, figure out the average rating of the "target" photo from subjects in Group A and compare it to the average rating of the "target" photo from subjects in Group B. Is there at least a 1–point difference in the ratings? If so, is it in the predicted direction—that is, did subjects in Group A, on average, rate the "target" photo as more attractive, compared to subjects in Group B? If so, you have demonstrated the contrast effect, showing that the same photo was rated as less attractive when seen in the context of photos of more highly attractive men. Whatever your results, bring a report of your findings to class and be prepared to discuss them.

2. PROJECT: Search through newspapers and magazines for "advice" columns in which people ask for help with personal problems or discuss their experiences and insights about life. Collect several examples and conduct an analysis of the kinds of attributions people make when discussing their own behavior and the behavior of others. Also, examine the attributions contained in the columnist's responses. In performing your analysis, draw upon your knowledge of attributional biases discussed in Chapter 4. For example, be on the look out for illustrations of the fundamental attribution error, attributions based on stereotypes, the actor-observer bias, the self-serving bias, etc. Bring your examples to class and give a report of your investigation.

3. PROJECT: With a little help from your friends, you can do an informal demonstration of Asch's "primacy effect on impression

formation." Tell your friend you are going to describe a person and that, following the description, you want him or her to tell you how much they think they would like this person—based on a 1 (not at all) to 10 (very much) scale. For half of your "subjects," use description A: "Steve is intelligent, industrious, impulsive, critical, stubborn, and envious." For the other half, use description B: "Steve is envious, stubborn, critical, impulsive, industrious, and intelligent." (Note: Be sure not to read the adjectives too rapidly.) Compare the average ratings from Description A and Description B. Did you find a tendency for people to prefer Steve as portrayed in Description A? Share your findings with your classmates.

4. DISCUSSION: Social psychologists have noted that people tend to behave in accordance with their social roles—acting differently in different situations, depending on which "role" the situation demands. Thus, one reason we often perceive other people's behavior as stemming from their stable personality traits is that we usually see them in only one role—say, as a friend or teacher.

Looking at your own behavior, are you the "same" person with all the different people in your life? Make a list of several of the social roles you occupy—for example, friend, son/daughter, brother/sister, wife/husband, student, worker, romantic partner, etc. Next, list some of the persons who typically "see" you in one of these different roles, but not all of the others. If these people all got together to discuss what kind of person you are and how you usually act, would they completely agree in their assessments of you? If not, how might their perceptions of you differ? To what extent are you aware of behaving differently in different situations?

Finally, try to recall an occasion or two when someone you knew fairly well seemed to be acting "out of character"—that is, in a manner that was at odds with your customary notion of his or her personality. How did you react to this "inconsistent" behavior? Did it surprise you? Looking back, can you think of possible situational factors or role requirements that might account for this person's behavior? Compare your observations and experiences with others in your discussion group.

Additional Readings

Fiske, S. & Taylor, S.E. (1984). *Social cognition.* Reading, MA: Addison-Wesley.

Fowler, R.D. (Ed.). (1994). *American Psychologist, 49,* 439–445. (Six commentaries on Loftus' 1993 article.)

Harvey, J.H. & Weary, G. (1985). *Attribution: Basic issues and applications.* New York: Academic Press.

Lindsay, D.S. (1993). Eyewitness suggestibility. *Current Directions in Psychological Science, 2,* (3), 86–89.

Loftus, E. (1993). The reality of repressed memories. *American Psychologist, 48,* 518–537.

Loftus, E.F. (1979, May–June). The malleability of human memory. *American Scientist,* pp. 312–320. (How subsequent information can distort memory for an event and the implications of this phenomenon for theory and research on memory processes.)

Loftus, E.L. (1992). When a lie becomes memory's truth: Memory distortion after exposure to misinformation. *Current Directions in Psychological Science, 1,* (4), 121–123.

Messick, D.M. & Asuncion, A.G. (1993). The Will Rogers illusion in judgments about social groups. *Psychological Science, 4,* (1), 46–48.

Offir, C.W. (1975, April). Floundering in fallacy: Seven ways to kid yourself. *Psychology Today,* pp. 66–68. (Covers common errors in human thinking.)

Perlmutter, L.C. & Monty, R.A. (1977). The importance of perceived control: Fact or fantasy? *American Scientist, 65,* pp. 759–765. (A review of experimental evidence regarding the benefits of the "illusion of control" for performance and well-being.)

Rubin, D.C. (1975, September). The subtle deceiver: Recalling your past. *Psychology Today*, pp. 38–46. (Current beliefs have a distorting impact on how we remember the details of our personal past.)

Slovic, P., Fischhoff, B. & Lichtenstein, S. (1980, June). Risky assumptions. *Psychology Today*, pp. 44–48. (Offers several examples of problems posed by errors in human thinking and judgment.)

Snyder, C.R. (1985, September). Excuses, excuses. *Psychology Today*, pp. 50–55. (Discusses self-protective attributions and other strategies people use to sustain a positive self-image.)

Taylor, S.E. (1989). *Positive illusions: Creative self-deception and the healthy mind.* New York: Basic Books.

Multiple-Choice Questions

Answer: a
Page: 120

1. Jane is trying to decide whether she should marry Jim. She sits down with a piece of paper and makes a list of all the positive aspects about marrying Jim, and then a list of all the negative aspects. After looking at both lists, she can see that the good things outweigh the bad. So, she calls Jim up and says, "OK, let's set a date for the wedding!" Jane's way of making up her mind is an example of:
   a. felicific calculus.
   b. using "distinctiveness" information in making a decision.
   c. decisional framing.
   d. the contrast effect.

Answer: b   2. Judy decides to withdraw from her psychology
Page: 120   class because she believes she must drop one of
                 the classes she is taking, and the psychology
                 class is the most boring and meets at 8:00 a.m.,
                 a time of day during which she would rather
                 sleep. Judy's behavior is best thought of as an
                 example of:
                 a. the halo effect.
                 b. felicific calculus.
                 c. the actor-observer bias.
                 d. the fundamental attribution error.

Answer: d   3. Harold Kelley's view of social cognition is that
Page: 120   people attempt to function as:
                 a. cost accountants.
                 b. cost-benefit analysts.
                 c. amateur social psychologists.
                 d. naive scientists.

Answer: c   4. According to Kelley, people look for which of
Page: 120–121   the following kinds of information in explaining
                 behavior?
                 a. continuity, consensus, and distinctiveness.
                 b. contiguity, consensus, and distinctiveness.
                 c. consistency, consensus, and distinctiveness.
                 d. consistency, covariation, and distinctiveness.

Answer: c
Page: 120–121

5. Richard asked his friend John if he could borrow $15 to buy his girlfriend a birthday present. John replied, "No problem. Are you sure you don't need more? Here, take $20." In attempting to explain this event, you consider the fact that a) John isn't wealthy; b) John doesn't often lend money to friends; and c) Richard was turned down earlier by two friends who didn't lend him the money. Based on Kelley's theory of how we use covariation information, which of the following conclusions would you be most likely to draw?
   a. John is a very generous person.
   b. John is the kind of person who can't manage his money.
   c. John really likes Richard.
   d. Richard is the kind of person who brings out generosity in others.

Answer: c
Page: 120–121

6. Suppose you notice that Fred becomes very embarrassed when the subject of knives comes up. In fact, he is the only person you have ever seen react in this way when you talk about knives, and he has never before expressed any concern about knives. According to Kelley, Fred's behavior is very high in:
   a. consistency.
   b. consensus.
   c. distinctiveness.
   d. reactance.

Answer: c
Page: 121–122

7. Kelley sees social cognition as a more _____ process: Aronson argues it is more _____.
   a. logical; logical
   b. illogical; illogical
   c. logical; illogical
   d. illogical; logical

Answer: c
Page: 122

8. The term "cognitive miser" refers to our tendency:
   a. to meticulously count up all the pros and cons of a particular decision.
   b. to expect others to do our thinking for us.
   c. to take shortcuts in processing complex information.
   d. to put self-interest over the interests of others when processing information.

Answer: d
Page: 125

9. Jill is in the market to buy a used car. She visits a car lot and tells the salesperson she is looking for something under $4,000. The salesperson first shows her a car that has very high mileage, a dented fender, and needs a new clutch. The asking price is $3,700. Shocked, Jill wonders, "Who on earth would pay that much for this piece of junk?" The salesperson then shows her a much nicer car—in fact, one that she thinks would suit her needs perfectly. Jill really needs to get a car as soon as possible, so she decides to buy it right then and there—even though it costs $4,800. Jill's decision has been influenced by:
   a. the representativeness heuristic.
   b. the availability heuristic.
   c. the context effect.
   d. the contrast effect.

Answer: c
Page: 125–126

10. Suppose you are ready to buy your textbooks for your first semester in college. You are unsure as to how much these books will cost, and when your bill is rung up at the register, the total is $200. According to the context effect, you will more likely think that the books are a bargain if the person ahead of you in line:
    a. pays $150 for her books.
    b. pays $200 for her books.
    c. pays $400 for her books.
    d. finds a mistake in her bill.

Answer: b
Page: 125

11. In an experiment by Kenrick and Gutierres, male college students were asked to evaluate a potential blind date before or after watching the television show *Charlie's Angels* (which features three glamorous actresses). Compared to subjects who rated the blind date before watching the show, those who gave their ratings *after* the show:
   a. found her more attractive, due to the halo effect.
   b. found her less attractive, due to the contrast effect.
   c. found her equally attractive, due to the consensus effect.
   d. found her less attractive, but only if they themselves were highly attractive—due to the availability heuristic.

Answer: d
Page: 125

12. If you were a young woman and were about to go out with a male blind date, you should hope that he has just been watching a movie that starred:
   a. attractive men.
   b. unattractive men.
   c. attractive women.
   d. unattractive women.

Answer: d
Page: 127

13. Aronson argues that recently activated or frequently activated concepts are more likely to readily come to mind and thus be used in interpreting social events. This phenomenon is called:
   a. context effects.
   b. reactance.
   c. heuristics.
   d. priming.

Answer: c
Page: 127–129

14. The effects of category priming on social judgment are illustrated by the tendency:
    a. for "gain" information to be more influential than "loss" information.
    b. for "loss" information to be more influential than "gain" information.
    c. for the public to see as most important those social and political issues that receive the most media coverage.
    d. for people to base their first impressions of another person on inaccurate information.

Answer: b
Page: 128

15. Heath and her colleagues asked a group of physicians to imagine themselves being exposed to the AIDS virus while working. A similar group of physicians received no such instruction. Heath's major result was that, compared to physicians who had not imagined exposure to AIDS, those who had imagined being exposed were more likely to:
    a. actually get AIDS.
    b. believe they were at a higher risk for getting AIDS.
    c. be extra careful with procedures that posed an AIDS risk.
    d. refuse to treat AIDS patients and those infected with HIV.

Answer: a
Page: 128–129

16. Iyengar and Kinder conducted a study in which subjects watched specially edited news programs for a week. Generalizing from their results, if you wanted to have college students focus on the issue that tuition is too expensive, you would:
   a. run articles in each issue of the college newspaper, thereby keeping the issue in front of the students.
   b. present the tuition issue in a high-fear campaign.
   c. present the issue only in one or two early issues, thereby depending on the primacy effect.
   d. link tuition-setting to corruption in the President's office, thereby using the halo effect.

Answer: c
Page: 129–130

17. John, a car salesman, is trying to persuade a customer to trade in his gas-guzzling, 8-cylinder car for a new 6–cylinder model. So he says to his customer, "Think of all the extra money you'll have if you buy this fuel-efficient model!" According to Kahneman and Tversky, John's sales pitch would be much improved if he had said:
   a. "Not only is this model fuel-efficient—it has a great safety record, too!"
   b. "Look at this article by *Consumer Report*. No other model in its class gets this kind of mileage on the freeway!"
   c. "Think of all the money you're losing on that gas-guzzler—dollar bills are flying right out of the exhaust pipe every time you drive!"
   d. "Buying this fuel-efficient model is a good way to show your concern for the environment!"

Answer: b 18. Aronson reports the results of an experiment in
Page: 130–131 which people who were asked to insulate their
homes were given information either about how
much money they would save, if they insulated,
or lose, if they didn't insulate. Based on results
of this study, if you were trying to sell insulation,
you would be wise to:
a. emphasize how much is saved by insulating.
b. emphasize how much is lost by not insulating.
c. emphasize both savings and losses, based on the halo effect.
d. emphasize neither savings or losses, since money is not something people are reluctant to discuss.

Answer: d 19. Asch's study on the primacy effect on impression
Page: 132 formation indicates that:
a. positive information is more influential than negative information in determining overall impressions of another person.
b. negative information is more influential than positive information in determining overall impressions of another person.
c. first impressions are usually more accurate than impressions based on later information.
d. information received first is more influential than later information in determining overall impressions of another person.

Answer: a 20. You are a college professor grading the exams of
Page: 132   students in your class. Student A and Student B
               both got 25 correct out of a total of 40 multiple-
               choice questions. However, Student A got the
               first 15 items correct, but missed 10 out of the
               last 25 items. Student B, on the other hand, got
               the first 15 items wrong, but had correct answers
               for the last 25 questions. According to research
               by Jones and his colleagues, what kind of
               impression would you be likely to have of these
               students?
               a. Student A is smarter than Student B.
               b. Student B is smarter than Student A.
               c. Student A and Student B are equally
                  intelligent.
               d. Student A became overconfident while taking
                  the exam, while Student B started off
                  insecure but gained confidence over time.

Answer: a 21. Suppose you are planning to take a class from a
Page: 132   professor about whom you know nothing. Just
               before class starts, a friend of yours describes the
               professor as inflexible, wordy, an easy grader,
               and kind to students. If the primacy effect is
               operating, you are most likely to think of the
               professor as:
               a. inflexible.
               b. wordy.
               c. an easy grader.
               d. kind to students.

Answer: b　　22.　Which of the following explanations have been offered to account for research findings on the *primacy* effect in impression formation?
Page: 133
　　a.　the latter items on a list receive more attention and, thus, have more impact on judgment.
　　b.　the first items on a list create an initial impression that is then used to interpret subsequent information.
　　c.　the first items on a list have a "priming effect" on subsequent items.
　　d.　the latter items on the list are more easily remembered than the first items.

Answer: a　　23.　The attention decrement explanation attempts to explain the basis for which of the following?
Page: 133
　　a.　the primacy effect
　　b.　the illusory correlation
　　c.　the hindsight bias
　　d.　the contrast effect

Answer: b　　24.　The tendency for neutral or irrelevant information to weaken a judgment or impression is referred to as:
Page: 134
　　a.　the priming effect.
　　b.　the dilution effect.
　　c.　the primacy effect.
　　d.　the halo effect.

Answer: b
Page: 134

25. A politician running for re-election is suspected of having misused campaign funds during the last election. Based on the "dilution effect," he or she can reduce the impact of this negative public image by:
   a. appearing in ads designed to defend his or her good character.
   b. appearing in ads that include irrelevant information—such as a story about his or her childhood.
   c. appearing in ads that cast doubt on the honesty of his or her opponent.
   d. appearing in ads with film or TV celebrities who believe in his or her innocence and will say so on camera.

Answer: a
Page: 135

26. One way that we make sense out of the vast and dizzying array of information that comes our way is through the use of heuristics, which are
   a. simple, but often only approximate, rules for solving problems.
   b. simple, but highly accurate, rules for solving problems.
   c. complex, but often only approximate, rules for solving problems.
   d. complex, but highly accurate, rules for solving problems.

Answer: b 27. You and a friend are visiting a new city and
Page: 135 would like to splurge and go out for a fine meal.
You look at the restaurant listings in the
newspaper and find one that is very expensive.
Your friend says, "Let's go for it. With prices
like that, we're bound to have an incredible
dining experience." In making her decision, your
friend most likely was guided by:
a. the "priming" effect.
b. the representative heuristic.
c. the contrast effect.
d. the primacy effect.

Answer: d 28. John is described as being introverted, shy,
Page: 135–136 logical, hard-working, not much fun, very
intelligent, and having a weird sense of humor.
These characteristics match your stereotype of
accountants. If you are asked whether John is
more likely to be an accountant or a salesman,
you are very sure he must be an accountant. This
result is predicted from:
a. the contrast effect.
b. the primacy effect.
c. the attitude heuristic.
d. the representative heuristic.

Answer: d 29. The representative heuristic helps to explain why,
Page: 137–138 in some instances, we tend to base our judgments
of other people on:
a. a careful consideration of their individual
characteristics.
b. their actual behavior, even when it conflicts
with their personalities.
c. how well they have treated us, or others, in
the past.
d. stereotypes regarding their gender, race,
appearance, etc.

Answer: d   30. Elizabeth, a literature major, believes that the author James Joyce was the most brilliant writer since Shakespeare. A friend asks her if Joyce had positive attitudes about women, or whether he was very sexist. Elizabeth has no knowledge whatsoever about Joyce's private life. Based on the attitude heuristic, which of the following responses would Elizabeth be likely to give?
Page: 138–139
   a. "He was probably a real sexist—most men of his time were."
   b. "I'm not sure. When I read his biography, I'll let you know."
   c. "If he was sexist, he was probably only conforming to the norms of his time."
   d. "No—he couldn't have been a sexist. I'm sure of it."

Answer: b   31. Suppose Pat believes that President Clinton is a wonderful President and Mike believes he has gross deficiencies. Both are asked to assess the truth of these two statements: A. President Clinton has had many lurid affairs with a wide variety of women, including several members of his staff; and B. President Clinton, although admitting to an extramarital affair early in his life, has since that time remained a faithful husband. Based on the attitude heuristic, we would predict that Pat would believe _____ to be true and Mike would believe _____ to be true.
Page: 138–139
   a. statement A; statement B
   b. statement B; statement A
   c. neither A nor B; neither A nor B
   d. none of the above since the attitude heuristic does not apply to this example

Answer: a　　32.　The false consensus effect implies that we:
Page: 139–140
　　a. overestimate the number of people who agree with us.
　　b. underestimate the number of people who agree with us.
　　c. rely too heavily on the primacy effect.
　　d. don't rely heavily enough on the primacy effect.

Answer: d　　33.　The tendency to overestimate the percentage of other people who agree with us on a given issue is referred to as:
Page: 139–140
　　a. the conformity bias.
　　b. the representativeness heuristic.
　　c. the hindsight bias.
　　d. the false consensus effect.

Answer: c　　34.　The halo effect occurs when:
Page: 139
　　a. we like a person whose attitudes are similar to our own.
　　b. we gain a favorable impression of a person who reminds us of someone we already know and like.
　　c. a favorable or unfavorable impression of someone biases our future expectations and inferences about that person.
　　d. we like a person whose actions make us look good.

Answer: c　　35.　Suppose you see Mary do very poorly on a classroom test. From this you conclude that Mary is not only stupid, but also has few friends, a poor personality, a difficult family life, and a hard time in everything she does. You have committed an error called:
Page: 139
　　a. the primacy effect.
　　b. the context effect.
　　c. the halo effect.
　　d. the attitude heuristic.

Answer: d 36. Under which of the following conditions are we
Page: 140   least likely to use heuristics in making decisions
               about social events?
               a. when we are overloaded with information
               b. when the decisions are not very important
               c. when we have little information to use in
                  making the decision
               d. when we have plenty of time to make the
                  decision

Answer: a 37. Which of the following words comes closest in
Page: 142   meaning to "category."
               a. stereotype
               b. heuristic
               c. halo effect
               d. illusory correlation

Answer: b   38. In a study by Darley and Gross, in which
Page: 142–143   subjects were exposed to different stories about
                   a fourth-grader named "Hannah," the effects of
                   stereotypes on social judgment were apparent
                   when:
                   a. Hannah was depicted as coming from a poor
                      background.
                   b. Hannah's performance on an achievement
                      test was ambiguous, *and* she was also
                      depicted as coming from a poor background.
                   c. Hannah's performance on an achievement
                      test indicated low ability.
                   d. Hannah was depicted as not trying hard to
                      achieve.

Answer: b   39. In informal surveys, people consistently overestimate the extent to which Lesbians are likely to contract the AIDS virus—when, in fact, Lesbians have the lowest rate of HIV infection, compared to male homosexuals and heterosexual men and women. This example illustrates:
Page: 143–144
   a. the false consensus effect.
   b. illusory correlation.
   c. in-group favoritism.
   d. the attitude heuristic.

Answer: a   40. One of the most common ways of categorizing people is to divide the world up into two groups—the in-group (one's own group) and the out-group. This tendency leads to:
Page: 144
   a. the perception that one's own group is "better" and more deserving than the out-group.
   b. the perception that greater similarity exists among members of the out-group, than among members of one's own group.
   c. a primacy effect when dealing with in-group members and a recency effect when dealing with out-group members.
   d. a primacy effect when dealing with out-group members and a recency effect when dealing with in-group members.

Answer: a   41. In Tajfel's research (in which subjects are randomly assigned to Group X or Group W) subjects who are total strangers, but who share the same meaningless label, tend to:
Page: 144–145
   a. express greater liking for, and allocate more rewards to, others in their own group.
   b. compete against members of their own group—as a form of "sibling rivalry."
   c. perceive greater similarity among members of their own group than among members of the other group.
   d. fabricate elaborate reasons to explain why they feel a sense of "belonging" to their own group.

Answer: b   42. Loftus conducted a study in which subjects saw
Page: 146–147   a film clip of a car accident. Some subjects were
                     asked about how the cars "hit" each other and
                     others were asked about how they "smashed into"
                     each other. The main result of this study was that
                     subjects who were asked about how the cars "hit"
                     were more likely to:
                     a. refuse to answer.
                     b. estimate a lower rate of speed for the cars.
                     c. rely extensively on stereotypes.
                     d. experience cognitive dissonance.

Answer: b   43. Research on social cognition indicates that human
Page: 146–148   memory:
                     a. is a literal translation of past events.
                     b. is reconstructed from bits of information that
                        we recall, as well as our expectations about
                        what should have been.
                     c. functions according to the "cognitive miser"
                        principle.
                     d. operates very much like a computer program.

Answer: a   44. Research by Loftus on eye-witness testimony has
Page: 146–147   revealed that:
                     a. "leading" questions can distort both a
                        witness's memory and his or her judgments
                        of the facts in a given case.
                     b. conformity pressures created in the
                        courtroom lead witnesses to say whatever
                        they think is expected of them.
                     c. "leading questions" are confusing to
                        witnesses, which makes them change their
                        testimony.
                     d. the courtroom atmosphere makes witnesses
                        nervous, which leads to memory deficits and
                        distorted testimonies.

Answer: a
Page: 148

45. The main point of the Ross, McFarland and Fletcher article that studied attitudes about bathing and teeth brushing was that:
   a. attitudes we hold can influence how we remember our own behavior.
   b. we generally see ourselves as having better attitudes but worse behaviors than our friends.
   c. we generally see ourselves as having worse attitudes but better behaviors than our friends.
   d. people can be persuaded to bathe and brush their teeth if they can be convinced that bathing and teeth brushing are beneficial to them.

Answer: b
Page: 150

46. The confirmation bias refers to the human tendency:
   a. to believe that other people share our views.
   b. to verify our pre-existing knowledge, hypotheses, and beliefs.
   c. to perceive persons or events that are similar on one dimension as being similar in all other dimensions.
   d. to find "loss" information more compelling than "gain" information.

Answer: a
Page: 151

47. Although Alex had no idea who would win a particular football game, after the game was over he claimed to have been "99% certain" that the winning team would be victorious. Alex's behavior is best thought of as an example of:
   a. the hindsight bias.
   b. priming.
   c. the representativeness heuristic.
   d. a context effect.

Answer: c
Page: 152

48. According to Greenwald, a positive feature of cognitive conservatism is that:
    a. it keeps inaccurate information from influencing our realistic and well-established categories for understanding the world.
    b. it helps us to make decisions in a rational and efficient manner.
    c. it allows us to perceive the social world as a stable, coherent place.
    d. it helps us to remain open to new information that will enhance our functioning in the world.

Answer: b
Page: 153

49. LaPierre conducted a study in the 1930s in which he wrote to restaurants and hotels to ask if they would allow Chinese people to eat or sleep there. He later visited these same establishments with Chinese friends and observed whether or not the friends were served. His results showed that about _____ percent of the places said they would not serve Chinese and that in reality about _____ percent of them actually did serve the Chinese.
    a. 90; less than 1
    b. less than 1; 90
    c. 50; 50
    d. 60; 40

Answer: b
Page: 155

50. Tom explains his wife's success in her job as being the result of her intelligence and determination, thus explaining her behavior in terms of her traits that are like the behavior. The text would consider Tom's explanation to be an example of:
    a. hindsight bias.
    b. correspondent inference.
    c. priming.
    d. a contrast effect.

Answer: c   51. One condition under which attitudes are a fairly
Page: 155–156   good predictor of behavior is when:
     a. we hold positive attitudes toward the particular behavior.
     b. we want to look good in the eyes of others.
     c. the attitude relevant to a given behavior is highly accessible.
     d. we are under strong pressure to conform to the behavior of others.

Answer: c   52. The general human tendency to overestimate the importance of personality or dispositional factors when explaining the causes of social behavior is called:
Page: 159
     a. the halo effect.
     b. the hindsight bias.
     c. the fundamental attribution error.
     d. the actor-observer bias.

Answer: d   53. Julie sees a stranger do poorly on a test. She automatically assumes that the stranger is stupid. She has committed an error best thought of as:
Page: 159–160
     a. a context effect.
     b. an attitude heuristic.
     c. a representative heuristic.
     d. the fundamental attribution error.

Answer: d 54. In the "quiz show" study conducted by Ross,
Page: 161–162   Amabile and Steinmetz, subjects were randomly assigned to serve as "questioners" or "contestants." Observers who watched the simulated quiz show tended to perceive the "questioners" as more knowledgeable than the "contestants." The observers committed the error of:
a. assigning favorable characteristics to high-status persons as compared to low-status persons.
b. equating intelligence with verbal skills.
c. making situational attributions for behavior, rather than dispositional ones.
d. underestimating the impact of social roles in explaining behavior.

Answer: a 55. The actor-observer bias involves the tendency for
Page: 163   actors to attribute their own actions to _____ and to attribute the actions of other people to those peoples' _____.
a. situational factors; personal dispositions
b. personal dispositions; situational factors
c. positive heuristics; negative heuristics
d. negative heuristics; positive heuristics

Answer: b 56. Suppose you and a classmate take your biology
Page: 163–164   test and both get A's. According to the actor-observer bias, you are more likely to attribute your own performance to _____ and your classmate's performance to _____.
a. an easy test; a difficult test
b. your intelligence; her studying hard
c. your studying hard; her intelligence
d. your studying hard; good luck

Answer: a
Page: 166

57. Although Susan was only peripherally involved in getting her friend elected as the president of the senior class, she felt her friend could never have won without Susan's support. Susan's feeling is best thought of as an example of:
   a. egocentric thought.
   b. the fundamental attribution error.
   c. the hindsight bias.
   d. the actor-observer bias.

Answer: b
Page: 167

58. Jim is concerned about his future, so he visits a "psychic" who tells him: "You are a person who can succeed in life. You have many talents that could be developed—ones that could bring you great prosperity. Sometimes you're afraid of taking risks, but you can spot a good opportunity when you see one." Jim leaves the psychic's office convinced that he has what it takes to be a success in life. The psychic's message
   a. is an example of decision-framing on the part of the psychic.
   b. is an example of a "Barnum statement."
   c. has made Jim fall prey to the effects of illusory correlation.
   d. probably indicates nothing true about Jim.

Answer: d
Page: 168–169

59. Rifka takes two tests for which she studies equally hard. She gets an A on one and a D on the other. She explains that she got the A because she is "smart" in that subject and got the D because the test was unfair and too difficult. Rifka's explanation is best thought of as an example of:
   a. the contrast effect.
   b. the actor-observer bias.
   c. the fundamental attribution error.
   d. the self-serving bias.

Essay Questions

1. Some theorists have proposed that people are rational thinkers and decision-makers, while others believe social cognition is often subject to biases and other distorting influences. Compare and contrast some of the central ideas that characterize these two perspectives, indicating which you find more convincing. What conditions are necessary for human cognition to operate on a thoroughly rational basis? How common are these conditions in everyday life?

2. In general, how does the "social context"—the way things are presented and described—influence our social judgment and cognition? Discuss the significance of TWO of the following contextual factors: a) contrast effects, b) priming, c) decision-framing, d) the order in which information is presented. Describe how these factors influence social judgments in everyday life and provide research evidence to support your answer.

3. What is the "primacy effect" and how does it influence the impressions we form of other people? Describe one piece of research that demonstrates this phenomenon. What two explanations have social psychologists offered in an effort to account for the existence of this effect?

4. What are heuristics? Under what circumstances are we likely to rely on them when making social judgments? Select two heuristics and discuss how they influence our thinking in daily life. Support your answer with examples of relevant research.

5. "Human memory is primarily reconstructive in nature." What does this statement mean? What are its implications for social cognition? How does research on eyewitness testimony demonstrate this point?

6. It's New Year's Eve, and you've been invited to a large party where there will be lots of people you've never met before. When you arrive, the person hosting the party hands you a blue party hat to wear and you put it on. As you mingle through the crowd, you notice that some people are wearing blue hats like yours, and other people are wearing green party hats. By the end of the evening, you realize you have spent most of your time with people wearing blue hats. Somehow, they just

seemed to be nicer people—they even dance better than those other people wearing green hats. Moreover, a guy with a green hat bumped into you at one point during the evening and spilled your drink! Given your knowledge of social cognition (and despite the somewhat far-fetched nature of this scenario), how could you explain your perceptions and judgments? If this were a costume party, how might you act if you were in change of awarding prizes for the best costume? Be sure to support your answer with examples of relevant research.

7. To what extent do cognitive processes operate in a conservative fashion? What are the benefits and drawbacks of this tendency in human cognition? What steps can be taken to reduce the negative consequences of cognitive conservatism?

8. How do cognitive biases involving the self contribute to the goal of maintaining and enhancing our view of ourselves? Of what value are such biases, and what are the potential consequences of not having them? Describe two self-biases, providing research evidence that demonstrates their effects.

5

Self-Justification

I. Introduction

    Self-justification and rumors (Prasad; Sinha)
    Cognitive dissonance theory (Festinger)
    Perceptual distortion (Hastorf & Cantril)

II. Dissonance Reduction and Rational Behavior

    Biased information-processing (Jones & Kohler; Lord, Ross, & Lepper)

III. Dissonance as a Consequence of Making a Decision

    Postdecision dissonance (Brehm; Johnson & Rusbult)
    Foot-in-the-door technique (Freedom & Fraser; Pliner)

IV. Irrevocability of decisions

    Low-balling (Cialdini)
    Immoral behavior (Mills)

V. The Psychology of Inadequate Justification

    A. Inadequate rewards

        Internal and external justification
        Saying is believing (Festinger & Carlsmith; Cohen)
        Eating grasshoppers (Zimbardo)
        Cheating (Mills)

    B. What is inadequate justification?

- C. Dissonance and the Self-Concept (Nel, Helmreich, & Aronson; Cialdini & Schroeder)

- D. Inadequate Rewards Applied to Education

    Turning play into work (Deci; Lepper & Greene)

- E. Insufficient Punishment

    Mild versus severe threat of punishment (Aronson & Carlsmith; Freedman)

VI. The Justification of Effort

Mild versus severe initiation (Aronson & Mills)
Snake phobia (Cooper)
Revising memory (Conway & Ross)

VII. The Justification of Cruelty

Derogating the victim (Jones & Davis; Glass)

VIII. The Psychology of Inevitability

Making the best of things (Brehm; Darley & Berscheid)
Denying danger (Lehman & Taylor)

IX. The Importance of Self-Esteem

Self-esteem and cheating (Aronson & Mettee)

X. Physiological and Motivational Effects of Dissonance

Pain perception (Zimbardo)
Hunger and thirst (Brehm)

XI. A Critical Look at Cognitive Dissonance as a Theory

    A. The refinement of dissonance theory

        Violations of the self-concept
        Freedom of choice (Linder)

    B. Alternative explanations of dissonance effects

        Bem's "self-reference" analysis
        Well-defined prior beliefs (Piliavin et al.)

    C. Dissonance as a state of arousal

        Task interference (Pallak & Pittman)
        Misattribution of arousal (Zanna & Cooper)

XII. Practical Applications of Dissonance Theory

    Three Mile Island
    Weight loss (Axsom & Cooper)
    AIDS prevention
    Water conservation
    The Waco and Jonestown tragedies

XII. "Man" Cannot Live by Consonance Alone

Terms & Concepts

cognitive dissonance
foot-in-the-door technique
low-balling
irrevocable decisions
internal justification
external justification
inadequate justification

inadequate rewards
turning play into work
justification of effort
justification of cruelty
self-fulfilling prophecy
psychology of inevitability

Chapter Overview

The social-psychological process of self-justification, which involves our tendency to justify our actions, behaviors, and feelings, is the topic of Chapter 5. The main tenets of cognitive dissonance theory are presented briefly and provide a framework for understanding the cognitive and motivational components that underlie self-justification processes. Throughout the chapter, the broad implications of the theory are discussed, as well as its application to a multitude of real-world situations and social phenomena. Highlights of the chapter are covered below.

In formal terms, cognitive dissonance (Festinger, 1957) is defined as a state of tension that occurs whenever an individual simultaneously holds two cognitions (attitudes, beliefs, etc.) that are psychologically inconsistent or contradictory. Because dissonance is unpleasant, people are motivated to reduce it—much as they are motivated to reduce hunger or thirst. Dissonance may be reduced by changing one or both cognitions in such a way as to render them more compatible (or consonant) with each other, or by adding more cognitions that help to reconcile, or bridge the gap between, the original cognitions.

In simpler terms, dissonance or self-justification processes generally occur when we find ourselves acting in a manner that contradicts our beliefs and attitudes—in particular, our conceptions of ourselves as good, decent, wise, and intelligent individuals. In order to justify our contradictory actions, we tend to change our attitudes or behaviors to make them more consistent with our previous behavior. For example, confronted with the health hazards associated with smoking, an inveterate smoker who can't or won't quit may reduce dissonance in a variety of ways—by discounting research on cancer as inconclusive or by stressing the benefits of smoking ("I may lead a shorter life, but it will be a more enjoyable one."). Thus, cognitive dissonance theory does not picture people as entirely rational beings; instead, it pictures them as rationalizing beings. We humans are motivated not so much to BE right; rather, we are motivated to believe we are right (and wise, good, intelligent, etc.).

Dissonance often occurs following a difficult or important decision. Once people have committed themselves to a particular choice, they typically justify their decisions by viewing the chosen alternative more positively, and the rejected more negatively, as compared to before the decision was made.

When people have inadequate external justification for a particular dissonance-arousing behavior, they tend to look for internal justification for the behavior in order to reduce dissonance. The search for internal justification often leads to changes in relevant attitudes and behaviors. This principle is illustrated in the classic Festinger and Carlsmith experiment, in which subjects lied to a "fellow student" by telling him that a boring task was interesting. Subjects who were paid only $1 for telling the lie rated the task as more interesting than subjects who were paid $20 for lying. Unlike the $1 subjects, the $20 subjects had sufficient external justification for lying and, thus, had no need to reduce dissonance by changing their perceptions of the task.

The phenomena of justification of effort is also associated with a lack of adequate external justification for one's behaviors. Thus, the Aronson and Mills experiment on mild versus severe "initiation" demonstrates that when we suffer or work hard for a goal, we come to place a high value on that goal—in order to justify the expenditure of effort and the sacrifices we have endured. Similarly, justification of cruelty occurs when we have acted in a cruel or unkind manner toward someone who does not deserve such treatment. Lacking sufficient justification, we tend to devalue the innocent victim of our unkind actions.

Refinements of Festinger's original formulation of dissonance theory have highlighted the role of the self-concept, pointing out that dissonance is greatest when individuals act in a manner inconsistent with their customary notions of themselves as good and competent. As a result, relatively higher levels of dissonance are likely to occur when we have done something "stupid" or immoral. In addition, freedom of choice plays a central role in dissonance arousal. When people perceive their actions as constrained by some external source, little dissonance is aroused.

Bem's "self-reference" analysis of dissonance effects offers an alternative interpretation of dissonance theory. Bem's notion is that the results of dissonance experiments reflect nothing more than reasonable inferences people make about their attitudes, based upon their perceptions of their own behavior. Where the inconsistency between attitudes and behavior is significant and clear, however, research evidence supports dissonance theory over Bem's self-reference interpretation.

Lecture Ideas & Teaching Suggestions

Self-presentation Strategies. Theory and research on self-justification rests on the notion that people are often motivated to avoid unpleasant information about themselves and will engage in acts of cognitive distortion in order to accomplish this goal. A related area of research you may wish to cover in lectures involves our tendency to represent ourselves to others, as well as ourselves, in the best possible light. The various ways that people attempt to create a desired social image are referred to collectively as self-presentation or impression management strategies. Jones and Pittman have developed a useful taxonomy of such strategies, each of which facilitates the achievement of a different self-presentational goal. These general strategies are:

Ingratiation, in which the main goal is to present the self as likable. Ingratiation tactics include paying compliments or conforming to the opinions of others.

Intimidation, in which the main goal is to arouse fear in others, thereby allowing the actor to control the outcome of the interaction to his or her advantage. Intimidation may involve the use of threats or the exercise of power within a relationship of unequal authority.

Self-promotion, in which the actor attempts to impress others with his or her competence, in regard to either a specific skill or general ability (e.g., intelligence). In promoting the self, the individual tends to focus on personal strengths and accomplishments, while downplaying or ignoring weaker areas. The self-promoter is vulnerable, however, to having to "make good" when claims of competence are put to the test.

Exemplification, in which the main goal is to display an image of integrity by appearing noble or as a long-suffering martyr in the pursuit of a worthy goal. The use of exemplification is frequently designed to make others feel guilty or morally inferior to the actor.

Supplication, in which the goal is gaining the sympathy of others. Presenting the self as weak or dependent often evokes feelings of protectiveness or obligation from others. As a result, the actor may reap practical or psychological benefits that might not be offered if he or she displayed a competent self-image.

In addition to the above strategies, researchers have explored other tactics for achieving self-presentational goals. For example, self-handicapping (Berglas & Jones, 1978) is employed when a person wishes to maintain the appearance of competence in the face of a likely threat to that competence. In such instances, people prearrange convenient excuses for failure so their later failure can be attributed to external causes. Thus, a tennis player who is unsure of her ability to beat her opponent may announce prior to the match that she only got three hours of sleep the night before. Basking in reflected glory (Cialdini et al., 1976) is another self-presentation tactic, which allows the individual to feel competent as a result of his or her association with successful others. For example, Cialdini and his colleagues (1976) found that students were more likely to wear clothing that announced their campus affiliation the day after their college football team won a game, compared to after a defeat. Further details on these self-presentation strategies may be found in: Jones, E.E. & Pittman, T.S. (1982). Toward a general theory of self-presentation. In J. Suls (Ed.), *Psychological perspectives on the self.* Hillsdale, NJ: Erlbaum; Berglas, S., & Jones, E.E. (1978). Drug choice as an externalization strategy in response to noncontingent success. *Journal of Personality and Social Psychology, 36,* 405–417; Cialdini, R.B., Borden, R.J., Thorne, A., Walker, M.R., & Freeman, S. (1976). Basking in reflective glory. Three (football) field studies. *Journal of Personality and Social Psychology, 34,* 366–375.

The Importance of Theory. In reviewing research on self-justification processes, you may wish to take advantage of the opportunity to discuss the importance of theory to the scientific enterprise. Cognitive dissonance theory provides a useful illustration of the properties of a good theory in its ability to: 1) organize and integrate existing empirical findings within a simple framework; 2) explain a broad range of phenomena; and 3) provide a fertile source of testable hypotheses that otherwise might not have occurred to researchers. An effective way to illustrate the integrative power of dissonance theory is to describe briefly the results of several dissonance studies, each representing a social-psychological phenomenon that—on the surface—bears little resemblance to the others. Experimental findings from different sections of the chapter can be presented, such as: 1) Prasad's rumor study; 2) Brehm's post-decision study; 3) Mill's cheating study; 4) Deci's research on "turning play into work"; 5) Aronson & Mills' justification of effort study; and 6) Glass's study of victim derogation. After presenting the results of each of these studies, the basic principles of cognitive dissonance theory can be set forth. The studies you have previously described can then be reviewed, with the goal of showing how these diverse findings are all predictable from the theory's basic tenets.

Finally, to give students a sense of the historical context of scientific discoveries, you might also wish to discuss the "revolutionary" nature of dissonance theory. In the late 1950s, when dissonance theory appeared on the scene, reinforcement theory was the prevailing framework for understanding behavior. In many instances, however, predictions based on dissonance theory were at direct odds with reinforcement principles. For example, Aronson and Mill's experiment on the effects of mild versus severe initiations demonstrates that people tend to prefer a goal for which they have suffered or expended great effort. Reinforcement theory would have predicted the opposite result: greater hardship or effort should have made the goal less, rather than more, attractive.

Projects and Discussion Topics

1. PROJECT: For about a week, keep a journal of instances in which you find yourself experiencing dissonance and engaging in efforts to reduce it. Refer back to Chapter 5 to gain some insight into the kinds of situations that are likely to arouse dissonance and elicit self-justifying thoughts and behaviors. Some of these are: a) after making a decision; b) after working hard for a goal that might not have been worth the effort; c) after succumbing to the temptation to do something against your beliefs; d) after resisting the temptation to do something against your beliefs; e) after hurting someone's feelings; f) having to "make the best" of an inevitable situation. (Make a special note of times when you felt dissonance under circumstances that were not covered in the chapter, if such situations occur.) For each entry in your journal, describe what provoked the dissonance, how it made you feel, and how you reduced it. Finally, if you did not reduce dissonance in a given situation, do your best to explain why you failed to do so.

2. PROJECT: Imagine that you are the parent of a 5-year-old girl named Lisa. It's the beginning of the summer and you've decided it's time for Lisa to learn how to swim. So, you enroll her in swimming lessons that a couple of her friends will be also attending. Unfortunately, the swimming lessons are rather expensive and the location is a fairly long drive from your home. Still, you figure, the goal of teaching Lisa to swim is well worth the trouble and expense. Lisa, however, is not crazy about the idea. When the morning of the first class arrives, Lisa puts her little foot down and says she doesn't want to go. This is a real dilemma. On the one hand, you don't want to force her to go to the classes—even though you've already paid for them. However, you also know that Lisa possesses a great deal of natural athletic talent and is sure to be a good swimmer. Moreover, you are convinced that once she gets over her initial hesitation, she will thoroughly enjoy being able to swim and play in the water with her friends. You also suspect she will feel really proud of herself for having learned a new skill.

   Based on your knowledge of cognitive dissonance, how would you handle this problem? Write a scenario describing the steps you would take to persuade Lisa to give swimming a try and how you think she would respond. In devising your strategy, pay special attention to the implications of the psychology of inevitability, the "foot-in-the-door" technique, and the effects of rewards on intrinsic motivation. Finally, looking back on your behavior as a parent, do you suspect there might have been times when you were experiencing dissonance and engaging in self-justifying behavior? If so, what was dissonance-arousing and why?

3. DISCUSSION: How would self-justification processes be engaged during a time of war? Here are a couple of situations to consider.

   A. First, put yourself in the shoes of a hypothetical combat soldier. You think of yourself as a good person—you love your family and friends—and they all love you. Suddenly, you are in the midst of a war zone and are faced with a situation of killing or being killed on a daily basis. You're 19 years old, you're far from home, and you're scared. Now, imagine you are that soldier and you find yourself in the following situations:

1. Face-to-face with an armed enemy who is about to kill you. You shoot first, killing him instead.

2. Face-to-face with a civilian who, in your eyes, physically resembles "the enemy." He has something in his hand—you're not sure what it is, but you think it might be a grenade and that he might be about to kill you. He takes a step toward you. Panic grips you, and you shoot him. You look at what he was holding and find it was not a weapon after all. You have killed an innocent civilian.

Under which of these two circumstances are you more likely to experience dissonance? Why? How would you be likely to reduce it?

B. Consider a different scenario. Imagine you are in the Army Reserves. You enlisted during a time when jobs were scarce, you had no money for an education, and your country had not been involved in armed conflict for a number of years. You figure it's your best chance of getting some kind of job skills, and perhaps a college education when your period of enlistment has ended. Considering these very real benefits, you block from your mind the possibility that a war could break out and you would be called upon to serve in it. The thought scares you and, besides, you grew up hearing about Vietnam and feel that it was an immoral war. Then, just six months before your period of enlistment is to end, a war breaks out in the Middle East and you are called up on "active duty." How do you suppose you would feel about this war and your involvement in it? Would you tend to think it was a "just" cause? How would you feel about people who opposed the war? In particular, how do you think you would feel about those who took the position, "I support our troops, but I oppose the war"? What would their view imply about your involvement in the war?

Share your reflections on these scenarios with members of your discussion group. Can you think of any other situations associated with war that would be likely to arouse dissonance? For example, consider the public's reaction to hearing that, contrary to early reports of war casualties, a great number of innocent civilians had been killed by our bombs. How would this information tend to influence public support for the war and the conclusion that our actions were morally correct and necessary? How might this impact differ for people who were consistently opposed to the war from the start, compared to those who, after some doubt and soul-searching, had decided they supported the war?

4. DISCUSSION: Aronson has stated that people "cannot live by consonance alone." Discuss your interpretation of this statement and its implications. What are the limitations of protecting our egos through dissonance reduction? Why might it be important to admit our mistakes? Why is it that we are usually so reluctant or unable to do so? What steps could we take in order to facilitate the chances of learning from our mistakes? Drawing on your personal experience, try to recall a situation in which it was relatively easy for you to admit a mistake. Discuss and analyze this situation with others in your group to see if you can determine the conditions that facilitate being able to face the truth about your behavior in a fairly non-defensive manner. Are these conditions the same for others?

5. DISCUSSION: Elementary-school teachers often use a reward system (such as offering children small prizes) in order to motivate their students to do well on their schoolwork and to maintain discipline in the classroom. Based on your knowledge of dissonance theory, what are the possible drawbacks of relying on such a system? What steps could teachers take to avoid or counteract these potential negative effects? How might dissonance theory be applied to other practical issues in real life? For example, consider such issues as teen-age pregnancy, substance abuse, water conservation, AIDS prevention, or any other problem that interests you. Can you think of ways that dissonance theory might shed light on such problems—either by deepening our understanding of them, or helping to solve them?

Additional Readings

Aronson, E. (1978). The theory of cognitive dissonance: A current perspective. In L. Berkowitz (Ed.), *Cognitive theories in social psychology*. New York: Academic Press.

Aronson, E. (1980). Persuasion via self-justification: Large commitments for small rewards. In L. Festinger (Ed.), *Retrospections on social psychology*. New York: Oxford University Press.

Bem, D.J. (1967, June). When saying is believing. *Psychology Today*, pp. 21–25. (Bem offers an alternative explanation for cognitive dissonance findings.)

Greene, D. & Lepper, M.R. (1974, September). How to turn play into work. *Psychology Today*, pp. 49–54. (A discussion of the use of rewards can undermine intrinsic motivation.)

Saxe, L. (1991). Lying: Thoughts of an applied psychologist. *American Psychologist, 46*, (4), 409-415.

Sinclair, R.C., Hoffman, C., Mark, M.M., Marlin, L.L. & Pickering, T.L. (1994). Construct accessibility and the misattribution of arousal: Schachter and Singer revisited. *Psychological Science, 5*, (1), 15-19.

Wicklund, R.A. & Brehm, J.W. (1976). *Perspectives on cognitive dissonance*. Hillsdale, NJ: Erlbaum.

Multiple-Choice Questions

Answer: c
Page: 177

1. The combined results of rumor research conducted by Prasad and Sinha were that following a natural disaster, people who lived in the towns directly affected by the event were more likely to _____ the possibility of impending disaster, while those living in relatively undamaged, neighboring towns tended to _____ the possibility of impending disaster.
   a. be prepared for; be unprepared for
   b. be anxious about; be unconcerned about
   c. downplay; exaggerate
   d. think about; repress

Self-Justification 121

Answer: c
Page: 178

2. Cognitive dissonance is defined as a state of tension:
   a. that occurs whenever a person is motivated to change his or her attitudes.
   b. that occurs when a person thinks and acts irrationally.
   c. that occurs when a person simultaneously holds two cognitions that are psychologically inconsistent.
   d. that occurs when a person is unaware of his or her conflicting cognitions.

Answer: c
Page: 178

3. The main idea behind cognitive consistency theories, such as dissonance theory, is that incompatible attitudes:
   a. are easily extinguished.
   b. are easy to change.
   c. make us feel uncomfortable.
   d. are very rare.

Answer: c
Page: 180

4. According to a survey gauging people's reactions to scientific evidence that smoking cigarettes causes cancer:
   a. smokers who were planning to quit believed the report even more than nonsmokers did.
   b. smokers believed the report, but nonsmokers rejected it.
   c. smokers were far less likely to believe the report than nonsmokers were.
   d. smokers were likely to believe the report, but still refused to quit smoking.

Answer: b
Page: 186–187

5. Lord, Ross, and Lepper showed articles favoring and opposing capital punishment to groups of students who either opposed or were in favor of it. The results of this study showed that reading articles on both sides of the controversial issue:
   a. brought the attitudes in the students closer together in a "middle" position.
   b. actually increased the difference in attitudes between the two groups.
   c. increased the self-esteem of members of both groups.
   d. decreased the self-esteem of members of both groups.

Answer: c
Page: 184

6. The responses of students from both campuses to a film of a roughly played football game between Dartmouth and Princeton indicated that _____ may be one important means of reducing dissonance.
   a. vicarious expression of aggression
   b. revenge-taking strategies
   c. actual perceptual distortion
   d. blaming the victim

Answer: a
Page: 185–188

7. According to dissonance theory, people are generally more motivated to:
   a. believe they are right, rather than to actually be right.
   b. be right, rather than simply believe they are right.
   c. have others believe they are right, rather than actually being right.
   d. be rational, rather than simply subjective.

Answer: d
Page: 188–190

8. Which of the following is *not* cited by Aronson as a possible way for people to reduce dissonance?
   a. changing their attitudes
   b. distorting their perceptions
   c. selectively exposing themselves to only certain information
   d. worrying more about the inconsistency that gives rise to the dissonance.

Answer: a
Page: 189–190

9. After choosing between two equally attractive appliances, women in Jack Brehm's study rated the appliance they selected:
   a. as more attractive than the one they rejected.
   b. as less attractive than the one they rejected.
   c. as equally attractive as the one they rejected.
   d. as less attractive than a group of similar appliances they were not allowed to choose from.

Answer: a
Page: 189–190

10. Suppose you decide to replicate Brehm's experiment in judgment of appliances. You ask a subject to rank order 10 candy bars according to her preferences with 1 = most preferred. Now you ask her to choose whether she would rather receive as a gift a box of Hersheys (ranked 6) or Heaths (ranked 7). For whatever reasons, she chooses the Heaths. After two weeks you ask her to re-rank the 10 candy bars. You would expect her to rank the Hershey as _____ and the Heath as _____.
    a. 5; 7
    b. 5; 6
    c. 7; 6
    d. 7; 8

124 *The Social Animal*

Answer: a
Page: 189–190

11. Joe is given the choice between two record albums he has already ranked as numbers 4 and 5 on a 1–10 scale. Joe chooses #4. Two weeks later when Joe is asked to rerank the ten albums, he reranks #4 as #2. This example is best predicted by:
   a. cognitive dissonance theory.
   b. reactance theory.
   c. stereotyping.
   d. the "just-world" hypothesis.

Answer: b
Page: 189–190

12. Suppose you are ready to buy a new car. You have great difficulty choosing between Brand A and Brand B. Finally, you buy Brand A. According to dissonance theory, after you have driven the car for a few weeks, you will be most likely to emphasize:
   a. the poor mileage you are getting in Brand A.
   b. how convenient the Brand A car is to park and drive.
   c. how pretty the Brand B car was.
   d. how you should have taken more time to make this difficult decision.

Answer: a
Page: 190

13. Suppose Bob and Tom are asked to rate the attractiveness of a group of young women about their same age and a group of women about the same age as their mothers. Bob is engaged to be married, whereas Tom is dating many women. Generalizing from an experiment conducted by Simpson and his colleagues, you should expect that, in comparison to Tom, Bob would see the younger women as _____ attractive and the older women as _____ attractive.
   a. less; equally
   b. more; equally
   c. equally; more
   d. equally, less

Answer: a   14. Jim has trouble deciding whether to buy a good-mileage, poor-maintenance MGB or a poor-mileage, easy-care Camaro. Finally, he buys the MGB. According to cognitive dissonance theory, he will probably spend most of his time concentrating on:
Page: 189–190
   a. the good mileage he gets.
   b. wondering when his car will break down.
   c. the unimportance of good mileage.
   d. the advantages of a low-maintenance car.

Answer: c   15. According to dissonance theory, we tend to experience dissonance after making an important decision because:
Page: 189–190
   a. we often feel forced into choosing a particular alternative.
   b. the rejected alternative seems more attractive than the chosen alternative.
   c. the chosen alternative is seldom entirely positive, while the rejected alternatives are seldom entirely negative.
   d. we hardly ever have enough time to make a good decision.

Answer: c   16. Carole has two boyfriends, Tim and Craig, whom she likes very much. Both of them really like her, too. She has decided, however, that dating both of them is making her life too complicated. After careful consideration, she decides to stop seeing Tim and to continue dating Craig. According to dissonance theory, which of the following is most likely to happen as a result of her decision?
Page: 189–190
   a. She and Tom will continue to be good friends.
   b. Tim will develop an intense dislike for Craig.
   c. Craig will seem more attractive than ever.
   d. Tim will seem more attractive, making her regret her decision.

Answer: b 17. Bill and Mary are concerned because they feel
Page: 189–190   their 13-year-old son spends too much time
   playing video games. One day, they came across
   a magazine article describing the positive and
   negative effects of video games on child
   development. After reading the article, Bill and
   Mary decided to show it to their son. According
   to dissonance theory, what would be the most
   likely impact of reading the article?
   a. Bill and Mary would stop worrying, now that
      they knew that video games had positive
      effects.
   b. Bill and Mary would be more convinced than
      ever that video games are a bad influence on
      their son.
   c. Their son would be more convinced than
      ever that video games were a bad influence
      on him.
   d. Bill and Mary, as well as their son, would
      develop a more balanced view of video
      games.

Answer: a 18. Freedman and Fraser, in their door-to-door study
Page: 193   in which housewives were asked to sign a
   petition or put an ugly sign in their yard, found
   that subjects who agreed to a _____ request
   first were _____ likely to comply with another
   request.
   a. small; more
   b. large; less
   c. small; less
   d. large; more

Answer: c
Page: 193

19. The foot-in-the door technique:
   a. is a method of encouraging people to do a small favor after they've refused to comply with a larger request.
   b. is a method of encouraging people to do a favor for us after we have granted them a small request.
   c. is a method of encouraging people to do a larger favor after they've agreed to an initially small request.
   d. is a method of using increasingly larger rewards to encourage people to comply with increasingly larger requests.

Answer: b
Page: 194

20. Bettors at a race track who were asked how confident they were about their chances of winning:
   a. were more confident the more money they bet.
   b. were more confident right after having placed their bets.
   c. were less confident right after having placed their bets.
   d. were equally confident both before and after placing their bets.

Answer: d
Page: 193–195

21. All other things being equal, cognitive dissonance following a decision is *greatest* when:
   a. the decision was not engaged in freely, but was coerced.
   b. the consequences of the decision were not foreseeable.
   c. the decision-maker has low self-esteem.
   d. the decision is irrevocable.

Answer: b   22. According to Mills's study of cheating among
Page: 197   sixth-graders, students _____ after having
                   resisted the temptation to cheat on an exam.
                   a. developed more tolerant attitudes toward cheating
                   b. adopted harsher attitudes toward cheating
                   c. were more tempted to cheat in the future
                   d. actually performed better on later exams

Answer: b   23. In Freedman's study, children who were given
Page: 212   mild threats of punishment for playing with a robot toy:
                   a. were more likely to play with the toy than those who received severe threats.
                   b. refused to play with the toy even after Freedman had left and several weeks had passed.
                   c. refused to play with the toy while Freedman was present but began playing with it as soon as he left.
                   d. played with the toy, but liked it less than the children who received severe threats.

Answer: a   24. Suppose you conduct an experiment in which a
Page: 212   child is placed in a room with a highly attractive toy. Generalizing from Freedman's research, you could diminish the child's attraction to the toy by:
                   a. using a mild threat of punishment for playing with the toy.
                   b. using a severe threat of punishment for playing with the toy.
                   c. using no threat of punishment for playing with the toy.
                   d. using a mild promise of reward for playing with the toy.

Answer: b   25. According to dissonance theory, as the external justifications for performing an act *decrease*, the need to find internal justifications for performing the act tends to:
Page: 198–200
- a. decrease.
- b. increase.
- c. remain the same.
- d. decrease rapidly, followed by a gradual increase.

Answer: a   26. Festinger and Carlsmith (1959) performed an experiment in which subjects were asked to lie to a "fellow student" for either $1 or $20. For subjects in the $1 condition, dissonance was created by the cognitions "I am an ethical person" and "I have told a lie." Based on the results of this study, which of the following statements best expresses how subjects probably reduced this dissonance?
Page: 201–202
- a. "I did not really tell a lie—what I said is quite true."
- b. "Though I told that person a lie and I know it, what she doesn't know won't hurt her."
- c. "Lying is a terrible thing."
- d. "I guess I'm not really a very ethical person at all."

Answer: a   27. In a study discussed in the text, students were paid either $20 or $1 for telling collaborative subjects that a dull task was actually interesting. Which group showed greater attitude change in actually rating the task as interesting?
Page: 201–202
- a. the group that told the lie for $1
- b. the group that told the lie for $20
- c. the group that refused to tell the lie for $1
- d. the group that refused to tell the lie for $20

Answer: d 28. The amount of dissonance produced when a
Page: 201–203 person engages in an attitude-discrepant act is *greatest* when the rewards are:
a. much greater than would be needed to induce the act in question.
b. so small that the act fails to occur.
c. secondary reinforcers.
d. just sufficient to induce the act.

Answer: b 29. As part of a psychology experiment, Ed and
Page: 201–203 Todd write essays saying that seat belts are unnecessary and laws requiring them should be abolished. From a questionnaire given several weeks before, it is known that both Ed and Todd are actually in favor of laws requiring seat belts. In the experiment, Ed is given a very small reward for writing an essay, while Todd is given a large reward for writing the essay. If their attitudes are subsequently measured, what is the most likely result?
a. Todd will favor seat belts more strongly than before; Ed will be more opposed.
b. Todd's attitude about seat belts will not change; Ed's will become more strong that seat belts are unnecessary.
c. Todd's attitude about seat belts will not change; Ed's will become more strong that seat belts are necessary.
d. Todd will favor seat belts more strongly than before; Ed's attitudes will not change.

Answer: b
Page: 201–203

30. Ginny is asked to give a speech in favor of requiring all students to take two years of a foreign language, although her personal position is for no such requirement. Under which of the following circumstances would you expect her attitude to undergo the most change in favor of the requirement?
   a. She agrees and is paid $1,000.
   b. She agrees and is paid $10.
   c. She decides not to give the speech, even though she is offered $1,000.
   d. She decides not to give the speech, even though she is offered $10.

Answer: c
Page: 201–203

31. Suppose you wanted to convince someone who is opposed to marijuana that it should be legalized. According to cognitive dissonance theory, what would be the best way to change that person's attitude?
   a. Give him or her a substantial reward to openly endorse the legalization of marijuana.
   b. Provide that person with as many convincing arguments and facts as possible in favor of marijuana until he or she changes his or her attitude.
   c. Offer the person a small reward to openly endorse legalization, but one just large enough to get him or her to endorse it.
   d. Create the illusion that everyone else favors legalization, so that disagreeing will make the individual feel uncomfortable.

Answer: a
Page: 201–203

32. According to cognitive dissonance theory, a disadvantage of the use of large rewards is:
    a. the intrinsic value of the rewarded behavior may be reduced.
    b. work may be turned into play.
    c. people will assume that their behaviors have an internal source.
    d. people will eventually grow tired of the rewards and will refuse to perform the behavior.

Answer: c
Page: 201–203

33. Which of the following is *not* an important element is activating dissonance reduction processes?
    a. The person's decision cannot be changed—it is irrevocable.
    b. The person's action was voluntary—it was not forced.
    c. The person was given large rewards.
    d. The person's self-concept is threatened by the decision or action.

Answer: d
Page: 203–204

34. Imagine that someone asked you to do something you found very distasteful—such as eating a handful of sugar-coated beetles. For the sake of argument, let's say that you complied and ate the beetles. According to dissonance theory, under which of the following conditions would you be most likely to find the experience of eating beetles enjoyable?
    a. when your best friend offered you a large reward for eating them
    b. when a person you disliked offered you a large reward for eating them
    c. when your best friend offered you a small reward for eating them
    d. when a person you disliked offered you a small reward for eating them

Answer: b
Page: 205

35. Aronson argues that the key to understanding whether or not dissonance will be aroused is whether or not the subject:
    a. is aware of his original attitude.
    b. feels his behavior violates his self-concept.
    c. has time to think about his actions or must act spontaneously.
    d. hurt another person.

Answer: b
Page: 205

36. Aronson argues that typically when dissonance arises it is because the subject:
    a. has a low self-concept.
    b. has done something stupid or immoral.
    c. cannot internally justify his or her actions so must seek external justification.
    d. all of the above

Answer: a
Page: 207

37. Dissonance effects are *greatest* when:
    a. people feel personally responsible for their actions and their actions have serious negative consequences.
    b. people feel personally responsible for their actions and they have low self-esteem.
    c. the person's actions have serious negative consequences whether the person feels responsible or not.
    d. the person's actions have serious negative consequences and the person has low self-esteem.

Answer: a
Page: 207

38. Suppose the fund-raising chairperson of a non-profit organization tells you he has heard of a new fund-raising approach in which, when people are asked for contributions, they are also told, "any amount you contribute will be appreciated, even a penny will help." Being a student of social psychology you should respond that, if he uses this technique, he can expect that:
   a. more people will give and the average size of the gifts will not decrease.
   b. more people will give, but the gifts will be smaller.
   c. fewer people will give, but the gifts will be larger.
   d. fewer people will give, and the gifts will be smaller.

Answer: c
Page: 208–209

39. Deci discovered that if you are rewarded for performing a fun and interesting puzzle:
   a. the puzzle becomes easier to solve than if you are not rewarded.
   b. the puzzle becomes harder to solve than if you are not rewarded.
   c. you become less likely to play with it later, when you are not rewarded.
   d. you grow more likely to play with it later, when you are not rewarded.

Answer: c
Page: 208–209

40. George bought his 6-year-old grandson, Pete, a set of paints for his birthday. Hoping to encourage the little artist, George told him he would give him $1 for every painting he made, which Pete thinks is a lot of money. According to Deci's research on the effects of rewards, which of the following is most likely to happen as a result of George's offer?
   a. Pete will love painting and will want to grow up to become an artist.
   b. George will have to start paying Pete more and more money, to justify his original decision to pay Pete.
   c. Pete will see painting as a way to make money, not as something enjoyable in itself.
   d. Pete will refuse to paint, due to feelings of reactance.

Answer: b
Page: 209–210

41. According to cognitive dissonance theory, if Abby wanted her roommate Rachel to pick up her clothes instead of leaving them on the floor, Abby would get the most behavioral change if she:
   a. severely punished Rachel when she threw her clothes down.
   b. used a very mild punishment that was enough to get Rachel to pick up her clothes.
   c. used a very mild punishment that was not enough to get Rachel to pick up her clothes.
   d. did not use any punishment whatsoever.

Answer: c 42. Which of the following conclusions is supported
Page: 214 by Aronson and Mills's experiment in which
subjects underwent either a severe or a mild
initiation in order to join a boring discussion
group?
a. The more you like something, the harder you will work for it.
b. The less you like something, the harder you will work for it.
c. The harder you work for something, the more you will like it.
d. The harder you work for something, the less you will like it.

Answer: c 43. Why is it, according to dissonance theory, that
Page: 215 we evaluate favorably those goals we've had to suffer for?
a. The goals themselves *are* valuable; otherwise we wouldn't go to all that time and trouble.
b. Deep down, people really like to work hard for what they get.
c. We are motivated to justify the time and effort we've spent.
d. Reaching the goal ends our suffering and, thus, is rewarding.

Answer: a 44. Suppose you are responsible for planning the
Page: 214–215 initiation of new members to a group to which you belong. Generalizing from Aronson and Mills's study on the effects of initiation on liking of the group, you would do well to make the initiation process:
a. difficult or unpleasant.
b. easy and pleasant.
c. closely resemble the activities of the group.
d. very different from the regular activities in which the group engages.

Answer: a
Page: 215

45. In Cooper's study of snake phobia, he found that which of the following groups improved the most:
   a. high effort-high choice
   b. high effort-low choice
   c. low effort-high choice
   d. low effort-low choice

Answer: b
Page: 220

46. In a study by Davis and Jones, subjects volunteered to insult a "fellow student" by telling him he was a shallow, untrustworthy and dull person. How did these subjects justify their hurtful behavior toward the other student, who had done nothing to deserve criticism?
   a. By agreeing to help the other student with a difficult task.
   b. By finding the other student less attractive than before they had insulted him.
   c. By convincing themselves that they had been forced to deliver the insults.
   d. By promising themselves they would never again perform such an unkind act.

Answer: b
Page: 220

47. Dissonance reduction processes can make:
   a. us like a person we hurt, in order to compensate the person for our mistake.
   b. us dislike a person we hurt, in order to justify hurting the person.
   c. us dislike a person we do a favor for, because we come to resent doing the favor.
   d. people with high self-esteem cheat more, because they feel less guilty.

Answer: a 48. In comparison to people with low self-esteem,
Page: 220 cognitive dissonance theory suggests that persons
of high self-esteem are _____ likely to
experience dissonance if they hurt someone and
they are _____ likely to derogate a victim
whom they have hurt.
a. more; more
b. less; less
c. more; less
d. less; more

Answer: b 49. Suppose you had volunteered to be in an
Page: 222 experiment in which you believe you have just
given painful electric shocks to another person.
According to cognitive dissonance theory, you
would:
a. estimate that the shocks were more painful
than they actually were.
b. have a lower opinion of the victims after the
experiment than before.
c. have a higher opinion of the subjects after
the experiment than before.
d. experience a temporary increase in your self-
esteem.

Answer: b 50. Lucas believes that, because women take longer
Page: 222 to learn mechanical skills at his factory, they
have less mechanical aptitude, and therefore he is
justified in not hiring any women. Lucas's belief
system is best thought of as an example of:
a. the inoculation effect.
b. the self-fulfilling prophecy.
c. the initiation effect.
d. the "turn about is fair play" effect.

Answer: c
Page: 224

51. Darrin Lehman and Shelley Taylor studied college students who lived in Los Angeles, the site of an impending earthquake. In their interviews with students, they found that:
    a. students living in seismically unsafe buildings planned to move to safer structures.
    b. students living in seismically unsafe buildings tended to be less familiar with safety measures than those living in safe buildings.
    c. students living in seismically unsafe buildings tended to underestimate the damage that would result from a major quake.
    d. students living in safer buildings spread more rumors about impending earthquakes.

Answer: c
Page: 226–227

52. In a study by Mettee and Aronson, subjects whose self-esteem had been temporarily lowered were more likely to cheat at a card game than subjects whose self-esteem was temporarily increased. According to Aronson, the results of this study suggest that:
    a. low self-esteem reinforces the belief that cheating is worth the risk of getting caught.
    b. high self-esteem reinforces the belief that cheating is worth the risk of getting caught.
    c. behaving in an immoral fashion is more dissonance-arousing for people with high self-esteem than for those with low self-esteem.
    d. behaving in an immoral fashion is less dissonance-arousing for people with high self-esteem than for those with low self-esteem.

Answer: b
Page: 226–227

53. How did Aronson and Mettee manipulate self-esteem in their article on self-esteem and dishonest behavior?
   a. They selected subjects who rated themselves as either high or low on a standardized test of self-esteem.
   b. They gave subjects false feedback about their personalities based on results of a personality test they had taken.
   c. They made the cheating task much more tempting for those subjects in the low self-esteem condition.
   d. They told people in the low self-esteem condition that others found them to be physically unattractive.

Answer: c
Page: 228

54. Zimbardo's experiment on the effects of dissonance arousal on pain, in which subjects received a series of intense electric shocks under different conditions, found that:
   a. subjects felt less pain when they were allowed to deliver the shocks to themselves, rather than receiving them from the experimenter.
   b. subjects felt more pain when they were allowed to deliver the shocks to themselves, rather than receiving them from the experimenter.
   c. subjects felt less pain when they volunteered to receive the shocks.
   d. subjects felt less pain when they received a large reward for receiving the shocks.

Answer: b   55.   Zimbardo put hungry subjects in a state of high
Page: 228–229   or low dissonance. According to his results,
                       subjects in the low-dissonance condition said they
                       were _____ hungry and actually ate _____
                       food than those in the high dissonance condition.
                       a.   more; less
                       b.   more; more
                       c.   less; more
                       d.   less; less

Answer: c   56.   In his restatement of dissonance theory, Aronson
Page: 231   stressed the need to make the theory:
                       a.   more precise by using quantitative measures
                            of change.
                       b.   more widely applicable by including self-
                            perception processes.
                       c.   more specific by stressing the role of
                            cognitions involving the self-concept.
                       d.   more well-known by publicizing its effects.

Answer: b   57.   Processes of dissonance reduction and self-
Page: 226–227;   justification can be beneficial:
      244   a.   because they cause people to be more rational.
                       b.   because they help protect a person's self-
                            concept.
                       c.   because they usually help us to adopt better
                            attitudes.
                       d.   because they lead to better self-understanding.

Answer: b   58. Most self-perception theorists such as Daryl Bem
Page: 233–234   believe that we come to infer our own attitudes by:
    a. asking people about ourselves.
    b. observing our own behavior.
    c. giving careful thought to what kind of people we are.
    d. taking cues from our parents about what kind of people we are.

Answer: c   59. Bem's self-perception theory differs from
Page: 233–234   cognitive dissonance theory in that it:
    a. predicts opposite results.
    b. is more humanistic and less deterministic.
    c. often predicts similar results but explains them differently.
    d. none of the above; Bem's theory is an extension of dissonance theory.

Answer: d   60. Suppose you conduct an experiment designed to
Page: 235–236   compare dissonance theory and self-perception theory. You do the experiment, and find that subjects supposedly experiencing dissonance perform worse at complex tasks but better at simple tasks than do the subjects in the control group. This finding is _____ a cognitive dissonance theory prediction and _____ a self-perception theory prediction.
    a. supportive of; supportive of
    b. contradictory to; contradictory to
    c. unrelated to; supportive of
    d. supportive of; contradictory to

Answer: a 61. Suppose a researcher discovered that when
Page: 235–237 subjects hold two conflicting attitudes, their
physiological responses parallel those of anxiety.
This new evidence would be _____ cognitive
dissonance theory and _____ self-perception
theory.
a. supportive of; contradictory to
b. supportive of; supportive of
c. contradictory to; contradictory to
d. contradictory to; supportive of

Answer: c 62. In comparing dissonance theory to Bem's theory
Page: 236–237 of self-judgment or self-reference processes,
Aronson concludes:
a. dissonance theory emerges as preferable, because it is a simpler, more cognitively oriented analysis.
b. Bem's theory emerges as preferable, because it is a simpler and more cognitively oriented analysis.
c. dissonance theory emerges as preferable, because it can better account for situations in which a person knows and acts against his or her attitudes.
d. Bem's theory emerges as preferable, because it can better account for situations in which a person knows and acts against his or her attitudes.

144 *The Social Animal*

Answer: a
Page: 237–238

63. According to dissonance theory, the people living nearest to the Three Mile Island nuclear plant during the crisis should:
    a. perceive the Nuclear Regulatory Commission's reassuring statements as more credible because they were committed to staying.
    b. perceive the Nuclear Regulatory Commission's reassuring statements as more credible because they were in favor of nuclear power.
    c. perceive the Nuclear Regulatory Commission's reassuring statements as less credible, because they had the most to lose.
    d. spread around the most frightening rumors, because they had the greatest reason to be scared.

Answer: c
Page: 239

64. According to Axsom and Cooper, what may well be the critical factor in therapy that accomplishes the recovery of the person?
    a. the empathy of the therapist
    b. whether or not the person enters the therapy under a doctor's care
    c. how much effort the person expends in the therapeutic process
    d. the particular type of therapy that is delivered

Answer: d
Page: 239

65. In Axsom and Cooper's study of weight reduction, they found that women in the ____ effort condition reported significant weight loss at ____.
    a. low; 4 weeks but not at 12 months
    b. low; 12 months but not at 6 weeks
    c. high; 4 weeks but not at 12 months
    d. high; 12 months but not at 4 weeks

Answer: b   66. Aronson and his colleagues found that he was
Page: 240–241   best able to convince students to use condoms
                       regularly when:
                       a. they were exposed to a high-fear campaign detailing the awful consequences of getting AIDS.
                       b. they were reminded of their own failures to use condoms and they made a speech advocating condom use.
                       c. they could obtain condoms for free by simply asking for them.
                       d. they were given an embarrassing "lesson" on how to use and remove them.

Answer: a   67. In his text, Aronson argues that Jim Jones was
Page: 242–243   able to persuade people to comply with his demands by first making small demands and then increasing them. This analysis is most similar to the research conducted by:
                       a. Freedman and Fraser on the "foot-in-the-door" technique.
                       b. Freedman on the threat of punishment.
                       c. Aronson and Mills on the severity of initiation.
                       d. Hastorf and Cantril on the Princeton-Dartmouth football game.

Essay Questions

1. According to cognitive dissonance theory, making an important decision is likely to arouse considerable dissonance. Let's say you were in the market to buy a new car. You are torn between buying a compact model—fuel-efficient, inexpensive and reliable—and a foreign sports car, which would be fast, flashy and impressive. Applying the theory of cognitive dissonance, describe what kinds of information you would seek (e.g., what kinds of ads or other information you would attend to) and what your attitudes would be (e.g, about fuel-efficiency, cost, safety, performance, etc.) both: a) before making your decision, and b)

after deciding to buy the sports car. Explain the reasoning behind your response, using relevant research examples to support your arguments.

2. What is meant by "the psychology of inevitability"? How can it be explained by cognitive dissonance theory? Illustrate your answer with an example from real life and describe at least one piece of research that demonstrates this phenomenon.

3. Imagine that you are approached by a member of a prominent cult in this country. On his or her invitation, you attend several cult meetings. As a result, you begin to believe that this group has some good ideas, but you still have some doubts about becoming a member. You are asked for a financial contribution, which you give. After several months, you find that you have donated a great deal of time and money to the group. Eventually, without even hearing any new arguments or propaganda, you believe everything the group stands for—they can do no wrong. You have become a devout member of the cult. How would a social psychologist explain this phenomenon? Be sure to cite research to support your answer.

4. Suppose you were a subject in Milgram's experiment on obedience, but for some reason, you were never debriefed. In other words, you were never told that the other person in the experiment was a confederate who didn't really receive the electric shocks you delivered. Suppose that the next day you ran into the other person at the college coffee shop. All other things being equal, how would you feel about that person if: a) you had gone all the way in delivering shocks to him or her? b) you had disobeyed the experimenter and refused to continue after delivering only a few mild shocks? Support your answer with relevant research and theory.

5. Imagine that you volunteered (for no pay) to spend a few hours each day teaching arts and crafts to young children in a day-care center. After several weeks, you discover that you really enjoy working with the children even though they sometimes make a mess and don't follow directions—which occasionally gets a little annoying. Now, suppose a paid position opened up at the center, and you began to receive a fairly good salary for performing the same kinds of work you had previously done for free. How might your attitudes toward your work—and,

perhaps, toward the children themselves—change as a result? Explain the reasoning behind your answer, making sure to discuss the distinction between internal and external justification. Support your response with relevant research and theory.

6. Suppose a mother was trying to get her oldest son to stop beating up on his younger brother. Given your knowledge of dissonance theory, what advice would you give this parent on how to proceed? Compare the likely result of your plan with one based solely on compliance (i.e., simple reward and punishment). Discuss research evidence that supports your reasoning.

7. Given what you know about cognitive dissonance, explain why direct efforts to change someone's mind about an important issue are often doomed to failure. Similarly, why would offering someone a reward to change his or her opinion be unlikely to produce real attitude change? Support your answer with relevant research.

8. One of the reasons dissonance theory has attracted great interest is its ability to explain and predict real-world phenomena that are not easily understood in common-sense terms. Describe two "practical applications" of dissonance theory, drawing upon relevant research examples to illustrate your discussion.

6

Human Aggression

I. Aggression Defined

Hostile versus instrumental aggression

II. Is Aggression Instinctive?

Thanatos and the "hydraulic" analogy (Freud)
Animal studies (Kuo; Eibl-Eibesfeldt; Scott; Lorenz)
The effects of learning (Berkowitz)

III. Is Aggression Necessary?

A. Survival of the fittest

Breeding for aggression (Lagerspetz)
Evolutionary value (Lorenz; Washburn & Hamburg; LeBoeuf)
Value of nonaggressive behavior (Ashley Montagu; Kropotkin)
America as a competitive culture

B. Catharsis

Sports (Patterson; Russell)
Fantasy (Feshbach; Hokanson & Burgess)
Direct aggression (Geen; Kahn; Doob & Wood)

C. Catharsis, public policy and the mass media

Effects of war (Archer & Gartner)
Imitation (Bandura)

Television and movies (Gerbner; Liebert & Baron; Parke; Eron & Huesmann)
Desensitization (Thomas)
Prizefights (Phillips)
Are violent shows preferred? (Diener & DeFour)

D. Media, pornography and violence against women

Violent pornography (Donnerstein; Malamuth)

E. Aggression to attract public attention

IV. Frustration and Aggression

Effects of frustration (Barker, Dembo & Lewin; Kulik & Brown)
Relative deprivation vs. social learning and aggression attributions (Mallick & McCandless)
Rewarding aggressive models (Bandura)
Aggressive cues (Berkowitz)—Deindividuation (Zimbardo; Mullen)

V. Toward the Reduction of Violence

A. Pure Reason

B. Punishment

Severe and frustrating forms of punishment (Hamblin)
Harsh prison sentences (*Gideon* v. *Wainwright*; Zimbardo)
Mild punishment (Aronson & Carlsmith; Freedman)

C. Punishment of aggressive models

D. Rewarding alternative behaviors

Reinforcing positive behaviors (Brown & Elliot)
Inhibiting the effects of frustration (Davitz)

E. Presence of nonaggressive models

   Conformity and nonaggression (Baron & Kepner)

F. Building empathy towards others

   Perspective-taking (Feshbach & Feshbach)

Terms & Concepts

hostile aggression
instrumental aggression
Eros
Thanatos
survival of the fittest
catharsis
frustration-aggression hypothesis

relative deprivation
deindividuation
aggressive cues
social learning
nonaggressive models
empathy

Chapter Overview

Chapter 6 discusses theory and research on aggression, which is defined as a behavior aimed at causing harm or pain. A further distinction is also made between hostile aggression, which serves as an end in itself, and instrumental aggression, an act of aggression that is performed as a means to achieving some other goal besides harm or pain. Important issues and questions covered in the chapter include:

Is human aggression instinctive? The answer to this question is still controversial, and much of the evidence comes from studies of non-human species rather than studies of humans. Although aggression may have an instinctual component in humans, the important point for the social psychologist is that it is modifiable by situational factors.

Is aggression necessary for human survival? It is possible that in the early history of human evolution, highly competitive and aggressive behaviors were adaptive. Given the violent and troubled state of human affairs in recent history, however, the survival value of aggressive behavior is questionable.

Does watching, enacting, or fantasizing about aggression serve a useful function in helping people to "blow off steam," thus preventing future, more extreme acts of violence? The weight of research evidence contradicts Freud's "catharsis" hypothesis, and instead indicates that violence breeds future violence. This is especially the case when aggression is unleashed against an innocent victim, largely due to the kinds of self-justification processes discussed in Chapter 5. Under special circumstances, however, aggressive retaliation can reduce the need for further aggression if something akin to equity has been restored.

Research on the impact of media violence suggests that watching violent programming not only increases aggressive behavior among children but leads to reduced sensitivity to aggressive acts in the real world. Studies using adult subjects—including research on the impact of violent pornography and "slasher" films—demonstrate that these effects are not restricted to children.

The finding that frustration leads to aggression is well-documented. Although frustration is one of the major causes of aggression, other social-psychological factors can intervene either to induce aggression in a person who is experiencing little frustration, or to inhibit aggressive behavior in a person who is frustrated. For example, knowing that the cause of one's frustration was unintentional tends to reduce the likelihood of an aggressive response. Factors that increase the probability of aggression include the presence of aggressive cues in the person's immediate environment. Similarly, the phenomenon of deindividuation, which occurs when a person's actions are cloaked by a sense of anonymity (e.g., as in a large crowd) tends to facilitate aggressive behavior.

Can human aggression be eliminated? Although there are no easy solutions to this problem, various possibilities for reducing violence and aggression have been proposed. These include the use of "pure reason," harsh punishment, punishment of aggressive models, rewarding alternative behavior patterns and building empathy toward others. Of these strategies, developing the capacity for empathy and rewarding nonaggressive behaviors are among the most promising.

Lecture Ideas & Teaching Suggestions

Aversive States and Aggression. In addition to the frustration-aggression relationship that is examined in Chapter 6, you may also wish to discuss the link between aggression and other unpleasant states. Research on human subjects has demonstrated that aggression is heightened in response to several aversive factors, including pain, high temperatures, foul odors, and cigarette smoke. These findings are consistent with the results of a large number of experiments conducted on animals. They also ring true with our everyday experiences. Thus, in introducing a discussion of the effects of aversive states on aggression, you may want to ask your students to think of situations in which they felt more irritable or reacted to others with greater hostility while suffering from an illness or injury. You may also wish to provide an example or two from your own experience.

A thoughtful review and analysis of this body of research may be found in Berkowitz, L. (1983). Aversively stimulated aggression: Some parallels and differences in research with animals and humans. *American Psychologist, 38,* 1135-1144. In this article, Berkowitz also examines the role of cognition in mediating the impact of aversive events on aggression. Moreover, in reconsidering the frustration-aggression hypothesis, he argues that frustrating experiences provoke aggression because they are aversive in nature. In his view, then, the instigation to aggression lies in the aversiveness of the experience, not simply the frustration of having failed to attain a desire goal. Finally, Berkowitz concludes that, while it is clearly impossible to eliminate all aversive events from our daily existence, human beings can learn to refrain from acting on the aggressive impulses stimulated by these events.

The Effects of Alcohol and Drugs. Do alcohol and drugs increase the tendency to engage in aggressive behavior? This question, which may be of interest to your students, has been explored in research conducted by Stuart Taylor and his colleagues. In their experiments, subjects consumed either small or large doses of alcohol and then interacted with a confederate who either did or did not make them angry. Next, they were given an opportunity to aggress against the confederate. The results were that, regardless of the dosage, alcohol did not increase aggression among subjects who had not been provoked by the confederate's behavior. Thus, alcohol, by itself, does not appear to stimulate aggression. For provoked subjects, however, consuming a large dose of alcohol did lead to heightened aggression, while low doses did not have this effect. This same procedure was conducted using small or large doses of marijuana (in the form of THC, the major active ingredient in marijuana). The results of marijuana use were different from the effects of alcohol. Among subjects who had been provoked by the confederate, those who ingested large doses of THC were significantly less aggressive than subjects who received either large alcohol doses or low THC doses. Moreover, subjects with high THC doses even responded less aggressively than subjects who had not consumed any drugs at all. Although based on a fairly small body of research, these findings seem somewhat consistent with the common stereotype of the "violent drunk" and the "mellow" pot-smoker. Further details on this topic are available in: Taylor, S.P. & Gammon C.B. (1975). Effects of type and dose of alcohol on human aggression. *Journal of Personality and Social Psychology, 32*, 169–175. Taylor, S.P., Gammon, C.B., & Capasso, D.R. (1976). Aggression as a function of the interaction of alcohol and threat. *Journal of Personality and Social Psychology, 34*, 938–941. Taylor, S.P., Vardaris, R.M., Rawitch, A.B., Gammon, C.B., & Cranston, J.W. (1976). The effects of alcohol and delta-p-tetrahydrocannibol on human physical aggression. *Aggressive Behavior, 2*, 153–162.

Gender Differences in Aggression. Throughout history and across cultures, aggressive activities such as hunting and waging war have been the special, if not sole, province of men. Thus, the issue of gender differences in aggression constitutes an important, and controversial, realm of social-psychological inquiry. In their 1974 review of the findings in this area, Maccoby and Jacklin concluded that males are more aggressive than females, and that these behavioral differences are partly the result of biological factors. More recently, Eagley and Steffen (1986) have noted that gender differences found in social-psychological research tend to be small and are often inconsistent. This is especially true when verbal and other forms of psychological aggression are the focus of study. When it comes to inflicting physical harm, however, these differences tend to be more pronounced, with men displaying higher levels of aggression. For a review and analysis of these findings, see Eagley, A.H., & Steffen, V.J. (1986). Gender and aggressive behavior: A meta-analytic review of the social psychological literature. *Psychological Bulletin, 100*, 309–330.

Projects and Discussion Topics

1. PROJECT: Find a television show that has a reputation for violent themes (detective or police dramas are a good choice). As you watch this program, pretend you are Paxman, an alien from the peaceful planet Pacifica, who has been sent on a mission to learn about life on Earth. Based on what you've seen on this television show—and nothing else—you must transmit a preliminary report back to your planet, describing what you've learned thus far. In your report, describe your observations and conclusions regarding what life is like on Earth, the basic nature of earthlings, and how and why they act as they do. Compare these creatures and their behavior with your own experience of living in a violence-free society.

2. PROJECT: Visit a playground at a time when lots of young children are playing. Look for instances of hostility and aggressive interactions among children, and see if you can determine what provoked them and how they were resolved. Write up your observations and analyses, and share them with your classmates.

3. PROJECT: Collect newspaper or magazine articles describing a violent crime or other incident involving aggression. What factors are described as having provoked the incident? What kinds of attributions concerning the incident are made by the writer, the witnesses, authorities, or other people quoted in the article? Does the article contain any explicit or implicit theories regarding the causes of aggression or its solution? Bring your articles to class and describe your findings.

4. DISCUSSION: Based on research evidence presented in Chapter 6, what are the effects of violent pornography? Given this evidence, do you think steps should be taken to make such pornography illegal? Why or why not? Similarly, research has demonstrated that watching televised violence increases aggressive behavior in children. Should there be policies or laws implemented that restrict the levels of violence contained in children's television shows? Why or why not? Is your opinion the same regarding pornography and children's shows? Why or why not? Share your views on these issues with members of your discussion group.

5. DISCUSSION: You are the parent of a young child whom you would like to see become a peaceful, affectionate, and cooperative adult. To achieve this goal, to what extent would you consider taking the following steps? a) preventing your child from watching violent television shows; b) preventing your child from playing with "violent" toys such as guns, swords, etc.; c) preventing your child from playing with "aggressive" children; d) preventing your child from fighting back, if another child kept bullying him or her. Finally, would you want to eliminate all aggressive behavior in your child? Why or why not? Discuss your decisions, and the reasoning behind them, with your classmates.

Additional Readings

Bandura, A. (1973). *Aggression: A social learning analysis.* Englewood Cliffs, NJ: Prentice-Hall.

Berkowitz, L. (1981, June). How guns control us. *Psychology Today,* pp. 11–12. (Review of field and laboratory research on the "weapons effect," offering support for gun-control legislation.)

Donnerstein, E.I., Linz, D. & Penrod, S. (1987). *The question of pornography: Research findings and policy implications.* New York: Free Press.

Feshbach, S. & Malamuth, N. (1978, November). Sex and aggression: proving the link. *Psychology Today,* pp. 110–117. (Explores the link between pornography and aggression.)

Fowler, R.D. (Ed.). (1993). *American Psychologist, 48,* (10), 1054-1087. (Five articles about violence against women.)

Geen, R.G. & Donnerstein, E.I. (1983). *Aggression: Theoretical and empirical reviews.* New York: Academic Press.

Gerbner, G. & Gross, L. (1976, April). The scary world of TV's heavy viewer. *Psychology Today,* pp. 41–45. (Heavy exposure to television leads people to view the world as a more dangerous place.)

Linz, D., Donnerstein, E. & Penrod, S. (1987). The findings and recommendations of the Attorney General's Commission on Pornography: Do the psychological facts fit the political fury? *American Psychologist, 42,* 946–953.

Lore, R.K. & Schultz, L.A. (1993). Control of human aggression: A comparative perspective. *American Psychologist, 48,* (1), 16–25.

Malamuth, N.M. & Donnerstein, E.I. (1984). *Pornography and sexual aggression.* Orlando, FL: Academic Press.

Satterfield, J.M. & Seligman, M.E.P. (1994). Military aggression and risk predicted by explanatory style. *Psychological Science, 5,* (2), 77-82.

Tavris, C. (1982, November). Anger defused. *Psychology Today,* pp. 25–35. (Contrary to catharsis theory, ventilating one's anger tends to increase feelings of hostility.)

Multiple-Choice Questions

Answer: c
Page: 249–250

1. Which of the following would most likely be considered an act of aggression by Aronson's definition?
    a. a football player tackling a practice dummy
    b. an actor rehearsing a fight scene who accidently punches a stuntman, breaking his nose
    c. a small child angrily, but harmlessly, punching his father
    d. a person whose comment unintentionally hurts a friend's feelings

Answer: c
Page: 250

2. Instrumental aggression differs from hostile aggression in that:
   a. instrumental aggression involves the intent to harm another person.
   b. instrumental aggression involves both emotional and physical harm to another person.
   c. instrumental aggression involves harming someone in order to achieve a goal, rather than for its own sake.
   d. instrumental aggression is an end in itself rather than a means to an end.

Answer: a
Page: 250

3. Which of the following is an instrumental act of aggression?
   a. dropping a bomb on a ball-bearing factory of the enemy during World War II
   b. the My Lai massacre
   c. a person who hits an enemy in anger
   d. watching a violent boxing match on TV

Answer: a
Page: 251

4. Sigmund Freud would most likely be associated with the idea that aggression:
   a. is instinctive.
   b. is a socially learned response.
   c. needs to be strictly controlled in order to protect a person's mental health.
   d. is a result of sexual drive.

Answer: c
Page: 251

5. According to Freud, society performs an essential and beneficial function in regulating the instinct of aggression by:
   a. forbidding opportunities for people to express their aggressive feelings.
   b. giving people free reign to express their aggressive feelings at those who provoke their anger.
   c. helping people to sublimate destructive energy into acceptable or useful behavior.
   d. helping people to direct their aggressive energy inward, in the form of self-punishment.

Answer: c
Page: 251

6. Freud believed that aggressive energy could be channelled so that the person's behavior actually worked toward the good of society. He called this process:
   a. catharsis.
   b. vicarious aggression.
   c. sublimation.
   d. Thanatos.

Answer: a
Page: 252

7. Kuo conducted a study in which he raised a kitten in the same cage as a rat. As an adult, the cat refrained from attacking the rat and, in fact, the two became close companions. The cat never chased or attacked any other rats as well. This study indicates that:
   a. aggressive behavior can be inhibited by early experiences.
   b. aggression is not instinctive.
   c. aggression is not instinctive in cats.
   d. the aggressive instinct does not operate when an animal is raised in captivity.

Answer: c 8. The Iroquois Indians lived in peace for hundreds
Page: 253–254 of years as a hunting nation, but in the seventeenth century, trade introduced by Europeans brought the Iroquois into competition with a neighboring tribe. A series of tribal wars developed, and the Iroquois ultimately became ferocious and successful warriors. This series of events suggest that:
   a. warlike behavior is the result of uncontrollable aggressive instincts.
   b. competition inevitably leads to violence.
   c. changing social conditions can lead to changes in aggressive behavior.
   d. aggressive behavior ensures evolutionary survival.

Answer: c 9. Overall, research indicates that:
Page: 254
   a. aggression is not instinctive among humans but is instinctive among other animals.
   b. aggression is not an instinct in either humans or nonhumans.
   c. aggression may have an instinctual component in humans, but it is also highly modifiable by situational factors.
   d. over the course of human evolution, aggression has changed from an instinct to a learned behavior.

Answer: c 10. According to Berkowitz, who stresses the role of
Page: 253 learning in human aggression:
   a. aggressive behavior is almost entirely the result of social influences.
   b. once learned, aggressive behavior is nearly impossible to modify.
   c. aggressive behavior is the result of an interplay between innate propensities and learned responses.
   d. once learned, aggressive feelings must be released through catharsis.

Answer: d   11. Kropotkin's study of chimpanzees documents that
Page: 256   when one hungry chimp begs for food from the
                  other, the other chimp reluctantly shares its food.
                  This research is cited to make which of the
                  following points:
                  a. like aggression, empathy is learned.
                  b. humans and chimps have many behaviors in
                     common; therefore animal studies are useful
                     in understanding human behavior.
                  c. aggression has been selected for according to
                     "survival of the fittest."
                  d. sharing may be an instinctual behavior.

Answer: a   12. The tension reducing properties of various types
Page: 258   of aggressive acts have been called:
                  a. catharsis.
                  b. repression.
                  c. deindividuation.
                  d. social facilitation.

Answer: a   13. Which of the following perspectives would
Page: 258–259   encourage you to let children watch violent TV
                  programs?
                  a. psychoanalytic
                  b. frustration-aggression
                  c. social learning
                  d. instinct

Answer: d   14. Catharsis refers to the idea that:
Page: 258   a. frustration results when a person can't attain
                     his or her goals.
                  b. frustration increases the drive, or activity,
                     state of the organism.
                  c. modeling increases the probability of
                     aggression.
                  d. violence reduces pent-up aggressive energy.

Answer: c 15. The analysis of the research on the catharsis
Page: 259–264 theory of aggression suggests that direct acts of
aggression:
a. generally reduce the tendency toward future aggression—Freud was right.
b. reduce the tendency toward future aggression, because they reduce the effect of social inhibitions.
c. reduce the tendency toward future aggression if they are done directly, are justified, and restore equity.
d. reduce the tendency toward future aggression if they are done indirectly, are not justified, and do not restore equity.

Answer: c 16. The catharsis theory of aggression holds that:
Page: 258
a. aggressive impulses, if kept bottled up, will eventually fade away.
b. one act of aggression usually leads to further aggression.
c. one act of aggression reduces the likelihood of further acts of aggression.
d. frustration leads to aggression.

Answer: d 17. John is frustrated by doing poorly on a college
Page: 258 chemistry test because he felt he really knew the material. After the test, he thought he would 'blow off steam' by going to his favorite bar and playing video games. This example highlights the principle underlying:
a. reinforcement.
b. punishment.
c. instinct.
d. catharsis.

Answer: a
Page: 259

18. Patterson measured the hostility of high-school football players both one week before and one week after the football season. He found that:
    a. players exhibited an increase in hostility over the course of the season.
    b. players exhibited a decrease in hostility over the course of the season.
    c. players from teams with losing records displayed higher rates of hostility over the course of the season.
    d. players from teams with winning records displayed higher rates of hostility over the course of the season.

Answer: b
Page: 260–261

19. In a "natural experiment" in the real world, some technicians who were laid off by their company were given a chance to verbalize their hostility against their exbosses, while other technicians did not have this opportunity. Later, when given a chance to talk about their exbosses, workers who had voiced their hostility were _____ than workers who had not voiced their hostility.
    a. less negative in their descriptions of their exbosses
    b. more negative in their descriptions of their exbosses
    c. more likely to feel empathy toward their exbosses
    d. less likely to feel socially inferior to their exbosses

Answer: a   20. Gordon Russell studied the hostility of spectators
Page: 259   during a violent ice hockey game. He found that, as the game progressed, the fans became increasingly more violent. This research is in direct conflict with the expected effects of:
                      a. catharsis.
                      b. high density on aggression.
                      c. the frustration-aggression hypothesis
                      d. social learning theory.

Answer: c   21. Feshbach conducted a study where students were
Page: 259–260   divided into three groups. Group 1 was insulted and given an opportunity to write a story about aggression. Group 2 was insulted but not allowed to write. Group 3 was not insulted. The results indicated that which group(s) were least aggressive later on?
                      a. Group 1
                      b. Group 2
                      c. Group 3
                      d. all groups were equally aggressive

Answer: a   22. Cognitive dissonance theory predicts that once a
Page: 261–262   person has hurt another, he will be _____ likely to hurt the person again in the future. This explanation is _____ the idea of catharsis.
                      a. more; contrary to
                      b. less; contrary to
                      c. more; consistent with
                      d. less; consistent with

Answer: b 23. According to a study by Archer and Gartner,
Page: 264   countries engaging in wars exhibit:
               a. greater hostility on the part of citizens toward all foreigners.
               b. higher rates of violence in their own country in the years following a war.
               c. lower rates of violence in their own country in the years following a war.
               d. higher rates of violence in their own country in the years prior to a war.

Answer: c 24. In Bandura's "Bobo doll" study, children who
Page: 265   watched an adult act aggressively toward a plastic, air-filled doll:
               a. admired the adult more than if the adult had not acted aggressively toward the doll.
               b. admired the adult less than if the adult had not acted aggressively toward the doll.
               c. not only imitated the adult's aggressive behavior, but also engaged in new forms of aggressive behavior toward the doll.
               d. wanted the adult to be punished for acting aggressively toward the doll.

Answer: b 25. Based on his work with children's play with
Page: 265–266 "Bobo dolls," the noted social learning theorist Albert Bandura has suggested that violence on TV should be:
               a. continued, since it supplies a healthy outlet for frustration and energy.
               b. discontinued, since it provides aggressive models for children to use and therefore increases aggressiveness in kids.
               c. discontinued, since it produces frustration which is then channeled into aggression.
               d. continued, since it suggests that violent behavior is always punished, thereby reducing aggression in these children.

Answer: b
Page: 265

26. "Bobo doll" studies found that:
    a. children will perform complex modeled responses for the reinforcement of being able to "beat-up a Bobo doll."
    b. children imitated adults who had been aggressive toward a "Bobo doll," and thus learned new forms of physical and verbal aggression through observation.
    c. children would not aggress against the "Bobo doll," especially after watching an adult do so.
    d. after aggressing against a "Bobo doll," children were less likely to engage in hostile behavior toward their playmates.

Answer: c
Page: 265

27. An analysis of television shows reveals that:
    a. violence prevails in about one out of every ten programs.
    b. an average of twenty to thirty violent incidents occur each hour.
    c. by the age of 12, the average child will have seen 100,000 acts of violence on TV.
    d. children's cartoons contain the fewest number of violent acts.

Answer: d
Page: 266

28. Eron and Huesmann looked at correlations between watching violence on TV and aggressive behavior. They found that there _____ a correlation at age 8 and that there _____ a correlation for the same boys at age 19.
    a. was; was not
    b. was not; was
    c. was not; was not
    d. was; was

Answer: b
Page: 267

29. Studies of the impact of violent movies and television shows on children's behavior indicate that:
   a. exposure to violent media is not associated with greater aggression.
   b. exposure to violent media is associated with reduced sensitivity to acts of violence in the real world.
   c. exposure to violent media increases aggression among young children, but this effect decreases as children mature.
   d. exposure to violent media has little impact on young children, but has an increasingly powerful effect as children mature.

Answer: b
Page: 269

30. In his study of the effects of televised prize-fights, sociologist David Phillips found that:
   a. the U.S. homicide rate increased after domestic fights, but *not* after overseas fights.
   b. the more publicity surrounding the fights, the greater the increase in homicides in the following days.
   c. the race of the losers of the fights was related to the race of homicide victims—when blacks lost fights, the rate of white (but not black) homicide victims increased.
   d. the effects of televised fights was more pronounced for older men than younger men.

Answer: b   31.   According to *The Social Animal*, research
Page: 270   comparing violent TV programs to nonviolent
                        programs suggests that:
                        a. viewers like violent programs more than
                           nonviolent programs.
                        b. viewers like nonviolent programs equally as
                           much as violent programs.
                        c. viewers like nonviolent programs more than
                           violent programs.
                        d. compared to female viewers, male viewers
                           are more likely to prefer violent programs
                           than nonviolent programs.

Answer: c   32.   In Donnerstein's study on the effects of
Page: 271   pornography, male subjects delivered more
                        intense shocks to a female confederate:
                        a. after viewing an erotic film with the female
                           confederate.
                        b. after being asked to describe their sexual
                           fantasies.
                        c. after viewing an erotic-aggressive film
                           involving rape.
                        d. after expressing their views on the "rape
                           myth."

Answer: b   33.   In experiments on the effects of violent
Page: 271–272   pornography, Malamuth found that:
                        a. men engaged in less violent sexual fantasies
                           after watching a film involving rape.
                        b. men were more accepting of violence against
                           women after watching violent pornography.
                        c. women were more accepting of violence
                           against women after watching violent
                           pornography.
                        d. women were more accepting of the "rape
                           myth" after watching violent pornography.

Answer: d   34.   The rape myth is the belief that:
Page: 272   a. rape occurs much more frequently than we believe.
                   b. rape is one form of catharsis.
                   c. when a woman says "no," she means "no."
                   d. women, deep down, want to be taken forcefully.

Answer: c   35.   Linz and his colleagues found that, compared to men who watched X-rated, but nonviolent, pornography, men who watched R-rated, violent "slasher" films:
Page: 274
                   a. were more likely to believe that women found "slasher" movies sexually arousing.
                   b. were less likely to believe that "slasher" movies could have harmful effects.
                   c. expressed less empathy for victims of rape.
                   d. expressed more empathy for victims of rape.

Answer: b   36.   The effect of violent pornography is:
Page: 274   a. similar to the effect of other violent media in that it tends to decrease the level of aggression.
                   b. similar to the effect of other violent media in that it tends to increase the level of aggression.
                   c. different from the effect of other violent media in that it tends to decrease the level of aggression.
                   d. minimal, except among men who have unusually high sex drives.

Answer: c   37. In the experiment by Barker, Dembo, and Lewin,
Page: 276–277   in which children were delayed or not delayed
       from playing with attractive toys, the greater
       aggression of children who were delayed from
       playing with the toys probably occurred because:
       a. of relative deprivation.
       b. they were angry at the children who weren't
          delayed from playing with the toys.
       c. they were frustrated at not getting what they
          had been led to expect.
       d. being delayed caused them to dislike the
          toys.

Answer: b   38. Barker, Dembo and Lewin's classic study of
Page: 276–277   children who were either delayed or not delayed
       from entering a room full of attractive toys
       showed that, with regard to aggression:
       a. children who were delayed from playing with
          the toys experienced dissonance and were
          thus less aggressive than children who were
          not delayed.
       b. children who were delayed from playing with
          the toys experienced frustration and were
          thus more aggressive than children who were
          not delayed.
       c. both groups were equally aggressive, but
          children who were delayed liked the toys
          more than children who weren't delayed.
       d. both groups were equally aggressive, but
          children who weren't delayed liked the toys
          more than children who were.

Answer: b   39. Which of the following hypotheses suggests that
Page: 276   the most potent means of inducing human beings
       to aggress is that of preventing them from
       obtaining various goals they seek?
       a. social learning theory
       b. frustration-aggression hypothesis
       c. catharsis
       d. survival of the fittest

Answer: c 40. Research on the relationship between frustration
Page: 277–278 and aggression indicates that
a. frustration always leads to aggression.
b. frustration increases aggressive feelings, but not aggressive actions.
c. frustration increases the probability of aggression.
d. both frustration and aggression decrease as we get closer to reaching a particular goal.

Answer: b 41. According to Aronson's analysis, the riots that
Page: 278 occurred in Watts and in Detroit *most clearly* exemplified the effects of:
a. frustration.
b. relative deprivation.
c. catharsis.
d. social learning.

Answer: a 42. According to a study by Mallick and
Page: 279–280 McCandless, in which children were kept from achieving a goal by another child's clumsiness, the amount of aggression we express after a frustrating experience is often reduced when:
a. we learn that the person who has frustrated us actually intended no harm.
b. we are not allowed to retaliate in an appropriate and moderate manner.
c. we are threatened with punishment if we retaliate.
d. we are exposed to an aggressive model just prior to being frustrated.

Answer: b 43. The results of Josephson's study, in which boys
Page: 280–281 watched violent movies of S.W.A.T. killings or
high-action movies and were later exposed to a
frustrating situation, indicate that:
a. exposure to violent stimuli reduces the tendency for frustration to provoke aggression.
b. exposure to violent stimuli strengthens the tendency for frustration to provoke aggression.
c. violent stimuli have no effect on the relationship between frustration and aggression.
d. the effects of violent stimuli on aggression are more powerful than the effects of frustrating situations.

Answer: c 44. Martha argues that children should not be
Page: 279–280 exposed to sex and violence on TV because it leads them to behave more aggressively. Martha's view is most consistent with:
a. psychoanalytic theory.
b. survival of the fittest.
c. social learning theory.
d. the frustration-aggression hypothesis.

Answer: d 45. The social learning theory of aggression does *not*
Page: 279–280 make which of the following assumptions:
a. children and adults can learn to be aggressive by observing others.
b. aggression can be maintained when its occurrence results in tangible rewards for the aggressor.
c. aggression can be maintained by social reward and approval.
d. human beings are constantly driven toward violence by built-in internal forces or ever-present external stimuli.

Answer: b 46. In a study by Berkowitz, subjects were made
Page: 281–282 angry in a room containing either a gun or a
badminton racket. Later, when given a chance to
administer shocks to a "fellow student," subjects
who had been in the room with the gun shocked
the other person more than those who had been
in the room containing the badminton racket.
This study demonstrates:
a. that anger increases the probability of
aggressive behavior.
b. the power of "aggressive cues" in facilitating
aggressive behavior.
c. that thoughts about playing nonviolent
sports—such as badminton—tend to reduce
the probability of aggression.
d. that the theory of "catharsis" is unable to
explain aggressive behavior.

Answer: d 47. Generalizing from Berkowitz's research, you
Page: 281–282 would predict that a subject who has just watched
a "slasher" movie (in which a beautiful young
woman gets brutally raped, beaten, and murdered
by a man who was an artist) would be more
likely to act aggressively against:
a. male artists.
b. female artists.
c. men who look like the murderer.
d. beautiful young women.

Answer: a
Page: 282

48. The results of Zimbardo's experiment on deindividuation and aggression, in which some subjects "shocked" a confederate while wearing hoods and loose-fitting robes, suggests that:
    a. anonymity reduces concern over social evaluation, and therefore tends to increase aggression.
    b. individuals are usually more aggressive when alone than in groups because there is no one around to make them feel guilty.
    c. individuals are less aggressive when anonymous because they feel more responsible for their behaviors.
    d. anonymity reduces self-esteem, and therefore increases the likelihood of aggressive behaviors.

Answer: c
Page: 282

49. Zimbardo's research suggests that "deindividuation" contributes to aggression. By this, he means that we are more likely to behave aggressively when we are:
    a. angered.
    b. frustrated.
    c. anonymous.
    d. rewarded for aggressive behavior.

Answer: c
Page: 282

50. Brian Mullen studied lynchings perpetrated from 1899 to 1946, and found that the larger the lynch mobs, the more violent the lynchings. This research suggests that:
    a. catharsis is more likely to occur in large crowds than in smaller groups.
    b. aggressive behavior studied in the laboratory differs greatly from behavior in the "real" world.
    c. being a "faceless" member of a crowd lowers inhibitions against destructive acts.
    d. the process of "groupthink" is less powerful in smaller groups.

Answer: d   51. The text describes a situation in which some
Page: 285–286   convicted criminals were released from prison
                      early due to a technicality, whereas others served
                      out their sentences. In comparing these two
                      groups, the primary finding was:
                      a. prisoners who were let out early were found
                         to be much less aggressive.
                      b. prisoners who were let out early were found
                         to be much more aggressive.
                      c. prisoners who served their full term were less
                         than half as likely to return to prison.
                      d. prisoners who served their full term were
                         twice as likely to return to prison.

Answer: b   52. The results of the Stanford Prison Study indicate
Page: 286   that:
                      a. unconscious aggressive impulses are
                         triggered by authority figures.
                      b. a powerful situation can overwhelm
                         individual differences in behavior.
                      c. prison guards choose their jobs because they
                         enjoy power and sadistic self-expression.
                      d. efforts to improve prison conditions are
                         unlikely to succeed.

Answer: a   53. According to Feshbach and Feshbach's corre-
Page: 292–293   lational study of empathy and aggression in
                      children:
                      a. as empathy increases, aggression decreases.
                      b. as empathy increases, aggression increases.
                      c. empathy eliminates aggressive feelings in
                         children.
                      d. there is no significant relationship between
                         empathy and aggression in children.

Answer: c 54. Several methods for reducing aggression were
Page: 288–293   discussed in *The Social Animal*. _____ would
seem to be the most effective.
a. Severe punishment or threats of severe punishment
b. Punishing aggressive models
c. Building empathy and rewarding alternative behavior patterns
d. Building empathy and punishing aggressive models

Answer: d 55. Five methods for reducing aggressive behavior
Page: 288–293   are discussed in Aronson's text. These are: (a) pure reason, (b) punishment, (c) punishment of aggressive models, (d) rewarding alternative behavior patterns, and (e) building empathy toward others. Of these, the two methods which presently seem to be the most effective are:
a. a and d
b. b and c
c. c and d
d. d and e

Essay Questions

1. Is aggression instinctive in non-human animals? Is aggressive behavior instinctive among humans—are we "hard-wired" from birth to behave aggressively toward members of our own species? If not, what other kinds of influences affect the human tendency toward aggression? Be specific and cite research evidence to support your arguments.

2. What arguments have been made to support the idea that aggression is necessary for the evolutionary survival of the human species? What research evidence is consistent with this notion of the "survival of the fittest?" Do you agree with this perspective? Why or why not?

3. There is a popular belief that exposure to, or participation in, aggressive behavior is beneficial because it allows people to release their pent-up aggression. What does research on aggression tell us about this view? What are the implications of this belief as it affects public policy and the mass media (e.g., pornography, children's television programs, sports, etc.)? Be sure to back up your answer with examples of relevant research.

4. Briefly discuss the relationship between frustration and aggression. What other social-psychological factors influence this relationship? Illustrate your discussion with examples of relevant research.

5. Most everyone would agree that reducing human aggression is a worthwhile goal—one that may be crucial to our survival as a species. Among several possible methods of achieving this goal are punishment of aggressive behavior, rewarding nonaggressive behavior, punishment of aggressive models, and building empathy toward others. Choose two of these methods and discuss their relative merits and limitations. Support your answer with relevant research.

7
Prejudice

    I.   The Effects of Prejudice

            Self-esteem (Clark & Clark; Goldberg)
            Task performance (Jemmott & Gonzalez)
            Stereotypes (Bond; Bodenhausen & Wyer; Steele & Aronson)

    II.   Stereotypes and Attributions

            "Ultimate attribution error" (Pettigrew)
            Gender roles and biased attributions (Feldman-Summers & Kiesler; Deaux & Emsweiler; Nicholls; Deaux & Taynor)

    III.   Blaming the Victim (Lerner; Fischhoff; Janoff-Bulman)

            Belief in a just world (Lerner)
            Hindsight bias (Fischoff; Janoff-Bulman)

    IV.   Prejudice and Science

            Biased IQ tests
            Women and persuasibility (Janis & Field; Sistrunk & McDavid)

    V.   Some Subtle Effects of Prejudice

            Biased interactions (Word)
            Belief creates reality (Snyder & Swann)
            Subtle racism (Frey & Gaertner)
            Sexism as a nonconscious ideology (Bem & Bem)
            The effects of gender stereotypes (Porter & Geis; Bem; Jackson & Cash; Horner)

VI. Prejudice and the Media

    Representation of minority groups (Thibodeau)
    Representation of women (Geis)

VII. Causes of Prejudice

    A. Economic and political competition

        Competition for limited resources
        Competition and intergroup conflict (Sherif)

    B. The "scapegoat" theory of prejudice

        Lynchings and cotton prices (Hovland & Sears)
        The Eta of Japan (Klineberg)
        Frustration and scapegoating (Miller & Bugelski)

    C. The prejudiced personality

        The Authoritarian Personality (Adorno et al.)

    D. Prejudice through conformity

        Conforming to prejudiced norms (Pettigrew; Watson)

VIII. Stateways Can Change Folkways (Reducing Prejudice)

    A. The effects of equal-status contact

        Integrated vs. segregated housing (Deutsch & Collins)

    B. The vicarious effects of desegregation

        Psychology of inevitability
        Importance of firm policies (Pettigrew; Clark)

C. But all other things are not always equal

Desegregation and self-esteem (Stephan)

IX. Interdependence: A possible solution

Mutual interdependence (Deutsch)
The cooperative classroom: Jigsaw technique (Aronson et al.)
Underlying mechanisms (Gaertner)
Cooperation and empathy (Bridgeman)

Terms & Concepts

stereotyping
attributions
"ultimate attribution error"
self-attributions
hindsight bias
self-fulfilling prophecy
nonconscious ideology

"scapegoat" theory of prejudice
authoritarian personality
equal-status contact
psychology of inevitability
mutual interdependence
jigsaw technique

Chapter Overview

Prejudice refers to a hostile or negative attitude toward a distinguishable group based on generalizations derived from faulty or incomplete information. Such generalizations are based on stereotypes, which result from the tendency to assign identical characteristics to any person in a group, regardless of the actual variation among members of that group. Chapter 7 examines the social-psychological processes involved in stereotyping and prejudice, as well as other causal factors associated with prejudiced attitudes and behavior. In addition, strategies for reducing prejudice are explored. Important issues covered in the chapter are described below.

Stereotyping is closely linked with the human tendency to make attributions, or causal inferences, about behavior. In ambiguous situations, people are especially likely to commit the "ultimate attribution error," which involves making attributions that are consistent with prejudiced attitudes. In a spiraling fashion, such biased attributions serve to reinforce stereotypes and further intensify a person's prejudice. Research on gender roles offers abundant evidence on the effects of stereotypes on attribution processes. For example, attributions regarding women's achievement typically stress the role of luck and effort, whereas male achievement is associated with high ability.

Prejudice can have a subtle, but potent, impact on the behavior of prejudiced individuals as well as the victims of prejudice. Research revealing major differences in the way white interviewers interact with white and black job applicants illustrates this point (Word et al.). Specifically, interviewers unwittingly engaged in a variety of discriminatory, largely nonverbal, behaviors that produced nervous and less effective behavior on the part of black job applicants. The subtle effects of prejudice are also reflected in the phenomenon of the self-fulfilling prophecy, which refers to our tendency to interact with others on the basis of our erroneous beliefs which, in turn, often causes them to act in ways that validate these mistaken beliefs.

The media play an important institutional role in sustaining prejudice. Although some progress has been made in recent decades, research indicates that underrepresentation and media stereotyping of women and minority group members remains fairly common.

Among the important causes of prejudice are political and economic competition for scarce resources, as well as the tendency for majority group members to "scapegoat" minority groups, particularly during troubled times or in the face of frustrating events.

Conformity processes are a key factor in prejudice. According to this view, when people act in a prejudiced manner, they are often simply conforming to the prevailing norms of their social world. Thus, research reveals that when people move to areas where norms are more prejudicial, their prejudice increases (and vice versa). The conformity hypothesis is also supported by evidence indicating that individuals who characteristically conform to a variety of social norms also show strong prejudice when they live in an environment in which bigotry is the norm.

The events surrounding the Supreme Court's 1954 decision calling for school desegregation provide a context for examining the problem of prejudice reduction. An analysis of these events, as well as evidence from social-psychological research, indicate that prejudice is more likely to be reduced when intergroup contact is based on equal-status relations, is clearly supported by authorities, and involves the interdependent pursuit of common goals. Incorporating these factors, the "jigsaw classroom" offers an effective strategy for reducing prejudice in the classroom. The technique involves the use of interdependent learning groups in which each student's academic performance rests on cooperating, rather than competing, with classmates. Carefully conducted field research has documented the success of the jigsaw technique in increasing self-esteem, academic performance, and facilitating the development of empathy.

Lecture Ideas & Teaching Suggestions

Face-ism. A subtle, but intriguing, manifestation of sexism in our culture is reflected in the phenomenon of "face-ism." Research on this topic by Archer and his colleagues has revealed that visual depictions of men and women differ in the extent to which facial features are given prominence. In several studies they found that, on average, male faces were depicted more prominently than female faces in a variety of visual media, including newspaper and magazine photos, works of art, and pictures drawn by college students. Conversely, in portrayals of women, relatively more space was devoted to the rest of the body. In discussing the implications of their findings, Archer and his colleagues note that they are consistent with gender stereotypes and serve to reinforce sexist notions regarding masculine and feminine domains in life: When it comes to the life of the mind, men are perceived as the natural leaders, whereas physical appearance is of greater importance for women.

To illustrate your discussion of face-ism, you might collect photos from newspapers and magazines that reflect this phenomenon. Before introducing the research findings, you can display these photos in class, asking your students if they detect anything unusual about the way men and women are portrayed. For details on how "face-ism" was measured in these studies, see Archer, D., Iritani, B., Kimes, D. D., & Barrios, M. (1983). Face-ism: Five studies of sex differences in facial prominence. *Journal of Personality and Social Psychology, 45*, 725–735.

The Effects of "Solo Status." Underrepresentation in employment, education, and other areas can cause women and minority group members to occupy a "token" status within an organizational setting. What are the effects of being the only member, or one of the few members, of an underrepresented group in a majority-group setting? Research by Shelley Taylor and her associates indicates that, for example, being the only Afro-American in an otherwise White group, or being the only woman in an otherwise all-male group, has considerable impact on how others perceive the person occupying this "solo status." In general, the minority person is perceived as more prominent and influential, is evaluated more extremely, and is more often categorized in stereotypic terms than a comparable individual within a sexually or racially integrated group. In addition, the minority person is typically perceived as playing a greater causal role in events that occur within the group. People also tend to remember more information about a person who occupies a minority position within a group. Taylor and her colleagues offer an information-processing interpretation of these effects: Because information about the solo individual is more salient, it engulfs one's field of attention. In explaining the effects of "solo status" to your students, you may wish to call their attention to the likely impact of tokenism on the minority person. Given what we know about the self-fulfilling prophecy and the confirmation bias (discussed in Chapter 4), how might the effects of salience influence the behavior of the solo individual? For a discussion of research on the effects of solo status, see Taylor, S.E., Crocker, J., Fiske, S.T., Sprinzen, M., and Winkler, J.D. (1979). The generalizability of salience effects. *Journal of Personality and Social* Psychology, 37, 357–368; and Taylor, S.E., & Fiske, S.T. (1978). Salience, attention, and attribution: Top of the head phenomena. In L. Berkowitz (Ed.), *Advances in experimental social psychology* (Vol. 11). New York: Academic Press.

Prejudice and Stereotypes. It is often difficult for people to acknowledge their stereotypes and prejudices about other people—especially for individuals who place a high value on eliminating prejudice from society. One way to stimulate discussion of personal experiences of prejudice is to ask students to describe the kinds of people who drive different makes of cars—such as Cadillacs, BMWs, Mercedes,

Volkswagens, Fords, and Hondas. After eliciting students' stereotypes, you can ask them several questions that pertain to stereotyping processes in general. What is the source of their "knowledge" about the drivers of these cars—advertising? family and friends? direct personal knowledge? How accurate do they think these stereotypes are? Do they believe these stereotypes are useful or destructive? Do they feel prejudiced against drivers of certain cars? For example, are they more likely to get angry if they are cut off in traffic by a Cadillac than a VW? If so, why? Finally, you might also want to illustrate in-group/out-group effects (covered in Chapter 4) by asking students if they feel a special sense of "kinship" or liking for others who drive the same kind of car. Do they perceive same-car drivers, as a group, as more unique and differentiated, whereas drivers of another make of car (e.g., Cadillac) are seen as highly similar to each other? In other words, from the in-group perspective, do out-group drivers "all look alike?"

Projects and Discussion Topics

1. PROJECT: Nearly everyone has been the target of blatant or subtle prejudice at some point in their lives. Whether this has been a frequent or rare occurrence for you, write about some of your experiences as a victim of prejudice. What kinds of stereotypes or labels were applied to you? What do you suppose was the cause of the other person's prejudice? How did being a victim of prejudice affect your self-esteem and behavior? What were your feelings and behavior toward the person who treated you in a prejudiced manner? How did you deal with the situation? Were you in any way able to counteract or defend yourself against their attitudes and behavior toward you? If so, how? Share some of these experiences with your classmates.

2. PROJECT: For one day, make a self-conscious effort to create "self-fulfilling prophesies" in your encounters with others by treating them as if you believed they were friendly, compassionate, competent, etc. (For the sake of ethics, restrict yourself to positive behaviors!) Keep a record of how people responded to your behavior, as well as your own reactions to their behavior. How often did they confirm your expectations, and how did you feel when they did? If and when they didn't, how did that make you feel? In general, what was it like to

conduct this "experiment"? Write a report of your findings and observations.

2. DISCUSSION: As you know from your readings, competition is one factor that appears to contribute to the problem of prejudiced beliefs and behaviors. Under what conditions is competition more likely to foster prejudice? Would you advocate eliminating all forms of competition as a strategy for reducing prejudice and aggression? Why or why not? Recall some experiences in your own life in which you felt highly competitive with another person or group of people. How did you feel about your "opponents," and how do you suppose they felt about you? If the period of competition ended or subsided, did your feelings change about this person or group? In what way? Share your experiences and reflections with others in your discussion group.

3. DISCUSSION: To what extent is prejudice a problem on your campus or in your community? If so, what are some subtle—or even blatant—ways that prejudice is expressed? What are the most common forms of prejudice in your social environment (e.g., racism, sexism, basic intolerance for different points of view, etc.)? Imagine you had the authority and resources to reduce prejudice on your campus or community. What kind of strategies would you implement to achieve this goal?

4. DISCUSSION: Is everyone prejudiced to one degree or another? That is, is it possible to be entirely free of prejudice in our society? Why or why not? How could people become more aware of the subtle ways in which they hold or express prejudiced beliefs and behavior? Describe any experiences you might have had in which you suddenly realized you were acting or feeling prejudiced toward another person or group. Were you surprised to discover this about yourself?

Additional Readings

Allport, G.W. (1979). (1954). *The nature of prejudice.* 25th anniversary edition. Reading, MA: Addison-Wesley.

Aronson, E. (1975, February). The jigsaw route to learning and liking. *Psychology Today*, pp. 43–50. (Discusses the prejudice-reducing effects of cooperative learning groups.)

Bem, S. (1975, September). Androgyny vs. the tight little lives of fluffy women and chesty men. *Psychology Today*, pp. 58–62. (Research on androgyny is discussed, as well as the benefits—for both sexes—of having a balance of masculine and feminine traits and qualities.)

Bentancourt, H., & López, S.R. (1993). The study of culture, ethnicity, and race in American psychology. *American Psychologist, 48*(6), 629-637.

Blanchard, F.A., Lilly, T., & Vaugn, L.A. (1991). Reducing the expression of racial prejudice. *Psychological Science 2*(2), 101-105.

Duckitt, J. (1992). Psychology and prejudice: A historical analysis and integrative framework. *American Psychologist, 47*(10), 1182-1193.

Fiske, S.T. (1993). Controlling other people: The impact of power on stereotyping. *American Psychologist, 48*(6), 621-628.

Jaynes, G.D., & Williams, R.M., Jr. (Eds.) (1989). *A common destiny: Blacks and American society*. Washington, D.C.: National Academy Press.

Kiesler, S., Sproull, L., & Eccles, J. (1983, March). Second-class citizens? *Psychology Today*, pp. 40–48. (Examines how girls are discouraged from using and learning about computers.)

Nelson, L.L., & Kagan, S. (1972, September) Competition: The star-spangled scramble. *Psychology Today*, pp. 53–56. (A discussion of the detrimental impact of competitive individualism on children, and the possibilities for learning how to cooperate.)

Rushton, J.P. (1991). Racial differences: A reply to Zuckerman. *American Psychologist, 46*, 983-986.

Sadker, M., & Sadker, D. (1985, March). Sexism in the schoolroom of the 80s. *Psychology Today*, pp. 54–57. (Research reveals that girls get less feedback and encouragement from teachers, as compared to boys.)

Snyder, M. (1982, July). Self-fulfilling stereotypes. *Psychology Today*, pp. 60–68. (When people act on the basis of their stereotypes, they elicit behavior that confirms and reinforces their prejudiced beliefs.)

Stephan, W.G., & Feagin, J.R. (1980). *School desegregation: Past, present and future*. New York: Plenum.

Sun, K. (1993). Two types of prejudice and their causes. *American Psychologist, 48*(11), 1152-1153. (A response to Duckitt.)

Taylor, D. (1984, January). Toward the promised land. *Psychology Today*, pp. 46–48. (A look at the impact of civil rights legislation in education, employment, and housing.)

Zuckerman, M. (1990). Some dubious premises in research and theory on racial differences: Scientific, social, and ethical issues. *American Psychologist, 45*, 1297-1303.

Multiple-Choice Questions

Answer: d
Page: 296

1. Kenneth and Clark conducted a study that found that even very young children preferred white dolls and thought they were prettier than black dolls. This study was used to make the point that:
   a. the authoritarian personality does exist.
   b. stateways change folkways.
   c. the psychology of inevitability is inescapable.
   d. separate is not equal.

Answer: b
Page: 296

2. In Goldberg's study, in which women read an article supposedly written by either John T. McKay or Joan T. McKay, it was found that:
   a. the women rated the article as better written when they thought a woman wrote it.
   b. the women rated the article as better written when they thought a man wrote it.
   c. the women rated the article as better written when they thought a woman wrote it, but were more persuaded by the message when they thought it was written by a man.
   d. the women thought the "male author" was more intelligent, but rated the "female author" as more likable.

Answer: c
Page: 296

3. In Golberg's study, in which women read an article supposedly written by either John T. McKay or Joan T. McKay, it was found that:
   a. changing one letter in the author's first name from an "h" to an "a" had no effect on the subjects' rating of the article.
   b. subjects rated the article as better written when the author was a woman than when he was a man.
   c. subjects rated the article as better written when the author was a man than when she was a woman.
   d. the quality of the article was rated equal in both conditions, but the subjects were more persuaded by it when the author was a woman.

Answer: a
Page: 296–297

4. Jemmott and Gonzalez found that children who were assigned to a low-status, minority position during an experiment performed poorly on a problem-solving task, compared to children who were not assigned to this low-status position. These findings indicate that:
   a. being singled out and labeled as "inferior," even on a temporary basis, has damaging effects on achievement.
   b. negative labeling, even on a temporary basis, has long-term damaging effects on self-esteem and empathy.
   c. being singled out and labeled as "inferior," even on a temporary basis, is equally damaging as a lifetime of negative labeling.
   d. negative labeling has damaging effects on achievement but only when the label is relevant to the particular task being performed.

Answer: a
Page: 298–300

5. Julia states, "all football players are just a bunch of thick-headed, beer-guzzling oafs." Her statement is best thought of as capturing the essence of:
   a. stereotyping.
   b. the self-fulfilling prophecy.
   c. the psychology of inevitability.
   d. scapegoating.

Answer: c
Page: 300–302

6. Which of the following is *not* a characteristic of a stereotype?
   a. Stereotyping provides a way of justifying our own biases.
   b. Stereotyping leads people to make attributions that are consistent with their prejudiced beliefs.
   c. Stereotypes are relatively flexible and change if individuals are provided with new information that is inconsistent with their beliefs.
   d. Stereotypes tend to generate self-fulfilling prophecies.

Answer: a
Page: 301

7. Bond and his colleagues investigated a psychiatric hospital that had a racially mixed population of patients but was run by an all-white staff. The results of this study revealed that:
   a. harsher methods of handling violent behavior were used against black patients than against white patients.
   b. black patients committed more violent acts while in the hospital than did white patients.
   c. black patients committed fewer violent acts while in the hospital than did white patients.
   d. the staff's prejudiced treatment toward blacks increased over time.

Answer: b
Page: 302

8. Suppose you are a subject in an experiment and are asked to make a parole decision about two criminals, a Latino, José Ortega, and an upper middle class white man, Matthew Smith. Both men were convicted of embezzling funds from the bank in which they worked. Generalizing from a similar study conducted by Bodenhausen and Wyer, you would most likely recommend parole for:
   a. José but not Matthew
   b. Matthew but not José.
   c. both José and Matthew.
   d. neither José nor Matthew.

Answer: d
Page: 303–304

9. Steele and Aronson administered the verbal portion of the GRE to black and white students, telling them either that the test was measuring their intellectual ability or that it had nothing to do with their intellectual ability. The results of this study revealed that:
   a. in general, students performed better when they thought the test was important, regardless of race.
   b. in general, students performed better when they thought the test was not important, regardless of race.
   c. black students did better than white, when they thought the test was important, but worse when they thought it was not important.
   d. white students did better than black when they thought the test was important, but not when they thought it was not important.

Answer: a
Page: 304–305

10. Attribution theory is most concerned with explaining the:
    a. tendency people have to infer the causes of behavior.
    b. tendency people have to make stereotypic statements about minority group members.
    c. tendency people have to derogate themselves.
    d. tendency people have to look for situational explanations for the behavior of others.

Answer: a
Page: 305

11. According to the ultimate attribution error, if subjects thought a harm-doer was black, they would be more likely to attribute his action to _____. When they thought he was white, they would be more willing to attribute his action to _____.
    a. his personality; the situation
    b. the situation; his personality
    c. the minority; the majority
    d. the majority; the minority

Answer: c
Page: 305

12. Frank has started working in an office recently where Mary has worked for several years. Mary is prejudiced against Jewish people, and Frank just happens to be Jewish. While eating her lunch at work one day, Mary noticed that Frank had saved his lunch bag after eating—rather than throwing it in the trash. "How cheap can you get?" Mary thinks. "Those Jews won't spend a nickel if they don't have to!" What Mary doesn't know is that Frank is an avid environmentalist who tries to recycle as many resources as he can. Mary's comment is an example of:
    a. scapegoating.
    b. the psychology of inevitability.
    c. the ultimate attribution error.
    d. the self-fulfilling prophecy.

Answer: b
Page: 305

13. The "ultimate attribution error" has been defined by Pettigrew as:
    a. the tendency to attribute one's own failures to the situation.
    b. the tendency for people to make attributions that are consistent with their beliefs or prejudices about others.
    c. the tendency to make situational attributions about another's behavior.
    d. the tendency to attribute another's behavior to both situational and dispositional factors.

Answer: b 14. Susan and Tim are college sophomores. One day
Page: 305–306 in physics class, the professor handed back the results of an exam they had taken the week before. Susan and Tim both received an "A" on their exams. According to research on attribution, which of the following statements would Susan be more likely to make?
- a. "That test was really tough, but I did a terrific job!"
- b. "Wow—what a lucky break!"
- c. "Boy, I'm glad I did well—I really blew it on the last two exams."
- d. "Dad was right—I *do* have a natural talent for science."

Answer: c 15. Summarizing the research on attribution and
Page: 307–308 gender roles, which of the following is true?
- a. When women fail, they are treated more harshly by society than men.
- b. When men succeed, they are seen as highly motivated.
- c. When men fail, they are treated more harshly by society than women.
- d. When men succeed, they are seen as deserving greater rewards than women.

Answer: c
Page: 307

16. Mary believes that she got her job as a lawyer because she has the potential to be a great lawyer. Her sister, Patty, believes she got her lawyer's job because her firm "needed to hire a woman." Suppose both women come up against a very difficult case. Which result would you be more likely to expect, based on research conducted by Turner and Pratkanis?
    a. Mary would work more hours, but be more likely to lose.
    b. Patty would work more hours, but be more likely to lose.
    c. Patty would be more likely to give up.
    d. Mary would be more likely to give up.

Answer: a
Page: 307–308

17. In comparison to women, men in our society are expected to be _____ successful; if they are not successful, men are treated _____.
    a. more; more harshly
    b. less; more harshly
    c. more; less harshly
    d. less; less harshly

Answer: b
Page: 308–309

18. In the Lerner experiment, in which subjects observed the experimenter flipping a coin to decide which of two people would be rewarded for his work, it was later found that:
    a. the nonrewarded person was seen as having engaged in the task for its own sake (dissonance effect).
    b. the rewarded person was seen as having worked harder on the task (just-world effect).
    c. the nonrewarded person was liked better than the rewarded one (compensation effect).
    d. the rewarded person came to believe that he had worked harder on the task (self-fulfilling prophecy).

Answer: c
Page: 309

19. Believing that the world is a "just place" tends to:
    a. create a more just world by inducing the person to treat others as responsible for their own outcomes.
    b. create a more just world by reducing prejudiced beliefs and attitudes.
    c. create a less just world by leading the person to derogate those who have received bad outcomes through no fault of their own.
    d. create a more just world by committing the person to the belief that it is.

Answer: b
Page: 309

20. Jorge states, "I always knew that that white guy Johnson was a sneak. I'm not at all surprised that they finally caught him stealing money out of the cash drawer." Jorge's statement is best thought of as an example of:
    a. an authoritarian personality.
    b. hindsight bias.
    c. the psychology of inevitability.
    d. mutual interdependence.

Answer: a
Page: 311

21. Suppose Fred and Margaret are both being persuaded about the best way to repair lawnmowers and the best way to choose paint colors to decorate a kitchen. Based on the recent work by Sistrunk and David, you would expect:
    a. Fred to be more persuaded about mower repair and Margaret about decorating.
    b. Margaret to be more persuaded about mower repair and Fred about decorating.
    c. Fred to be more persuaded about mower repair and decorating.
    d. Margaret to be more persuaded about mower repair and decorating.

Answer: b 22. Frey and Gaertner, in a study involving prejudice
Page: 314 and helping, found that:
   a. whites, wishing to look "open-minded," were actually more willing to help a black than a white person.
   b. whites discriminated against a black person only when such discrimination could be easily rationalized.
   c. whites and blacks discriminate against each other equally.
   d. whites discriminated against blacks when their self-esteem was threatened.

Answer: c 23. Research on the self-fulfilling prophecy conducted
Page: 313–314 by Mark Snyder and his colleagues has revealed that:
   a. women are more likely than men to be influenced by others' beliefs about them.
   b. introverts are less likely than extroverts to test their hypotheses about other people.
   c. even when we're "open-minded" enough to test our beliefs about others, we can inadvertently produce the very behaviors we expect.
   d. when people are offered large rewards for being correct, they are less likely to use a biased strategy in testing their hypotheses about others.

Answer: d 24. It's the first day of the semester, and a group of
Page: 314–315 students are sitting around a table in the
classroom, waiting for their seminar in social
psychology to begin. An attractive woman enters
the room and sits down next to George, a college
senior. In an effort to be friendly, George
immediately turns to the woman and says, "What
have you heard about this Jones guy? Is he a
boring instructor, or what?" The woman replies,
"I don't know what other people think, but I'm
Professor Jones and I think I'm a very interesting
instructor!" George's behavior is an example of:
a. androgynous ideology.
b. the self-fulfilling prophecy.
c. biased attributions.
d. nonconscious ideology.

Answer: a 25. According to a study by Jackson and Cash, men
Page: 318 and women described as "androgynous" were
liked more:
a. than those described as behaving in a gender-stereotyped manner.
b. by female subjects than by male subjects.
c. by male subjects than by female subjects.
d. when they were physically attractive, but less when they were unattractive.

Answer: b 26. Jeannine grows up with parents who believe that
Page: 313–314 women should be soft-spoken, gentle, content to
stay at home, and not involved in decision-making. Consequently, as an adult, Jeannine
conforms to their expectations. This situation is
best thought of as an example of:
a. an androgynous ideology.
b. a self-fulfilling prophecy.
c. the psychology of inevitability.
d. scapegoating.

Answer: a
Page: 318

27. In a series of experiments on fear of success, it was found that:
  a. women were likely to predict an unhappy future for a woman described as successful in a nontraditional role.
  b. men were likely to predict a happy future for a man described as successful in a nontraditional role.
  c. women tend to fear success regardless of the role, while men tend to fear success only when it is inconsistent with a traditionally male role.
  d. external conditions that block women's success are inconsequential compared to internal obstacles, such as the "fear of success."

Answer: b
Page: 320

28. According to research by Thibodeau, from the 1940s to the 1960s, the number of blacks depicted in stereotypic roles in *New Yorker* cartoons _____.
  a. increased
  b. decreased
  c. increased until about 1950, then decreased
  d. decreased until about 1950, then increased

Answer: d
Page: 322

29. A study by Florence Geis and her colleagues on the effects of television commercials on women's aspirations found that:
  a. women exposed to sex-stereotyped commercials expressed "fear of failure."
  b. women exposed to sex-stereotyped commercials expressed "fear of success."
  c. women who saw commercials in which men were subservient expressed the desire to have careers and never get married.
  d. women exposed to sex-stereotyped commercials displayed lower levels of achievement aspiration than women who saw commercials in which male-female roles were reversed.

Answer: b   30. Of the following, people are most likely to be
Page: 323   prejudiced if:
            a. they have no choice but to live in a racially integrated housing project.
            b. their social status is low or declining.
            c. they believe they are not prejudiced.
            d. they have high self-esteem.

Answer: d   31. Which of the following is probably *not* a major
Page: 324   cause of prejudice?
            a. personality needs, such as authoritarianism
            b. economic or political competition
            c. scapegoating—the displacement of aggression
            d. the fact that stereotypes about different groups are highly accurate

Answer: b   32. The subject in Sherif's study of two groups, the
Page: 326–327   "Eagles" and the "Rattlers" were:
            a. college students who volunteered to participate for extra credit.
            b. normal 11–12 year old boys.
            c. male college students.
            d. men age 24–27 from various occupations who volunteered to participate for money.

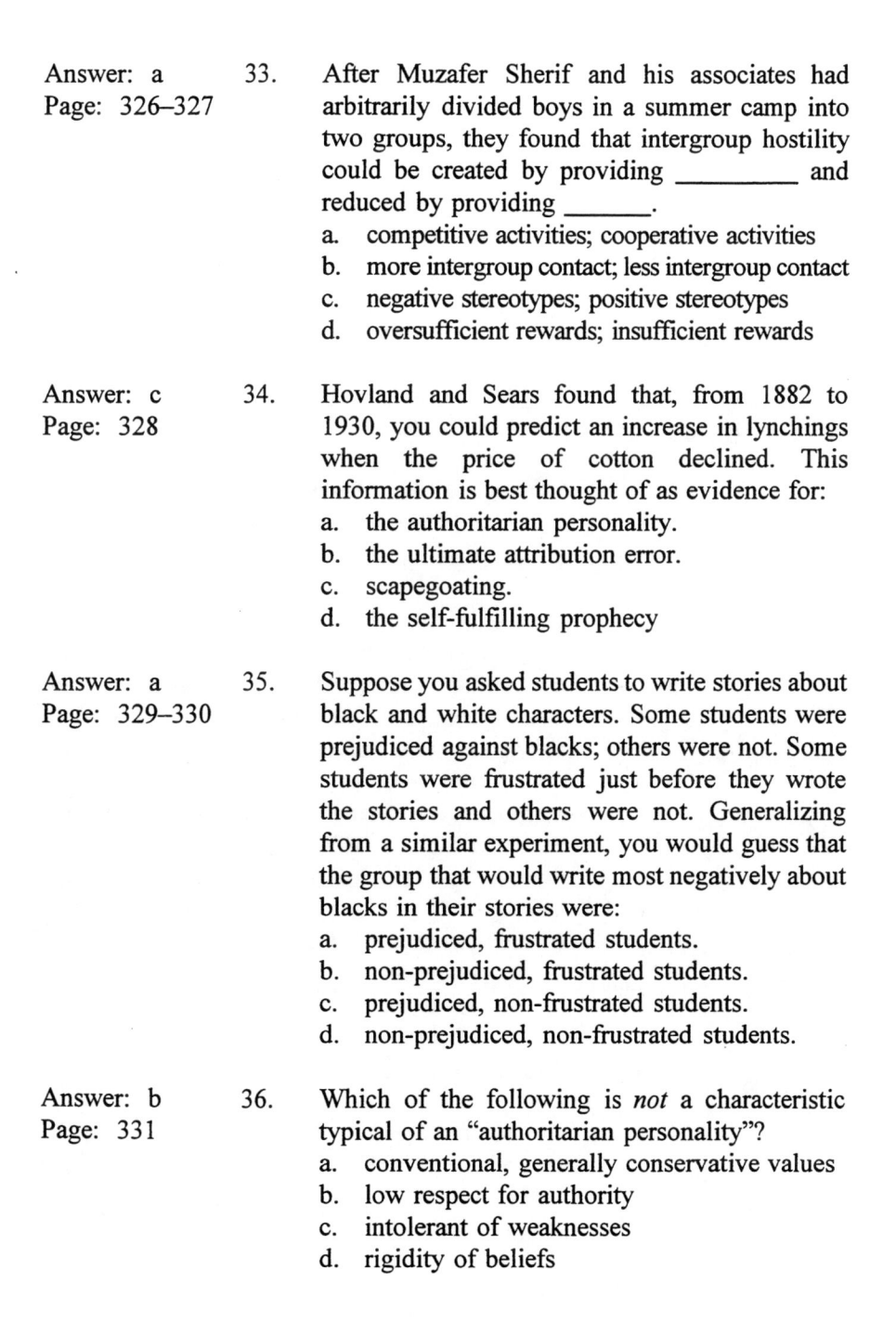

Answer: a   33. After Muzafer Sherif and his associates had
Page: 326–327   arbitrarily divided boys in a summer camp into
                      two groups, they found that intergroup hostility
                      could be created by providing _____ and
                      reduced by providing _____.
                      a. competitive activities; cooperative activities
                      b. more intergroup contact; less intergroup contact
                      c. negative stereotypes; positive stereotypes
                      d. oversufficient rewards; insufficient rewards

Answer: c   34. Hovland and Sears found that, from 1882 to
Page: 328   1930, you could predict an increase in lynchings
                      when the price of cotton declined. This
                      information is best thought of as evidence for:
                      a. the authoritarian personality.
                      b. the ultimate attribution error.
                      c. scapegoating.
                      d. the self-fulfilling prophecy

Answer: a   35. Suppose you asked students to write stories about
Page: 329–330   black and white characters. Some students were
                      prejudiced against blacks; others were not. Some
                      students were frustrated just before they wrote
                      the stories and others were not. Generalizing
                      from a similar experiment, you would guess that
                      the group that would write most negatively about
                      blacks in their stories were:
                      a. prejudiced, frustrated students.
                      b. non-prejudiced, frustrated students.
                      c. prejudiced, non-frustrated students.
                      d. non-prejudiced, non-frustrated students.

Answer: b   36. Which of the following is *not* a characteristic
Page: 331   typical of an "authoritarian personality"?
                      a. conventional, generally conservative values
                      b. low respect for authority
                      c. intolerant of weaknesses
                      d. rigidity of beliefs

Answer: d   37. Which of the following is *not* characteristic of
Page: 331   people to whom Adorno and his colleagues refer
                 as the "authoritarian personality"?
                 a. They tend to be rigid and set in their beliefs.
                 b. In general, they tend to be intolerant of
                    weakness.
                 c. They tend to possess conventional values and
                    standards.
                 d. They tend to be authority figures.

Answer: d   38. An "authoritarian personality" is closely linked to
Page: 331   which of the following dimensions?
                 a. mutual interdependence
                 b. the matching hypothesis
                 c. the self-fulfilling prophecy
                 d. prejudice

Answer: d   39. Joe was brought up in a household in which both
Page: 333   of his parents worked outside the home, and both
                 they and the children shared responsibilities for
                 housework. When Joe left home and went to
                 college, he joined a fraternity and became friends
                 with some members who held rather sexist
                 attitudes towards women's roles. When Joe came
                 home for the summer, his parents were surprised
                 to find that Joe expected his mother to do his
                 laundry and pick up after him. Joe's new
                 attitudes were most likely a function of:
                 a. scapegoating.
                 b. his authoritarian personality.
                 c. the psychology of inevitability.
                 d. conformity processes.

Answer: a   40.   Studies on conformity and prejudice have shown
Page: 333–334   that:
                      a. individuals who move into areas in which the
                         norm is more prejudiced show dramatic in-
                         creases in their levels of prejudice.
                      b. individuals who are least likely to conform to
                         a wide variety of social norms usually show
                         a higher degree of prejudice in environments
                         that are highly prejudiced.
                      c. individuals with nonconformist personalities
                         tend to become less prejudiced when they
                         move into areas that are high in prejudice.
                      d. conformity to general norms and specific
                         prejudices such as racism are not related.

Answer: b   41.   According to *The Social Animal*, when important
Page: 337   issues are involved, information campaigns:
                      a. have been successful in changing prejudiced
                         attitudes when given adequate media
                         coverage.
                      b. generally fail because people are unlikely to
                         listen to information that is incompatible
                         with their prejudiced beliefs.
                      c. are effective in eliminating distortions and
                         deep-seated prejudiced attitudes when indi-
                         viduals are forced to listen to the information.
                      d. are ineffective in changing prejudiced attitudes
                         unless both sides of the issue are presented.

Answer: a 42. According to the "psychology of inevitability," if
Page: 339 an individual anticipates close contact with a
group against which he or she is prejudiced:
   a. that individual will change his or her prejudiced attitude so that it becomes more favorable toward the group.
   b. it will tend to increase that individual's prejudice toward the group.
   c. there will be no change in the individual's attitude because he or she is being forced into the situation.
   d. that individual will pretend to be less prejudiced toward the group, but the real prejudice will not change.

Answer: a 43. When it comes to changing deeply rooted
Page: 339 attitudes and behavior, such as prejudice, the most effective strategy is to:
   a. place people in a situation in which they must change their behavior, then changes in attitudes will follow.
   b. give people lots of vivid and personal information that contradicts their attitudes, then changes in behavior will follow.
   c. offer people rewards and praise for changing their behavior, then changes in attitudes will follow.
   d. have a highly attractive and credible speaker present arguments that contradict the person's attitudes, then changes in behavior will follow.

Answer: b   44. In general, early efforts to desegregate the
Page: 342–343   schools resulted in:
a. an increase in the self-esteem of minority children, but a surprising decrease in the self-esteem of nonminority children.
b. an unanticipated decrease in the self-esteem of minority children.
c. reduced prejudice among minority children, but not among nonminority children.
d. better academic performance among non-minority children.

Answer: c   45. In their investigations of the early years of school desegregation, Pettigrew and other researchers found that violence tended to result when:
Page: 341–342
a. people were not given a choice about whether desegregation would occur.
b. desegregation took place in the South, rather than the North.
c. desegregation policies were implemented in a hesitant, gradual, or inconsistent manner.
d. no efforts were made to reduce prejudice prior to desegregation.

Answer: c   46. Aronson argues that the most effective way to reduce prejudice is to:
Page: 343
a. allow people to choose whether or not they will desegregate so that cognitive dissonance causes them to change their attitudes.
b. use information campaigns to change people's attitudes.
c. require people to desegregate with no options of going back to segregation.
d. try to keep prejudiced groups apart as much as possible to reduce frustration and competition.

Answer: c 47. Aronson points out that one failure of the jigsaw
Page: 345–346 group technique is that:
a. it diminishes the learning gains typically made by the white, middle-class majority.
b. even though it decreases competition in the larger classroom, it increases competition in the small groups.
c. not all situations reward cooperation.
d. although minority children learn more in school, their self-concept usually suffers.

Answer: c 48. Jane is a fifth-grader whose classroom operates
Page: 351 according to the cooperative principles of the "jigsaw" technique. One day on the school playground, Jane saw a second-grade girl trip and fall, scraping her knee badly. Which of the following would best characterize Jane's response to this incident?
a. "I better be careful, or I might trip, too."
b. "Too bad the teacher isn't here to help this kid."
c. "Ouch—that must really hurt. I'll go see if she needs some help."
d. "Hey, I saw the kid who tripped that little girl. I hope he gets caught!"

Answer: b 49. Mutual interdependence refers to a situation in
Page: 344 which:
a. you depend on someone else to help you accomplish your goals.
b. individuals need, and are needed by, one another to accomplish their goals.
c. individuals allow each other the freedom to accomplish their own independent goals.
d. individuals compete in a friendly way to accomplish a goal that each person values highly.

Answer: b 50. The major feature of jigsaw groups that Aronson
Page: 344–345   believes accounts for their success in reducing
the negative effects of prejudice is:
a. lack of competition among children.
b. the necessity of depending on all group members for vital information.
c. the forbidding of any teasing or abuse of minority children.
d. the breaking down of a large, formal classroom into small, informal groups so the children get a chance to know each other.

Answer: d 51. According to Aronson, which of the following is
Page: 350   a result of a jigsaw classroom?
a. Anglo children experienced a reduction in self-esteem
b. Anglo children learned less than in a traditional classroom
c. minority children experienced a reduction in self-esteem
d. minority children performed better than in a traditional classroom

Answer: d 52. Recent research has shown that children who
Page: 351   cooperate with each other in interdependent classroom situations:
a. like each other less.
b. show decreases in their self-esteem.
c. enjoy school less.
d. develop more empathy.

Answer: b　　53.　According to *The Social Animal*, the jigsaw
Page: 346–350　　technique was successful because:
　　a.　it appealed to natural altruistic tendencies in children before they outgrew them.
　　b.　it capitalized on children's self-interest to do well in school.
　　c.　teachers played little or no role in the learning process.
　　d.　cooperation allows everyone to perform equally well in school.

Answer: d　　54.　Suppose you know a black person who feels that
Page: 350–353　　he is the victim of sexual discrimination and prejudice. According to experimental data, which of the following strategies will be effective in reducing this prejudice?
　　a.　competing more aggressively with whites for economic and political power
　　b.　creating counter-stereotypes aimed at the prejudiced group, such as "whitey"
　　c.　drawing together with other blacks into highly cohesive groups which do not include whites
　　d.　working interdependently with white people in situations which allow both an equal status

Answer: a   55. Suppose you were a woman who felt she was the
Page: 350–353   victim of sexual discrimination and prejudice.
                    According to experimental data, which of the
                    following strategies will be effective in reducing
                    this prejudice?
                    a. working interdependently with men in situations which allow you both an equal status
                    b. drawing together into highly cohesive groups which do not include men
                    c. assigning women leadership roles to demonstrate they can perform as well as, or better than, men
                    d. changing people's attitudes by pointing out the injustice of prejudice against women.

Answer: d   56. Aronson's argument that "stateways change
Page: 336–338   folkways" is based primarily on:
                    a. reactance theory.
                    b. the "just world" hypothesis.
                    c. conformity pressures.
                    d. the theory of cognitive dissonance.

Essay Questions

1. What is prejudice and how is it related to the phenomenon of stereotyping? How do stereotypes influence the kinds of attributions that are made regarding the behavior or personalities of members of a stereotyped group? In your answer, provide research examples that illustrate the role of attributions in stereotyping and prejudice.

2. The year is 1954, and the Supreme Court has just made its ruling in the case of *Brown v. the Board of Education of Topeka, Kansas*. Desegregation of the schools will proceed. You've been called upon to provide expert social-psychological testimony on how best to implement desegregation. What specific advice would you give policy-makers? What factors should they consider in planning desegregation efforts so that the expected positive outcomes are more likely to occur? Cite research to support your recommendations.

3. Daryl and Sandra Bem suggest that prejudice against women in our society is an example of a "nonconscious ideology." What is meant by this term? Describe at least one piece of research that supports this position.

4. How can economic or political forces foster prejudice between different groups in society? What role does competition and conflict over resources play in this process? Provide one historical example and one piece of research evidence to support your answer.

5. What is meant by the term "authoritarian personality" and how is it used to explain the phenomenon of prejudice? What are the characteristics and origins of this personality type? What research evidence supports or casts doubt on the notion that an "authoritarian personality" is a strong determinant of prejudice?

6. Briefly describe the features of the "jigsaw" classroom by comparing it to the way classrooms traditionally operate. What are the principles underlying the jigsaw technique that promote positive outcomes for students? How is the jigsaw technique related to the development of empathy?

8

Liking, Loving, and Interpersonal Sensitivity

I. Introduction

   Reward theory of attraction

II. The Effects of Praise and Favors

   Praise and criticism (Amabile)
   Flattery (Jones)
   Favors (Jennings; Lott & Lott; Brehm & Cole; Jecker & Landy; Lerner & Simmons)

III. Personal Attributes

   A. Competence (Aronson, Willerman & Floyd; Deaux)

   B. Physical attractiveness

      Dating couples (Walster; White)
      Attributions (Dion; Dion & Berscheid)
      The business world (Frieze)
      Reactions to beautiful women (Sigall & Aronson; Sigall & Ostrove; Sigall & Landy; Dows & Lyons; Snyder, Tanke & Berscheid)

IV. Similarity and Attraction

   Attitude similarity (Byrne; Rosenbaum)
   The effects of "conversion" (Sigall)

V. Liking, Being Liked, and Self-Esteem

    The perception of being liked (Curtis & Miller)
    Self-esteem (Walster; Kiesler & Baral; Grube; Rubin)
    Similarity and being liked (Jones, Bell & Aronson)

VI. The Gain and Loss of Esteem

    Gain-loss theory of attraction (Aronson & Linder; Mettee et al.)

VII. Love and Intimacy

    A. Opposites do attract—sometimes (Winch)

    B. Defining love

        Liking and loving scales (Rubin)
        Passionate versus companionate love (Walster & Walster)

    C. The quest for communal relationships

        Exchange and communal relationships (Clark & Mills)

    D. Gain-loss theory: Implications for close relationships

        Friends and strangers (Harvey; Floyd)

VIII. Intimacy, Authenticity, and Communication

    A. Communication goals
    B. The problem of miscommunication

IX. Characteristics of Effective Communication

    A. The importance of immediacy
    B. Feelings versus judgment
    C. Feelings and intentions
    D. Communication in everyday life

Terms & Concepts

reward theory of attraction
the foot-in-the-door technique
transsituational rewards
the pratfall effect
gain-loss theory of attraction
Rubin's liking and loving scales
passionate love

companionate love
self-disclosure
straight talk
T-group
feelings vs. judgments
feelings vs. intentions

Chapter Overview

Chapter 8 examines a broad range of social-psychological processes and factors that influence why people like each other. The merits of the reward theory of attraction—that we like those whose attributes or behavior are in some way rewarding to us—are explored, as well as its limitations in covering the full spectrum of phenomena associated with interpersonal attraction. In addition, the characteristics of various forms of attraction and attachment, such as liking and loving, are discussed. Finally, the chapter addresses some of the problems in communication that crop up in long-term, close relationships. Strategies for enhancing communication and intimacy in such relationships are explored in detail. Major points covered in the chapter are outlined below.

Research indicates that, contrary to the common-sense advice of Dale Carnegie, praise and favors are not universally rewarding and, thus, do not always lead to greater attraction. If the praise seems unwarranted, or if we think someone has an ulterior motive in praising us, our liking for the praiser will not increase and, in fact, may even decrease. Similarly, although we do like people who do us favors, getting someone to do us a favor is a more certain way of using favors to increase our attractiveness.

Reward theory suggests that we will like people more if they have pleasant or positive characteristics. While often true, under certain conditions this prediction does not hold. For example, research on the effects of a "pratfall" indicates that a highly competent person is liked more when he or she commits a small blunder than if he or she performed in a perfectly competent manner.

Physical beauty plays an important role in determining whether people will be initially attracted to each other. People also tend to perceive physically attractive people as having more desirable personality traits than less-attractive individuals. These perceptions can have profound effects on how people are treated and how they, in turn, behave toward others. Thus, in a study by Snyder, Tanke, and Berscheid, men who thought they were talking on the phone with an attractive woman rated her more positively, compared to men who thought they were talking with a less-attractive woman. More interestingly, however, independent judges who listened to the woman's half of the conversation—but who did not see her photo—also rated the attractive woman more positively, indicating that the expectations and behavior of the male subject had a strong impact on the behavior of the woman with whom he interacted.

Generally speaking, the single most powerful determinant of whether we like someone is whether that person likes us. Moreover, research indicates that mere perception of being liked can initiate a spiraling series of events that promote increasingly positive feelings and behavior between two people. That is, when we believe someone likes us, we tend to act on those beliefs—treating that person in a friendly, warm manner. Our behavior, in turn, leads the other person to feel liked, and to treat us in a friendly manner.

Although there is a strong relationship between similarity and attraction, other factors can weaken this relationship. For example, research indicates that we are more inclined to like someone whose attitudes are dissimilar to ours, as long as we are secure in the knowledge that this person already likes us—despite our different beliefs. Similarly, when we feel strongly about an issue we tend to find a person more attractive when they initially disagree with us, but are later "converted" to our way of thinking. Research also suggests that, under certain limited conditions, marital satisfaction is greater in relationships in which partners have dissimilar, but complementary, needs and characteristics.

Research on the "gain-loss" theory of attraction reveals that we tend to like someone more if they initially express disliking for us, but gradually come to feel positively toward us. Contrary to reward theory, our attraction is greater under such conditions than if the person had consistently expressed positive views about us all along. Gain-loss theory has important implications for long-term relationships. Over time, the positive regard of people who love us becomes less rewarding; yet, because we have grown accustomed to their affection, their power to hurt us is all the greater when, for whatever reason, they become critical or withhold their affection from us.

Social psychologists draw a distinction between liking and loving, generally viewing these two experiences as qualitatively different. Liking is marked by admiration and friendly affection; loving generally includes feeling of strong attachment, intimacy, and a deep concern for the beloved's welfare. In addition, researchers have identified two forms of love: passionate and companionate. The former is characterized by strong emotions, sexual desire, and intense preoccupation with the beloved. In contrast, companionate love is a milder, more stable experience marked by feelings of trust, dependability, and warmth. Typically rapid in onset, passionate love may be a prelude to the eventual development of companionate love, which is more enduring and deepens over time.

A distinction can be made between communal relationships, where people respond to others based on the others' needs, and exchange relationships, where the focus is on equity between participants. The closer a relationship is, the more communal it is, as demonstrated in research studies.

Honest and sensitive communication plays a vital role in establishing and maintaining intimate relationships over time. Yet, this is no easy matter. A general lesson of our society is to protect ourselves by concealing our feelings and to react defensively to others when engaged in an interpersonal conflict. One strategy for effective communication lies in learning how to use "straight talk" in our dealings with others. Straight talk involves a clear expression of our feelings, rather than blaming or attacking the other person with our negative judgments. This form of communication facilitates conflict resolution by allowing the other person to react to our concerns in a nondefensive manner, thereby preventing negative feelings from escalating.

Lecture Ideas & Teaching Suggestions

The Importance of Self-disclosure. As discussed in Chapter 8, a major obstacle to resolving interpersonal conflicts is the reluctance to reveal one's vulnerabilities. This reluctance inhibits effective communication, making it difficult for people to state their feelings and concerns without becoming defensive and judgmental toward the other person. Similarly, research indicates that self-disclosure is a key ingredient in developing and maintaining a close relationship. One way to augment your coverage of material on intimacy and communication is to provide students with a closer look at the role of self-disclosure in close relationships.

For example, research suggests that in order for intimacy to develop, self-disclosure generally must be reciprocal: as one partner begins to open up and reveal personal information, the other person responds in kind, disclosing information of a similar level of intimacy. Sharing intimate information about oneself implies to the other person that you trust him or her, and it is gratifying to have that trust returned when the other person also self-discloses. An experiment by Chaiken and Derlega (1974) illustrates the importance of reciprocity in self-disclosure. In their study, subjects observed a conversation between two women in which the first woman either disclosed intimate information about a sexual relationship or merely discussed a superficial problem about school. In response, the second woman either disclosed equally intimate or superficial information about herself. Subjects rated the second woman as more likable when she responded in a reciprocal fashion to the first woman's disclosures. When her responses were not reciprocal, she was evaluated negatively. Specifically, subjects perceived her as cold when her self-disclosures were less intimate than the other woman's. When she disclosed more intimate information than the other woman, subjects perceived her as psychologically maladjusted and indicated that they would be unlikely to want her as a friend.

Taking a different approach to the topic of self-disclosure, Derlega and Grzelak (1979) have identified four basic functions it serves for the individual: 1) self-expression—it allows us "get things off our chests"; 2) self-clarification—it helps us to understand more clearly our own thoughts and feelings; 3) social validation—it provides feedback regarding the appropriateness of our feelings and perceptions; 4) social control—it allows us to influence the other person's impression of us, since we can control how much and what kinds of information we choose to reveal about ourselves.

Details of the above research may be found in: Chaiken, A.L., & Derlega, V.J. (1974). Liking for the norm-breaker in self-disclosure. *Journal of Personality. 42*, 112–129; Derlega, V.J., & Grzelak, A.L. (1979). Appropriate self-disclosure. In G.J. Chelune (Ed.), *Self-disclosure: Origins, patterns and implications of openness in interpersonal relationships.* San Francisco: Jossey-Bass. Finally, for a look at gender differences in self-disclosure, see Derlega, V.J., & Chaiken, A.L. (1976). Norms affecting self-disclosure in men and women. *Journal of Consulting and Clinical Psychology, 44*, 376–380.

Loneliness. In recent years, researchers interested in love and friendship have increasingly turned their attention to the problem of loneliness, the flipside of intimacy. Research suggests that loneliness is quite common in our society and is frequently experienced by college students, especially those who are living away from home for the first time. As a result, this topic may be of special interest to your students.

How can we tell if someone is lonely? Perlman and Peplau (1982) have defined loneliness as "the unpleasant experience that occurs when a person's network of social relations is deficient in some important way, either quantitatively or qualitatively" (p. 31). Although researchers have offered a number of other definitions, common to all of them is the notion that loneliness is a highly subjective experience that cannot be identified by merely observing someone's behavior. You may wish to illustrate this point by asking students to consider and describe the difference between being "alone" versus being "lonely." For most people, being alone can often be a welcome and enjoyable experience, while loneliness is always associated with negative states of emotion. What are some of these emotions? Rubenstein and Shaver (1982) asked people to describe in detail how they felt when lonely. An analysis of these descriptions yielded four factors: desperation (e.g., feelings of panic and helplessness), depression, impatient boredom, and self-deprecation.

Two forms of loneliness—social and emotional—have been distinguished by Weiss (1973). Social loneliness results from insufficient ties to social networks such as groups of friends, co-workers, clubs, etc. Emotional loneliness arises when a person lacks a deep emotional connection with someone, such as a romantic partner, parents or children, or an intimate friend. A study by Russell, Cutrona, Rose, and Yurko (1984) supports Weiss's distinction. In their survey of 1,000 college students, they found that social loneliness stemmed from a lack of satisfying friendships, while emotional loneliness was associated with the absence of a romantic relationship.

Focusing on situational sources of loneliness, Perlman and Peplau (1982) have identified four kinds of events that tend to precipitate loneliness in most people: 1) when a close relationship ends (e.g., death, divorce); 2) physical separation from loved ones (e.g., moving to a new geographical area); 3) various changes in status (e.g., loss of job, when one's children "leave the nest"); and 4) when, for any number of reasons, the quality of an existing relationship is reduced (e.g., illness of one's partner). As is evident, societal conditions including high geographical and social mobility, rising divorce rates, and chronic unemployment can play an important role in the otherwise very private experience of loneliness.

For more information on this research and other aspects of loneliness, see: Peplau, L.A., & Perlman, D. (1982). *Loneliness: A sourcebook of current theory, research, and therapy*. New York: Wiley; Perlman, D., & Peplau, L.A. (1982). Toward a social psychology of loneliness. In Duck, S. and Gilmur, R. (Eds.), *Personal relationships* (Vol. 3): *Personal relationships in disorder*. New York: Academic Press; Rubenstein, C., & Shaver, P. (1982). *In search of intimacy*. New York: Delacorte; Russell, D., Cutrona, C.E., Rose, J., & Yurko, K. (1984). Social and emotional loneliness: An examination of Weiss's typology of loneliness. *Journal of Personality and Social Psychology, 46*, 1313–1321; Weiss, R.S. (1973). *Loneliness: The experience of emotional and social isolation*. Cambridge, MA: MIT Press.

Romantic jealousy. What can social psychology tell us about jealousy in relationships? White (1981) has observed that two factors are generally involved in any jealous reaction: feelings of personal inadequacy and the desire for an exclusive relationship. In addition, he proposes that a person who experiences romantic jealousy is threatened with two basic losses: the loss of the actual rewards provided by the relationship, and the loss of self-esteem that results from rejection by one's partner. An investigation by Mathes, Adams, and Davies (1985) supports White's theory. They asked subjects to imagine losing a romantic partner due to several factors, including: a) a rival (partner leaves you for someone else), b) rejection (no rival, partner simply ends relationship), c) destiny (e.g., partner takes a new job in a distant city), or d) fate (death by car accident). In all cases, losing the partner involved the loss of the rewards provided by the relationship. However, they predicted that the self-esteem component of jealousy would be engaged when the relationship ended due to simple rejection or being replaced by a rival. This is exactly what they found. Jealous reactions were greatest when subjects imagined their partners leaving them for someone else, and least when the relationship was lost due to fate. Thus, a threat to the individual's self-esteem appears to play a central role in the experience of romantic jealousy. Mathes et al. also found that each component of White's theory of jealousy was associated with a different emotion. Loss of esteem tended to provoke anger, while loss of relationship-rewards generally produced feelings of depression. Details of this research may be found in: White, G.L. (1981). A model of romantic jealousy. *Motivation and Emotion, 5*, 295–310; Mathes, E.W., Adams, H.E., & Davis, R.M. (1985). Jealousy: Loss of relationship rewards, loss of self-esteem, depression, anxiety, and anger. *Journal of Personality and Social Psychology, 48*, 1552–1561.

Projects and Discussion Topics

1. PROJECT: Make a list of your attitudes and preferences in a variety of domains, including: music, movies, politics, religion, as well as a variety of social issues such as capital punishment, abortion, the environment, nuclear arms, affirmative action, etc. Ask a couple of close friends to indicate their attitudes and preferences on these issues. Next, ask a couple of people you have known for a while—but have not become friends with—to describe their views on these same issues. Compared to your acquaintances, are your friends' attitudes more similar to your own? What role do you think similarity plays in your relationship with your close friends? If they were to change their minds on some of the issues in which your views agreed, do you think it would affect your friendship and your feelings for them? If so, which issues would have the greatest impact on your relationship? If your

friends' attitudes are somewhat or highly dissimilar to your own, what other characteristics of your friendship do you think compensate for this fact? Write a brief report describing your observations and reflections on this exercise.

2. PROJECT: How common is the gain-loss effect in relationships? Have you ever experienced it? For example, have you ever started off knowing or believing someone didn't like you, but later found out that he or she did? Did his or her attraction to you seem particularly rewarding as a result? Similarly, have you ever felt "taken for granted" by a good friend and, then, after withdrawing your interest or affection, found your friend was especially eager to re-establish good relations with you? Have you ever found yourself on the "other end" of this kind of relationship—where you initially disliked someone, but later grew to like him or her? Or where you took a friend for granted, and later felt hurt or insecure when he or she seemed to be ignoring you? Write a report of your experiences, using the "gain-loss" theory of attraction to analyze them. Ask a few friends the same questions to see if their experiences are similar to your own, and include them in your report.

3. PROJECT: Research on physical attractiveness indicates that people tend to form long-term relationships with others whose level of physical attractiveness "matches" theirs. Search through copies of your local or regional newspaper for the wedding or engagement announcements, which are usually accompanied by pictures of the newlyweds or engaged couples. (These announcements are typically published once a week in the "features" section of the newspaper. If only a few photos are published, you may need to find several back copies of the newspaper at your campus or public library.) Look at the pictures of the couples carefully. Is there a tendency for both people to be equally attractive? Bring your newspaper clippings to class and report your findings.

4. PROJECT: Create a scenario in which you and someone you care about are involved in an interpersonal dispute. In writing the scenario, first describe why you and/or the other person are hurt and angry with each other. Then, go on to create a dialogue in which you and your friend communicate defensively about the problem—accusing, judging, making excuses, etc. Describe how the conflict ended, how do you felt

during and after the interaction, as well as how your friend felt. In the past, have you had real experiences similar to this one? Next, re-write the scenario, but in this version have you and your friend engage in "straight talk." How do you feel about the interaction this time around? How does your friend feel? What obstacles, if any, do you foresee in using "straight talk" with your friends and loved ones in your everyday life? In your report, present your scenarios and reflections on this exercise.

5. DISCUSSION: Based on the experiments you have read about, how important are "good looks" in determining whether one person is attracted to another? Do these findings correspond with your own personal experience? Apart from the research evidence, how important do you think physical attractiveness *should* be in friendship and love?

6. DISCUSSION: In our society, it is relatively uncommon for people to use "straight talk" in their relationships. Why do you think this is so? What are the personal and societal obstacles to using "straight talk," and how might they be overcome? For example, do you think children should be taught in school how to engage in effective communication and conflict resolution? Would it be feasible for them to practice such techniques with teachers and other authority figures, as well as peers? Finally, are there circumstances in which you feel it would be unwise to engage in "straight talk"? If so, what are those circumstances?

7. DISCUSSION: In small groups, students can take turns role-playing a scenario in which two friends or romantic partners are involved in a conflict. (For example, one friend/partner might be angry because the other showed up two hours late to go to a party they had planned to attend.) To begin with, the role-players should attempt to resolve their dispute by using defensive and ineffective forms of communication-accusing, blaming, and judging each other. After finishing, the actors should take turns describing their experience during the interaction, explaining how the other person's comments made them feel and why they responded as they did. Next, the same partners should "re-play" their scenario, this time using "straight talk" to the best of their ability. Again, the actors should discuss how they felt during the interaction, and whether they found themselves slipping back into ineffective patterns of communication. Meanwhile, the audience should observe the

interaction, reserving their comments until after each performance is completed and the actors have had a chance to speak. Using different scenarios, take turns with role-playing so everyone in the group who wants to participate can do so. (Note: If students have conducted Project 4, their scenarios can be used for this role-playing exercise.)

Additional Readings

Adams, V. (1980, May). Getting at the heart of jealous love. *Psychology Today*, pp. 38–47, 102–108. (Reviews research on types and causes of jealousy, as well as gender differences in jealous behavior.)

Batson, C.D. (1990). How social an animal? The human capacity for caring. *American Psychologist, 45*, 336-346.

Berscheid, E. (1985). Interpersonal attraction. In G. Lindzey & E. Aronson (Eds.) *Handbook of social psychology*. New York: Random House.

Brehm, S. (1985). *Intimate relationships*. New York: Random House.

Cash, T.F., & Janda, L.H. (1984, December). In the eye of the beholder. *Psychology Today*, pp. 46–52. (Examines the role of physical attractiveness in dating preferences, employment, and other areas.)

Chapdelaine, A., Kenny, D., & LaFontana, K. (1994). Matchmaker, matchmaker, can you make me a match? Predicting liking between two unacquainted persons. *Journal of Personality and Social Psychology, 67*(1), 83-91.

Davis, K.E. (1985, February). Near and dear: Friendship and love compared. *Psychology Today*, pp. 22–30. (Similarities and differences between love and friendship are explored.)

Hatfield, E., & Sprecher, S. (1986). *Mirror, mirror: the importance of looks in everyday life*. Albany, NY: State University of New York Press.

Hendrick, C., & Hendrick, S. (1983). *Liking, loving and relating*. Monterey, CA: Brooks/Cole.

Hogan, R., Curphy, A.J., & Hogan, J. (1994). What we know about leadership: Effectiveness and personality, *American Psychologist, 49*(6), 493-504.

McGue, M., & Lykken, D.T. (1992). Genetic influence on risk of divorce. *Psychological Science, 3*(6), 368-373.

Psychology Today. (1994, March/April). (Three feature articles are devoted to the study of love.)

Thompson, B., & Borrello, G.M. (1992). Different views of love: Deductive and inductive lines of inquiry. *Current Directions in Psychological Science, 1*(5), 154-156.

Trotter, R.J. (1986, September). The three phases of love. *Psychology Today*, September 1986, pp. 46–54. (A discussion of Sternberg's three-dimensional theory of love, which involves commitment, intimacy and passion.)

Walster, E., & Walster, W. (1978). *A new look at love.* Reading, MA: Addison-Wesley.

Multiple-Choice Questions

Answer: c
Page: 357–358

1. The general reward theory of attraction is based upon which of the following basic principles?
   a. The more often we see another person (repeated exposure), the more we will like him or her.
   b. The more control we can exert over another person, the more we will like him or her.
   c. We tend to like a person whose behavior provides us with maximum reward at minimum cost.
   d. We tend to like a person who grows to like us after initially disliking us.

Answer: b 2. Reward theory of attraction suggest that we
Page: 357–358   generally like people who:
　　　　　　　　　a. give us small rewards.
　　　　　　　　　b. give us big rewards.
　　　　　　　　　c. give us rewards that need to be reciprocated.
　　　　　　　　　d. leave us alone and don't give rewards except when we earn them.

Answer: d 3. The advice given by Dale Carnegie, if one
Page: 356–357   wishes to "win friends," is most consistent with which of the following theories?
　　　　　　　　　a. cognitive dissonance theory
　　　　　　　　　b. self-perception theory
　　　　　　　　　c. the gain-loss theory of attraction
　　　　　　　　　d. reward theory

Answer: d 4. Suppose you turn in a paper that is graded by
Page: 360   two professors. Professor Jones is very complimentary whereas Professor Smith is very critical of your work. Generalizing from the results of a similar experiment described in the text, you would believe that Professor _____ is more intelligent and you would like best Professor _____.
　　　　　　　　　a. Jones; Jones
　　　　　　　　　b. Smith; Smith
　　　　　　　　　c. Jones; Smith
　　　　　　　　　d. Smith; Jones

Answer: d 5. As Edward Jones says, "Flattery will get you
Page: 361   somewhere," except when:
　　　　　　　　　a. you are flattering a person with very high self-esteem.
　　　　　　　　　b. the person overhears you saying good things about him or her to somebody else.
　　　　　　　　　c. the person you are flattering is too often flattered by others.
　　　　　　　　　d. the person you are flattering thinks you are trying to manipulate him or her.

Answer: d
Page: 361–363

6. When people do favors for us, we:
   a. only like them better when our self-esteem is low.
   b. only like them better if the favor was unanticipated.
   c. don't like them better, because they seem superior and make us feel insecure.
   d. only like them if we don't feel indebted to return the favor.

Answer: b
Page: 361–363

7. If you persuade someone to do you a favor, it is likely that:
   a. he or she will like you less.
   b. he or she will like you more.
   c. you will like him or her less because you feel indebted.
   d. his or her self-esteem will decrease.

Answer: b
Page: 363

8. In general, getting someone else to do you a favor is _____ effective in increasing his liking for you than your doing a favor for him, due to _____.
   a. less, his negative reinforcement
   b. more, his dissonance reduction
   c. less, your dissonance reduction
   d. more, your positive reinforcement

Answer: b   9.   Aronson's text describes an experiment in which
Page: 364–365   subjects watch a victim supposedly receive
                      electric shocks. Subjects were given the
                      opportunity to vote as to whether the victim
                      should continue to receive the shocks, and the
                      shocks were either terminated or not. Which
                      group of subjects came to like the victim most?
                      a. those who voted to terminate the shocks, but
                          the shocks were not terminated
                      b. those who voted to terminate the shocks, and
                          the shocks were terminated
                      c. those who voted to not terminate the shocks,
                          but the shocks were terminated
                      d. those who voted to not terminate the shocks,
                          and the shocks were not terminated

Answer: a   10. When a near-perfect person commits a blunder,
Page: 365–368   his or her attractiveness generally _____.
                      When a mediocre person commits the same
                      blunder, his or her attractiveness generally ____
                      ___.
                      a. increase; decrease
                      b. stays the same; decreases
                      c. decreases; decreases
                      d. decrease; increases

Answer: b   11. Suppose you are observing a highly popular and
Page: 366–368   well-respected politician and a college student eat
                      lunch. Both proceed to spill gravy on their
                      neckties. Generalizing from research cited in
                      Aronson, your liking of the politician will most
                      likely _____ and your liking of the college
                      students will _____.
                      a. increase; increase
                      b. increase; decrease
                      c. decrease; decrease
                      d. decrease; increase

Answer: c
Page: 368

12. In studies of "the pratfall effect," Deux has shown that men prefer a _____, but women are more likely to prefer a _____.
    a. highly competent male blunderer; highly competent female blunderer
    b. highly competent female blunderer; highly competent male blunderer
    c. highly competent male blunderer; highly competent nonblunderer, regardless of sex
    d. highly competent blunderer, regardless of sex; highly competent nonblunderer, regardless of sex

Answer: b
Page: 369–370

13. In a study by Walster and her associates, in which students were randomly matched for a computer date after taking a battery of psychological tests, it was found that:
    a. intelligence and attitude similarity were significantly related to mutual liking.
    b. the physical attractiveness of the individuals involved was significantly related to mutual liking.
    c. complementary needs such as dominance/submissiveness were significantly related to mutual liking.
    d. comparable levels of self-esteem were significantly related to mutual liking.

Answer: c
Page: 369

14. Walster and her colleagues randomly matched incoming students to determine what they looked for in a potential blind date. Which of the following characteristics best determined whether or not subjects liked each other?
    a. a sense of humor
    b. intelligence
    c. physical attractiveness
    d. similarity of attitudes

Answer: a
Page: 369

15. From a study in which college freshmen were subjects in a "computer dating" experiment, the primary determinant of how much subjects initially liked their dates was:
    a. the date's physical attractiveness.
    b. the subject's physical attractiveness.
    c. the similarity of the date's and the subject's physical attractiveness.
    d. the similarity of attitudes and backgrounds of the experiment's participants.

Answer: a
Page: 369–370

16. Generalizing from research presented in the text, on a first date, the partner people like most is the one whose physical attractiveness _____; in long-term relationships, they prefer a partner whose physical attractiveness _____.
    a. is greatest; matches their own level of attractiveness
    b. is greatest; is greatest
    c. matches their own level of attractiveness; matches their own level of attractiveness
    d. matches their own level of attractiveness; is greatest

Answer: d
Page: 370

17. According to research on dating, people:
    a. with low self-esteem are more selective about whom they will accept as dates, because they are less willing to take risks.
    b. with low self-esteem are more likely to initiate interactions with attractive people, since they have less to lose by being rejected.
    c. with high self-esteem are less likely to initiate interactions with attractive people, because they want to protect their self-esteem.
    d. tend to have relationships with someone who matches their level of physical attractiveness.

Answer: d   18.   Dion and her colleagues showed subjects pictures of
Page: 370   attractive, average, and unattractive people. The
                        results of her study indicated that:
                        a. men prefer attractive men and women, but
                            women prefer average men and women.
                        b. men and women prefer attractive people of the
                            opposite sex but average people of the same
                            sex.
                        c. men prefer attractive women and average men
                            whereas women prefer average men and
                            attractive women.
                        d. all subjects preferred attractive people re-
                            gardless of sex.

Answer: a   19.   In an experiment by Karen Dion and Ellen
Page: 371–372   Berschied concerning physical attractiveness in
                        children, it was found that:
                        a. physically attractive boys were liked better
                            than unattractive boys.
                        b. unattractive boys were perceived as less
                            aggressive than attractive boys.
                        c. physically attractive children got better
                            grades than unattractive children.
                        d. teachers tended to feel more compassion for
                            the unattractive children.

Answer: c   20.   Dion asked teachers to examine reports of
Page: 372   behavior disturbances caused by attractive and
                        unattractive boys and girls. Which group of
                        children were most likely to be blamed for the
                        disturbance and thought to be chronic trouble
                        makers?
                        a. unattractive boys
                        b. unattractive girls
                        c. unattractive boys and girls
                        d. unattractive boys and attractive girls.

Answer: c
Page: 373

21. In comparison to unattractive men, if you were an attractive man, you could expect to:
    a. get dates more easily, but have a harder time maintaining a long-term relationship.
    b. buy more beauty and grooming products.
    c. make more money at your job.
    d. have a more troubled marriage.

Answer: d
Page: 373

22. Harold Sigall and Elliot Aronson conducted an experiment in which a female confederate was made up to appear either physically attractive or unattractive. Posing as a graduate student in clinical psychology, she interviewed college men and evaluated half favorably and half unfavorably. The results showed that:
    a. she was disliked more when she was homely than when she was attractive, regardless of the evaluation she gave.
    b. she was disliked more when her evaluation was negative than when it was positive, regardless of her physical attractiveness.
    c. she was well-liked in every condition except the one in which she was unattractive and also gave a negative evaluation.
    d. when she was attractive, the kind of evaluation she gave had a strong effect on men's liking for her, but when she was unattractive, it had virtually none.

Answer: a 23. Suppose you see two men. One is sitting with a
Page: 374–375   highly attractive woman. The other is with an
unattractive woman. Generalizing from research
presented in Aronson:
a. the man with the attractive woman will be seen as friendlier and more self-confident.
b. the man with the unattractive woman will be seen as friendlier and more self-confident.
c. there will be an interaction; only attractive men benefit from sitting with unattractive women.
d. the attractiveness of the woman does not generalize to the man.

Answer: a 24. The main reason we tend to like people whose
Page: 377   opinions are similar to our own is probably that they:
a. provide consensual validation for our beliefs.
b. have similar backgrounds to ours.
c. are better able to empathize with us.
d. keep us from having to consider alternative opinions.

Answer: a 25. What does Aronson say is the single most
Page: 378   powerful determinant of whether you will like another person?
a. if that person likes you
b. if that person and you are about equally attractive
c. if that person and you have similar attitudes
d. if you have high self-esteem

Answer: b 26. Suppose Susan is in an experiment and is led to
Page: 379   believe that Ted likes her but Bob does not. She
                 meets both Ted and Bob. Generalizing from a
                 study by Curtis and Miller, you would predict
                 that Susan would like ___ more and ___ would
                 like Susan more.
                 a. Bob; Bob
                 b. Ted; Ted.
                 c. Bob; Ted.
                 d. Ted; Bob.

Answer: b   27. In Walster's experiment in which women were
Page: 379–380   asked for a date by a young man prior to
                 receiving favorable or unfavorable personality
                 evaluations from a psychologist, the results
                 showed that subjects:
                 a. liked the young man more when the evaluation was positive, since he was associated with a reward.
                 b. liked the young man more when the evaluation was negative, because he gave their lowered self-esteem a greater boost.
                 c. liked the young man more when the evaluation was positive, because they felt they deserved to be asked for a date.
                 d. expected the date to be less enjoyable when the evaluation was negative.

Answer: c 28. Suppose you are a young man who asks a young woman for a date, and she accepts. Assuming that the following situations occurred prior to your date, which of them would probably cause your liking for her to increase?
Page: 380–381
   a. You just saw a psychologist, who gave you a positive evaluation of your personality.
   b. Because you felt indebted to her, you went to a lot of trouble to get tickets for the play you will see.
   c. She turned you down on two previous occasions before accepting this date.
   d. Some of her attitudes were similar to yours and some were not.

Answer: a 29. Suppose two young men had taken a test of intelligence. Ralph believed he did very well and Fred believed he did poorly. Both have the occasion to meet a young woman. Which of the following best describes how they would most likely react, based on her physical attractiveness?
Page: 380–381
   a. Ralph would like her more if she is attractive, Fred if she is unattractive.
   b. Fred would like her more if she is attractive, Ralph if she is unattractive.
   c. Ralph and Fred would both like her more if she is attractive.
   d. In this instance, attractiveness would not be related to how much the men like the woman.

Answer: a   30.   According to research conducted by Grube and
Page: 381   his colleague, compared to men with low self-
                     esteem, men who have a favorable view of
                     themselves tend to:
                     a. be attracted to women who are assertive and
                        independent.
                     b. be attracted to women who are willing to do
                        them favors.
                     c. be attracted to women who are submissive
                        and dependent.
                     d. be attracted to women who play "hard to
                        get."

Answer: b   31.   Generalizing from research conducted by Rubin,
Page: 381   if you were an unattractive man and wanted your
                     physical unattractiveness to not influence whether
                     women would date you or not, you would be best
                     advised to go into which of the following
                     occupations?
                     a. iron worker
                     b. physician
                     c. bartender
                     d. plumber

Answer: c   32.   Jones and his colleagues conducted an
Page: 382   experiment in which subjects were exposed to a
                     confederate who either liked or disliked them,
                     and whose attitudes were either similar or
                     dissimilar to theirs. The results showed that
                     subjects liked the confederate best when:
                     a. she liked the subject and held similar
                        attitudes.
                     b. she disliked the subject but held similar
                        attitudes.
                     c. she liked the subject but held dissimilar
                        attitudes.
                     d. she disliked the subject and held dissimilar
                        attitudes.

Answer: b 33. The gain-loss theory of attraction predicts that:
Page: 383–384
a. you like people more when they say all positive things about you than if they say some negative things.
b. you like people more when they begin by disliking you and gradually increase their liking for you.
c. you like people more when they initially like you and then gradually decrease their liking for you.
d. the more people like you, the less you like them.

Answer: c 34. When someone is initially critical of you and later becomes complimentary:
Page: 383–384
a. you tend to distrust him or her.
b. you like him or her less because you suspect flattery.
c. you like him or her more than someone who has always been complimentary.
d. you like him or her less than someone who has always been complimentary.

Answer: d 35. In Aronson and Linder's "gain-loss" experiment, subjects overheard a confederate give a series of evaluations of them which were (1) consistently positive, (2) consistently negative, (3) negative and then increasingly positive (gain), and (4) positive and then increasingly negative (loss). The results showed that, in terms of mean liking for the confederate, subjects rated (from positive to negative) the confederates as follows:
Page: 384–387
a. 1 4 3 2
b. 1 3 4 2
c. 3 1 4 2
d. 3 1 2 4

Answer: a   36.   You are at a party and are engaged in a
Page: 384–387   discussion with someone you just met. The topic
                         is capital punishment, an issue you feel very
                         strongly about. Based on your discussion, your
                         chances of liking this person will be greatest if
                         he or she:
                         a. initially disagrees with you, but ultimately
                            comes to accept your position.
                         b. shows integrity by refusing to be persuaded
                            to adopt your position.
                         c. consistently agrees with your position.
                         d. forces you to think up good arguments to
                            defend your beliefs.

Answer: b   37.   Suppose you take a class from each of the
Page: 384–387   following four professors: 1, 2, 3, and 4. You
                         write five papers and get the following grades:
                         1: A A A A A, 2: D D C B A, 3: A A B C F, 4:
                         D D C D D. Generalizing from Aronson, which
                         professor will you like the most?
                         a. 1
                         b. 2
                         c. 3
                         d. 4

Answer: d   38.   If college professors were sneaky and manipu-
Page: 384–387   lative, how might they get you to like them or
                         their courses more?
                         a. give you high grades first, and then
                            increasingly lower ones
                         b. make it very easy for you to register for their
                            courses
                         c. agree with many of your ideas about course
                            material, but express some disliking for you
                            as a person
                         d. induce you to do some noncredit work for
                            them as a favor

Answer: d   39.   Studies of couples engaged in long-term relation-
Page: 389   ships indicated that:
                   a. no evidence exists for the belief that "opposites attract."
                   b. differences in fundamental values keep a relationship from going stale.
                   c. if one partner is more dominant than the other, the relationship probably will not endure.
                   d. physical attractiveness is related to long-term happiness in a relationship.

Answer: c   40.   Compared to passionate love, companionate love tends to:
Page: 391   a. assume less importance in a long-term relationship.
                   b. decline over the course of a relationship.
                   c. deepen over the course of a relationship.
                   d. be rapid in onset.

Answer: c   41.   Your friend Ellen is talking to you about Jim, a guy she's been dating now for six months. In describing their relationship, Ellen says, "If Jim and I stopped seeing each other, I would be miserable. I feel I can confide in him about virtually anything!" Based on Rubin's research, which of the following conclusions would you be likely to draw?
Page: 391
                   a. Ellen is too dependent on Jim and may get hurt.
                   b. Ellen feels a "companionate" attachment to Jim.
                   c. Ellen loves Jim.
                   d. Ellen and Jim's love will endure if they can maintain this level of passion.

Answer: a   42.   Barb and Tom are very concerned that they each
Page: 392   share equally in the tasks related to living
                       together. They want to ensure that each partner
                       receives the same rewards and costs in the
                       relationship. According to Clark and Mills, their
                       arrangement is best thought of as an example of:
                       a.   an exchange relationship.
                       b.   a communal relationship.
                       c.   companionate love.
                       d.   the "gain-loss" theory.

Answer: c   43.   "I think you are an extremely attractive person."
Page: 393–394   From which of the following sources would this
                       statement probably have the greatest positive
                       effect on your self-concept?
                       a.   a close friend
                       b.   your spouse
                       c.   an attractive stranger
                       d.   someone who just did you a favor

Answer: c   44.   In Joanne Floyd's experiment, young children
Page: 395   were asked to share trinkets with another child,
                       who was either a close friend or a stranger. They
                       were led to believe that the other child was
                       acting in either a generous or a stingy manner
                       toward them. The results showed that:
                       a.   they were stingy to stingy strangers and to
                            stingy friends.
                       b.   they were generous to generous strangers and
                            to generous friends.
                       c.   they were generous to stingy friends and to
                            generous strangers.
                       d.   they were generous to generous friends and
                            to stingy strangers.

Answer: c   45. Higher levels of satisfaction in marriage tend to be
Page: 396   associated with:
                       a. long, uninterrupted periods of harmony, marked
                           by few disagreements.
                       b. a nontraditional attitude regarding the roles of
                           men and women.
                       c. a nonaggressive, but confrontational, style of
                           resolving conflicts.
                       d. the couple's willingness to frequently express
                           their positive feelings toward each other.

Answer: d   46. "Straight talk" refers to a style of communication
Page: 400   in which:
                       a. you tell a person directly what you think of
                           him or her, without beating around the bush.
                       b. people discuss their conflicts face-to-face
                           rather than complaining about each other to
                           someone else.
                       c. people can resolve all of their conflicts,
                           without any discomfort.
                       d. you offer a clear statement of your feelings
                           and concerns, without accusing or judging
                           the other person.

Answer: b   47. Which of the following statements provides the
Page: 400–401   best illustration of "straight talk"?
                       a. "You wouldn't act like that if you really
                           cared about me."
                       b. "I've been feeling competitive with you ever
                           since you got that promotion."
                       c. "If you want to act like a phony, the choice
                           is yours."
                       d. "Don't be upset—I didn't mean to hurt your
                           feelings."

Answer: a 48. The general lesson of our society is to hide one's
Page: 400–401 vulnerabilities from another person. This strategy:
- a. often results in defensiveness and poor communication.
- b. is seldom useful in some situations, especially when dealing with a true enemy.
- c. is essential for survival in our society.
- d. prevents us from understanding why we feel vulnerable.

Answer: a 49. According to Aronson, open and effective communication is especially difficult in many situations because:
Page: 400–402
- a. people are not fully aware of their own needs and feelings.
- b. people express their feelings without making sure the other person is ready to hear about them.
- c. people have no trouble expressing their negative feelings, but are less likely to express their positive feelings.
- d. one person almost always takes more blame and responsibility for the conflict than the other.

Answer: b 50. Aronson discussed the characteristics of sensitivity groups, also called T-groups. In a T-group, people learn by:
Page: 402–404
- a. doing what others tell them they should do.
- b. trying things out and getting feedback.
- c. receiving clear instructions and interpretations from the group leader about what motivates their behavior.
- d. learning to communicate with factual statements only, thereby reducing the emphasis on how they and others "feel" about things.

Answer: a   51.   Aronson has outlined the process of interpersonal
Page: 404   relations in terms of feelings, intentions,
                       behaviors, interpretations, and evaluations.
                       According to his analysis, T-groups attempt to
                       short-circuit many of these stages and allow the
                       people involved to focus primarily on their ___
                       ___.
                       a.   feelings
                       b.   behaviors
                       c.   interpretations
                       d.   evaluations

Answer: c   52.   In communicating effectively with another
Page: 404–406   person, giving that person immediate feedback
                       regarding your own feelings is useful:
                       a.   because it keeps the person from having his
                            or her feelings hurt.
                       b.   because it prevents disagreements from
                            occurring.
                       c.   because it increases the person's insight into
                            the impact of his or her actions.
                       d.   because it prompts disagreements to occur
                            that can be resolved.

Answer: c   53.   When we are angry or hurt about someone's
Page: 409   behavior, it is tempting to express our negative
                       judgments of the other person because:
                       a.   it's the quickest and surest way to get the
                            person to stop his or her negative behavior.
                       b.   it gives the person the clear option of
                            changing his or her behavior, or keeping
                            things as they are.
                       c.   it makes us feel less vulnerable than if we
                            expressed our feelings.
                       d.   we usually would rather be "right" than solve
                            the problem.

Answer: a 54. According to Aronson, expressing one's feelings,
Page: 409–412   rather than one's judgments about another person,
is important primarily because:
a. expressing feelings is less hurtful than expressing judgments.
b. people need to know whether their feelings are legitimate.
c. it's not right to feel judgmental about another person.
d. expressing our feelings makes the other person feel trusted.

Essay Questions

1. What does the reward theory of attraction predict regarding the probability that we will like people: a) who are similar to us? b) who do us favors? c) who evaluate us positively? d) who are highly competent? Given your knowledge of research on interpersonal attraction, to what extent are the above predictions supported or open to question? Illustrate your answer with specific examples of research.

2. Mary has just made a new acquaintance. She wants to be liked by this person and would like to see a friendship develop. What characteristics of interpersonal attraction might she want to consider to achieve her goals? Discuss three studies from your readings on interpersonal attraction and their implications for Mary's situation.

3. Describe both the reward theory of attraction and the gain-loss theory of attraction. How do these two theories differ in their predictions regarding the conditions under which people come to like each other? Discuss a research finding that supports one theory over the other.

4. To what extent are physically attractive people perceived and treated differently than less-attractive people? What effect, if any, does this treatment have on their behavior? In more general terms, what is the role of "good looks" in determining whether people are

attracted to each other? Support your answer with examples of relevant research.

5. What kinds of distinctions have social psychologists made between liking and loving, as well as different forms of love? What are the characteristics of these various forms of attachment and attraction? Are they mutually exclusive within a given relationship, or do they have the capacity to co-exist?

6. The gain-loss theory of attraction suggests that individuals are likely to face certain obstacles in maintaining a long-term, loving relationship. What is the nature of these problems? How, and to what extent, might these problems be reduced?

7. Define the term "straight talk" and discuss its relevance to interpersonal sensitivity and communication. What are the important characteristics of this form of "feedback" that make it effective? Why is it so often so difficult to engage in straight talk when communicating with other people? Give an example of how a person might deal with an interpersonal conflict by using "straight talk" and contrast it with how someone might approach the same problem using a less-effective approach to communication.

9

Social Psychology as a Science

I. Science as Art

II. From Speculation to Experimentation

    Why we do experiments
    Designing an experiment (Aronson & Mills)

III. The Importance of Random Assignment

    Why random assignment?
    Correlation and causation

IV. The Challenge of Experimentation in Social Psychology

    A. Control versus Impact
    B. Realism (experimental versus mundane)
    C. Deception
    D. Ethical problems (Dawes, McTavish & Shaklee; Milgram)
    E. The post-experimental session

IV. The Morality of Discovering Unpleasant Things

    The use of scientific findings
    The researcher's responsibility

Terms & Concepts

experimental condition
extraneous variables

independent variable
dependent variable
cause and effect
random assignment
third factors
correlated variables
experimental realism
mundane realism
cover story
debriefing

Chapter Overview

Chapter 9 provides a discussion of the major features and advantages of the experimental method in social psychology. The difficulties posed by laboratory experimentation—both methodological and ethical—are also addressed. To illustrate these important issues, experiments introduced in earlier chapters are examined in detail. Highlights of the chapter are summarized below.

The use of random assignment constitutes the crucial difference between experimental and nonexperimental approaches. Under conditions of random assignment, each subject has an equal chance to be in any condition in the study. Thus, if we find a difference between conditions in an experiment, it is unlikely that this would be due to individual differences in any single characteristic—since all of these characteristics were distributed randomly across all conditions. As a result, any differences between conditions could be attributed to the effects of the independent variables.

Unlike research involving correlational methods, experiments can determine the causal relationship between two variables. With correlational research, we cannot tell whether variable A is the cause of variable B, or vice versa. In fact, there may be no causal relationship at all between A and B; a third variable—often unknown to the researcher—may be the cause of both A and B.

Control over the experimental setting is important because it allows the researcher to draw valid conclusions about the experimental results. An experiment, however, must also have impact on subjects if its findings are to have any real meaning and not simply be the trivial results of an artificial situation. Impact, or experimental realism, occurs when a subject finds the events of an experiment interesting and absorbing and, thus, reacts in a natural manner. Mundane realism, the degree to which the experimental setting approximates real life, also can impact, although it is not always possible to attain. The difficulty for experimenters is that these two crucial factors—impact and control—often work in opposite directions. The challenge, then, is to maximize impact on subjects without sacrificing control over the experimental situation.

To achieve valid and meaningful results, it is frequently necessary to disguise the true purpose of the study through the use of a "cover story". If subjects are aware of the hypothesis before participating in the study, they are unlikely to act in a spontaneous manner. Rather, they will tend to perform in a way that makes them look good or "normal," or they may try to "help out" the experimenter by behaving in a way that confirms the hypothesis.

The use of deception in experiments, as well as the tendency for some experiments to cause discomfort for subjects, raises serious ethical problems for the researcher. First, it is simply unethical to tell lies to people. In addition, deception prevents subjects from giving their informed consent to participate in a study and, thus, can lead to an invasion of privacy. These issues are especially problematic when the experimental procedure involves unpleasant experiences.

Aronson proposes five ethical guidelines in deciding whether to conduct a given experiment: 1) Procedures that cause intense pain or discomfort should be avoided. 2) Experimenters should be alert to alternative procedures to deception, using them whenever viable. 3) Experimenters should give subjects the real option of quitting the experiment if their discomfort becomes too intense. 4) Experimenters should spend considerable time with each subject during the debriefing session, gradually and carefully explaining the experiment, its true purpose, and the reasons for any deception. They should make every effort to protect the dignity of subjects and to make sure they leave feeling good about themselves and their role in the experiment. 5) Before entering the lab, researchers should be certain their experiment is sound and important. They should not conduct an experiment involving deception or discomfort in order to address a trivial research question.

Social psychologists also face a moral dilemma regarding what they discover in the pursuit of a scientific understanding of behavior. For example, research findings can be used to develop sophisticated and efficient techniques for controlling people's behavior. There is always the possibility that some individuals will use such techniques to exploit others for their own gain. While there is no perfect solution, Aronson's personal approach to this moral dilemma is "to educate the public about how these techniques might be used and to remain vigilant against their abuse as I continue to do research aimed at furthering our understanding of us social animals—how we think and how we behave."

Lecture Ideas & Teaching Suggestions

Finding Flaws in Experiments. One approach to exploring the important features of experimental methodology is to present students with examples of flawed experiments, interspersed with some properly conducted studies. After describing each study, you can challenge students to try to determine what, if anything, is wrong with each one. For example, you might describe a two-condition study in which the experimenter ran all subjects in one condition during the first three weeks of the semester and then—due to an equipment or staffing problem—ran all subjects in the second condition during the last two weeks of the semester. If students understand the concept of random assignment, they should quickly spot the potential for systematic differences in subjects' behavior that would invalidate the experimental findings. (For example, subjects may be more distracted by exam pressures at the end of the semester, or there may be personality differences in the kinds of people who sign up for an experiment early in the semester, compared to those who sign up late in the semester—e.g., the tendency to procrastinate, attitudes toward science, etc.)

To take another example, you could describe a study that examined whether being insulted by someone leads to feelings of hostility and aggression. In this study, male and female subjects interact with a confederate who either does or does not insult them. The researcher then asks each subject if he or she felt like hitting the confederate at any point during the interaction. The results of the study reveal that, among subjects who were insulted, only male subjects indicated that they wanted to hit the confederate. Men who were not insulted, and females in both conditions, did not express a desire to hit the confederate. The researcher concludes that there is a strong gender difference in the effects of insults on aggressive feelings. Students who understand the problem of demand characteristics will be able to spot the flaw in this study: Admitting to aggressive feelings—especially those involving physical harm—is less acceptable for women than for men in our society. More generally, simply asking subjects how they feel is usually an ineffective procedure, especially when undesirable behaviors are being investigated. You might then ask students how the use of a good cover story and a different measure of aggressive feelings would help to improve this study.

Finally, you might describe a study on similarity and attraction, in which the researcher first determined each subject's attitudes on a variety of topics and then gave them a description of a person who held nearly identical attitudes. The researcher then asked subjects how much they thought they would like this person and, lo and behold, nearly all subjects said they would like this person very much and would like to have a chance to meet him or her. The researcher concludes that similarity does lead to attraction—"birds of a feather do flock together." Here, the simple point is there was no manipulation of the independent variable and, hence, no subjects who saw descriptions of dissimilar others to serve as a comparison group. As a result, the researcher has no basis upon which to draw any conclusions from his or her "experiment."

(NOTE: One way to generate more examples is to take existing experiments and create flaws in them. Another possibility is to ask students in small groups to come up with their own flawed studies to see if they can stump their classmates.)

Values and science. In their commitment to the goals of science, researchers typically strive to conduct their investigations in an objective, value-free manner. It is possible, however, for values to influence research in a variety of ways. In your discussion of scientific methods in social psychology, you might also wish to introduce your students to the more "subjective" side of the research enterprise.

For example, the impact of prejudiced beliefs on the conclusions drawn from research is reflected in the discussion of early studies on gender differences in persuasion, presented in Chapter 7. To briefly summarize, research conducted by Janis and Field in the 1950s indicated that women were more easily persuaded than men. Subsequent research, however, revealed that this apparent difference was due to the specific topics used as stimuli in the Janis and Field experiment. Because these topics were more reflective of masculine interests, female subjects evidently had little knowledge about them and, as a result, tended to conform to the opinions of others. In contrast, later research by Sistrunk and McDavid found that when topics involved traditionally feminine domains of interest, men were more easily persuaded than women. This example illustrates the unintended impact of values on how research is conducted, as well as how research findings are interpreted. Not only were the stimulus materials used in the Janis and Field study biased in favor of masculine performance, but the results of this study went unquestioned for several years—undoubtedly because they were consistent with stereotypes regarding women's greater gullibility and lack of firm convictions. To borrow Bem and Bem's terminology, such is the power of a "nonconscious ideology."

Values that are at odds with the those of the scientific community can also have implications for social-psychological research. For example, several years ago, Senator William Proxmire of Wisconsin publicly criticized research on love conducted by Ellen Berscheid and Elaine Hatfield, claiming that the American public would prefer to remain ignorant of the dynamics underlying the "mystery" of love and romance. Thus, in his view, certain domains of life are sacred and should be protected from the cold scrutiny of scientific inquiry. One way to stimulate discussion on this topic is to ask students if they agree with Proxmire's position. Should certain topics—such as love, religious faith, or the sublime effect of a beautiful poem—be off-limits to scientists? Will scientific knowledge of certain aspects of life destroy our capacity to participate fully and unselfconsciously in such experiences? Is it, as Proxmire has argued, a waste of public funds to support research on such topics?

Values are also implicit in the kinds of topics researchers choose to investigate. Often such decisions are influenced by the pressing social problems of the day, rather than some abstract set of scientific criteria. Thus, Latane and Darley's research on bystander intervention was stimulated by growing alarm regarding the potentially dehumanizing effects of urban life. Milgram's research on obedience to authority was a response to the horrors of Nazism. Similarly, waves of research interest in racial and gender prejudice, pornography, violence and aggression, and a host of other phenomena have been strongly influenced by current social values and concerns.

Finally, it is worth noting that certain values are implicit in the special emphasis that social psychologists place on "situational" causes of behavior. This focus has clear implications for the kinds of solutions to social problems that researchers are likely to propose. Policy recommendations based on social-psychological research are more likely to involve modifications of institutional arrangements or changes in the structural conditions of society, while individual-level interventions are apt to receive less attention.

Field experimentation. In your coverage of methods in social psychology, you may wish to supplement the chapter's treatment of laboratory experimentation with a discussion of other methods used by researchers. In particular, the topic of field experimentation may merit special attention since, in recent years, researchers have increasingly sought to test their hypotheses within natural settings. In part, this turn to the field reflects the desire of many experimenters to increase the generalizability of their findings beyond the lab and into the real world.

Field experiments resemble laboratory experiments in allowing the researcher to manipulate independent variables and to assign subjects to experimental conditions on a random basis. In addition, they offer the advantage of observing people in their natural environment. And, because subjects typically do not know they are in an experiment, they are likely to respond to the experimental manipulations in a spontaneous manner. (It should also be noted, however, that laboratory experiments that are high in experimental realism also achieve this effect.) Unfortunately, field experiments have their share of drawbacks as well. First, the control over extraneous variables that is easily achieved in the lab is usually more difficult to establish in a field setting. In a laboratory experiment, the researcher can ensure that the setting is virtually identical for all subjects. This is impossible in the field because any number of conditions can—and are likely to—change over the course of running the experiment. For example, other people (who are not in the study) may be present in the setting in some cases, but not others. Their presence may interfere with, or otherwise influence, the experimental procedure or subjects' behavior. In general, the best the researcher can do is to minimize the impact of such extraneous variables, taking steps to ensure that these factors do not have a systematic impact on the results of the study. Another disadvantage of field experimentation is that it is often difficult to conduct a study involving complex variables or several variables that must be manipulated simultaneously. As a result, some hypotheses cannot be easily or adequately tested in field settings. Additional background on field experimentation and other research methods used in social psychological research may be found in: Aronson, E., Ellsworth, P.C., Carlsmith, J.M., & Gonzales, M.H. (1990). *Methods of research in social psychology*. Reading, MA: Addison-Wesley; and Judd, C.M., Smith, E.R., & Kidder, L.H. (1991). *Research methods in social relations*. New York: Holt, Rinehart & Winston.

Projects and Discussion Topics

1. PROJECT: Examine several research reports describing experiments in the field of social psychology. Good sources of such articles are *The Journal of Personality and Social Psychology, Personality and Social Psychology Bulletin, The Journal of Experimental Social Psychology*, and *The Journal of Applied Social Psychology*. (These journals should be available at your campus library or the library of a nearby university.) Select two articles that you find interesting, one describing an experiment with high experimental realism, and another with low experimental realism. For each article, describe or identify: a) the title, authors, journal, and date of the article; b) the purpose of the study; c) the independent and dependent variables; d) the various experimental conditions or treatments; e) the "cover story," if any; f) the study's degree of experimental realism; g) the presence of "suspicious" subjects or other complications, if any, and how these problems were handled; h) how the experimenter controlled extraneous variables; i) ethical concerns raised by the study; j) the study's results. Finally, briefly summarize the conclusions drawn by the researchers, as well as any possible alternative explanations for the experimental findings.

2. PROJECT: Come up with a social-psychological question that interests you, develop a hypothesis, and design an experiment to test it. (If you have trouble coming up with a question, choose an experiment you are familiar with and design a new experiment to test the same hypothesis.) Write a report of your experimental design and procedure, and include the following information: a) the hypothesis or research question addressed in your study; b) the independent and dependent variables; c) the various experimental conditions; d) how you would assign subjects to conditions; e) how you would control for extraneous variables; f) your "cover story"; g) any ethical issues raised by your study; h) how you would protect the rights of your subjects; i) how you would conduct the post-experimental session. Finally, describe any difficulties you had in designing your experiment and any problems you think you might encounter if you were to conduct it. (Note: this project also works well in class as a discussion item.)

3. DISCUSSION: Select an experiment you have read about that you feel raises serious ethical concerns. Do you think this study should have been performed? That is, does the knowledge gained from this study justify the deception or discomfort experienced by subjects? If the experiment's negative impact on subjects was only temporary, does this fact diminish the ethical problems to an acceptable level in your opinion? In general, what standards of ethics would you follow if you were a researcher?

4. DISCUSSION: Would you question the ethics of the Milgram study if none of the subjects had administered shocks beyond the "moderate shock" level? One study found that when people were told that a high proportion of Milgram's subjects was obedient, they rated the procedure as more harmful than if they were told that only a low proportion obeyed the experimenter's orders. What do you make of these findings? Should researchers restrict themselves to conducting experiments that reveal flattering information about human nature and behavior? Would this even be possible? Why or why not?

5. DISCUSSION: Consider the issue of the researcher's moral responsibility for how her or his discoveries are put to use. For example, research on persuasion and self-justification has yielded a number of potent strategies for influencing people's behavior. These techniques

can be used for good or ill, depending on the purposes of those who possess the knowledge and resources to use them. Do you feel it is immoral or dangerous for researchers to develop this knowledge, without being able to control how it is used? Do you think some form of control over the use of research findings could or should be implemented? If so, how? Finally, do you think it is right for potent techniques of persuasion to be employed to change people's behavior, without their knowledge? Would you feel the same way if it were used "for their own good"—such as influencing people to stop smoking or to use condoms to prevent AIDS? If you were a researcher, how would you deal with this moral dilemma?

Additional Readings

Aronson, E., Ellsworth, P.C., Carlsmith, J.M., & Gonzales, M.H. (1990). *Methods of research in social psychology.* Reading, MA: Addison-Wesley.

Aronson, E., Brewer, M., & Carlsmith, J.M. (1985). Experimentation in social psychology. In G. Lindzey & E. Aronson (Eds.), *Handbook of Social Psychology.* New York: Random House.

Baumrind, D., (1964). Some thoughts on ethics of research: After reading Milgram's behavioral study of obedience. *American Psychologist, 19,* 421–423. See also: Milgram, S. (1964). Issues in the study of obedience: A reply to Baumrind. *American Psychologist, 19,* 848–852.

Berkowitz, L., & Donnerstein, E. (1982). External validity is more than skin deep: Some answers to criticisms of laboratory experiments. *American Psychologist, 37,* 245–257.

Estes, W.K. (Ed). (1994). *Psychological Science, 5*(3). (Special section including general article by Robert Rosenthal (pp. 127-134) and four commentaries regarding the current state of ethics in scientific research.)

Fisher, C.B., & Fyrberg, D. (1994). Participant partners: College students weigh the costs and benefits of deceptive research. *American Psychologist, 49*(5), 417-427.

Gibson, E.J. (1994). Has psychology a future? *Psychological Science, 5*(2), 69-76.

Pope, K.S., & Vetter, V.A. (1992). Ethical dilemmas encountered by members of the American Psychological Association: A national survey. *American Psychologist, 47*(3), 397-411.

West, S.G., & Gunn, S.P. (1978). Some issues of ethics in social psychology. *American Psychologist, 33*, 30–38.

Multiple-Choice Questions

Answer: d
Page: 415–416

1. According to the text, the first step in the scientific method is:
   a. assigning subjects randomly to groups.
   b. specifying the independent and dependent variables.
   c. answering the ethical questions implied by the research question.
   d. observation.

Answer: a
Page: 416

2. Aronson believes that the study of social psychology is:
   a. an art and a science.
   b. an art but not a full-blown science.
   c. science but not an art.
   d. an incomplete science.

Answer: b
Page: 420–421

3. In the Aronson and Mills experiment, the _____ was (were) the independent variable(s) and the _____ was (were) the dependent variable(s):
   a. severity of initiation; young women who participated.
   b. severity of initiation; women's liking for the discussion group.
   c. severity of initiation; boring discussion group.
   d. severity of initiation; women's liking for the discussion group.

Answer: a
Page: 420–421

4. Suppose you constructed an experiment to better understand the effect of the content of a speech on how persuaded people were by it. In this experiment, the independent variable would be:
   a. the content of the speech.
   b. how persuaded the subjects were.
   c. the characteristics of the subject.
   d. how the speech was delivered.

Answer: b
Page: 421

5. Suppose you conducted an experiment to study the effect of violence in television shows on aggressiveness in children. The dependent variable would be:
   a. the factors that distinguished between one group of children and another.
   b. how aggressive the children were.
   c. whether or not the children should be exposed to the violence.
   d. how violent the programs were.

Answer: c
Page: 420–421

6. The factor systematically varied by the experimenter is usually termed:
   a. the dependent variable.
   b. the extraneous variable.
   c. the independent variable.
   d. the control variable.

Social Psychology as a Science 257

Answer: b
Page: 421

7. The dependent variable in an experiment is used to measure:
   a. the effects of extraneous variables in the experimental setting.
   b. the effects of the independent variable.
   c. the degree of experimental realism achieved in the experiment.
   d. the degree of mundane realism achieved in the experiment.

Answer: c
Page: 422–423

8. In an experiment, extraneous (nonmanipulated) variables are controlled by:
   a. having more than one experimenter interact with all subjects in the study.
   b. using subjects who are similar to each other in nearly all respects.
   c. making all aspects of the procedure identical for all conditions, except for the independent variable manipulation.
   d. the assignment of subjects to experimental conditions based on the characteristics of the subjects.

Answer: c
Page: 420–421

9. In conducting an experiment, the researcher's goal is to:
   a. determine whether experimental findings also operate under real-world conditions.
   b. determine whether the theory of random assignment actually works when put into practice.
   c. determine whether manipulations of the independent variable cause systematic differences in subjects' behavior.
   d. predict whether subjects will believe the "cover story" used in the experiment.

Answer: b
Page: 424

10. Experimentation is used in social psychology primarily because:
    a. it allows for more precise quantification of the dependent variable than other research techniques.
    b. it allows for greater control of the relevant variables than other research techniques.
    c. it is less time-consuming than other research techniques.
    d. it presents fewer ethical problems than other research techniques.

Answer: c
Page: 422–423; 427

11. In social psychological experiments, the experimenter tries to:
    a. create an exact duplicate of conditions found in the real world.
    b. control conditions in natural, real-world situations.
    c. create of functional equivalent to conditions found in the real world.
    d. let the subject know what behavior is expected of him or her.

Answer: d
Page: 423

12. In the context of an experiment, "random assignment" means that:
    a. subjects are assigned at random to different "cover stories".
    b. subjects are selected at random from a large population of potential subjects.
    c. subjects are assigned to only one experimental condition.
    d. each subject has an equal chance to be in any condition in the study.

Answer: a   13. According to Aronson, the most important con-
Page: 423   dition which must be met before any experiment
                 can lead to definite cause-and-effect conclusions
                 is:
                 a. random assignment of subjects to groups.
                 b. the presence of a correlation between variables.
                 c. the presence of broad demand characteristics.
                 d. the manipulations of all dependent variables.

Answer: a   14. The essence of random assignments is that:
Page: 423   a. each subject has an equal chance of being
                    assigned to each treatment group.
                 b. subjects are chosen from the subject pool
                    randomly, so each subject has an equal
                    chance of being in the experiment.
                 c. levels of the independent variable are
                    presented in random order to subjects.
                 d. when statistics are used to analyze results,
                    they test the null hypothesis that the results
                    are due to random responses.

Answer: b   15. Which of the following word pairs corresponds
Page: 421   most closely to "cause-effect"?
                 a. experiment-correlation
                 b. independent variable–dependent variable
                 c. experimental realism–mundane realism
                 d. control-impact

Answer: d 16. An experimenter was conducting a study on
Page: 426–428 conformity. Frequently, subjects would show up
for the study accompanied by a friend. Wanting
to expose as many people as possible to the
research enterprise, the experimenter allowed
friends to watch the subject while he or she
participated in the study. Which of the following
conclusions can you draw regarding this
experiment?
a. Subjects could not be randomly assigned to
conditions.
b. The presence of friends increased the
mundane realism of the study.
c. The presence of friends probably made
subjects more relaxed, thus enhancing the
validity of their behavior.
d. The study failed to control for extraneous
variables in the experimental setting.

Answer: b 17. Generally, the relationship between control and
Page: 427 impact is such that:
a. as impact increases, control increases.
b. as impact increases, control decreases.
c. as impact increases, control shifts from the
independent to the dependent variable.
d. as impact increases, control shifts from the
dependent to the independent variable.

Answer: d 18. The crucial difference between experimental and
Page: 426 nonexperimental methods of investigation is that
experimental methods involve:
a. the quantification of empirical findings.
b. establishing a relationship between two or
more variables.
c. the use of deception.
d. the use of random assignment.

Answer: c   19.   Simply knowing that achievement is positively
Page: 425-426   correlated with happiness tells us:
                         a. that there is a casual relationship between
                            achievement and happiness.
                         b. that a third variable is the cause of both
                            achievement and happiness.
                         c. that as achievement increases, happiness also
                            increases.
                         d. that achievement causes happiness, *or* that
                            happiness causes achievement.

Answer: d   20.   If researchers find a positive correlation between
Page: 425–426   cowardice ad nosebleeds, it most likely means
                         that:
                         a. cowardice is a cause of nosebleeds.
                         b. nosebleeds are a cause of cowardice.
                         c. that a third variable—a genetic, hormonal
                            factor—causes both cowardice and
                            nosebleeds.
                         d. any, all, or none of the above.

Answer: c   21.   The main reason social psychologists want their
Page: 427   experiments to have impact on subjects is that,
                         without impact:
                         a. an exact duplicate or real-world situation
                            cannot be achieved.
                         b. subjects will be bored and, thus, will refuse
                            to participate in the experiment.
                         c. subjects' reactions will not be spontaneous
                            and, thus, the results of the experiment will
                            have little meaning.
                         d. subjects will probably guess the hypothesis
                            of the experiment.

Answer: d
Page: 428

22. _____ realism refers to the impact an experiment has upon a subject; _____ realism refers to the degree to which laboratory procedures are similar to commonly occurring events in the outside world.
   a. Experimental; dependent.
   b. Mundane; procedural.
   c. Independent; dependent.
   d. Experimental; mundane.

Answer: c
Page: 428

23. An experiment that gets the subject involved and interested but that does not represent events that occur in the real world is:
   a. high in experimental control, low in correlational control.
   b. high in mundane realism, low in experimental realism.
   c. high in experimental realism and low in mundane realism.
   d. high in correlational control and low in experimental control.

Answer: c
Page: 428

24. Suppose you volunteered to be a subject in a psychology experiment in which you were locked into a sound-proof booth and were told that your brain waves were being measured. Furthermore, you truly believed that your brain wave pattern was being used to predict your basic personality traits. According to Aronson, this experiment would have _____ mundane realism and _____ experimental realism.
   a. low; low.
   b. high; high.
   c. low; high.
   d. high; low.

Answer: a 25. Cover stories are used to:
Page: 429–430
a. mislead subjects about the true purpose of the experiment.
b. direct the subject's attention toward the specific behavior being studied.
c. decrease experimental realism.
d. decrease mundane realism.

Answer: c 26. If subjects know the true purpose of an experiment while participating in it, the most serious risk is if they:
Page: 430
a. refuse to continue their participation in the experiment.
b. tell the experimenter ways that the experiment could be improved.
c. act in ways that they believe will make them look good or "normal".
d. ruin the "cover story" by telling other subjects about the hypothesis of the experiment.

Answer: b 27. If deception is used, its negative effects best can be overcome by:
Page: 436
a. never telling the subject anything.
b. debriefing the subject.
c. using role playing techniques.
d. forming a T-group.

Answer: d 28. When deception has been employed in an experiment, one of the most important aspects of conducting a debriefing session is to:
Page: 436–438
- a. determine whether the truth will upset the subject and, if so, restrict the debriefing to aspects of the study that are not upsetting.
- b. praise the subject for not being suspicious and for being such a trusting person.
- c. tell subjects gently that the social benefits of the experiment outweigh any slight discomfort or embarrassment the deception might have caused.
- d. tell subjects that virtually everyone else who participated in the study was also fooled by the procedure.

Answer: c 29. In Asch's study of conformity, which involved a comparison of the lengths of different lines, subjects were told that the experiment was about perceptual judgment. Telling subjects this:
Page: 430–431
- a. involved the unnecessary use of deception, which Asch later regretted.
- b. aroused a great deal of suspicion because the line-judging task was too easy.
- c. was part of the experimenter's cover story.
- d. created a high level of mundane realism in the experiment.

Answer: d
Page: 432

30. Many subjects in a study by Robyn Dawes, Jeanne McTavish, and Harriet Shaklee experienced considerable discomfort after their participation in a study of how people respond to "social dilemmas". This study was included in *The Social Animal* to illustrate:
   a. the pitfalls inherent in doing research involving deception.
   b. the hazards of failure to carefully debrief subjects after their participation in an experiment.
   c. the need to screen subjects before conducting an experiment, to make sure they are good psychological health.
   d. that no code of ethics can anticipate all problems, even when an experiment is carefully planned and conducted.

Answer: d
Page: 433

31. According to the text, ethical dilemmas faced by experimental social psychologists stem from two conflicting values to which most researchers subscribe. These values are reflected in the belief _____, versus the belief _____.
   a. that they must advance their scientific careers; that research should address important social problems
   b. that informed consent is desirable; that deception cannot be avoided in research
   c. that most people benefit from participating in research; that some people may be harmed by experimental deception
   d. that free scientific inquiry is important; that the dignity of humans and their right to privacy should be respected

Answer: b
Page: 434

32. An important factor in deciding whether a particular experimental procedure is ethical or not is
    a. whether the experiment had sufficient mundane realism.
    b. whether the potential benefits to society outweigh the cost to subjects.
    c. whether the subjects are adequately compensated for their participation.
    d. whether it is similar to experiments done in the past.

Answer: b
Page: 434

33. Suppose you asked subjects how harmful Zimbardo's prison study was to subjects. One group of subjects (a) believed that Zimbardo's experiments went just as planned, with subjects spending the full two weeks as prisoners and guards. A second group (b) believed that the experiments had to be terminated early due to the extreme discomfort of the subjects. If the two groups (a and b) were asked how harmful the Zimbardo procedure would be, you would expect that:
    a. group a would rate it as more harmful.
    b. group b would rate it as more harmful.
    c. groups a and b would rate it as equally harmful.
    d. the results would depend on the particular subjects assigned to each group and are therefore unpredictable.

Social Psychology as a Science   267

Answer: c   34.   Which of the following is not an ethical guideline
Page: 434-435   proposed by Aronson in conducting an
                      experiment?
                      a. Procedures that cause intense pain or discomfort should be avoided.
                      b. Experimenters should be ever alert to alternative procedures to deception. If some other viable procedure can be found, it should be used.
                      c. Deception, in general, can be justified in all experiments, provided that the subjects are adequately debriefed at the end.
                      d. Experimenters should provide their subjects with the real option of quitting the experiment if their discomfit becomes too intense.

Answer: b   35.   Psychiatric interviews of subjects in Milgram's
Page: 436   obedience study (in which subjects believed they were delivering intense electric shocks to another person) conducted one year following the study, revealed:
                      a. that many subjects still had negative feelings toward the experimenter who deceived them.
                      b. that many subjects believed their participation in the study had been both instructive and enriching.
                      c. only a few subjects experienced long-term negative effects as a result of the study.
                      d. that some subjects still believed they had actually shocked the confederate.

Answer: a
Page: 428

36. Jane is a subject in Milgram's study of obedience. As she delivers increasingly severe shocks to the "learner," she feels a great deal of anxiety, engages in nervous laughter, and breaks out into a sweat. Caught in the grip of conflicting emotions, she would like to stop but feels she must continue to obey the orders of the experimenter. She has never encountered a situation like this before. Based on this description, what can we conclude about the Milgram experiment?
    a. It was high in experimental realism.
    b. It was worth conducting, even though it caused discomfort for subjects.
    c. It should not have been conducted, because it caused too much discomfort for subjects.
    d. It was high in mundane realism.

Answer: a
Page: 436–439

37. The postexperimental session(debriefing):
    a. allows the experimenter to determine the extent to which the procedure worked.
    b. should fool the subject in order to be effective.
    c. increases the mundane realism of the experiment.
    d. is when the independent variable is put into effect.

Answer: b
Page: 436–439

38. Debriefing a subject at the end of an experiment:
    a. is unethical if the subject already seems upset by the experimental procedure.
    b. is a valuable way of undoing some of the discomfort and deception that may have occurred during the experiment.
    c. has been shown to be relatively ineffective in undoing possible harmful effects to the subject.
    d. helps to keep the subject unaware of the true nature of the experiment.

Answer: b 39. When an experimenter knows that a subject has
Page: 436–437 been suspicious about the true nature of the
study, and thinks that this suspicion may have
influenced the subject's behavior, the
experimenter must:
a. ask the subject to run through the experiment
a second time.
b. discard the data obtained from that subject,
since it is probably invalid.
c. ask the subject to try not to be so suspicious
when participating in future experiments.
d. change the experimental procedure to
eliminate all possibility of suspicion.

Answer: a 40. At the end of an experiment, the experimenter asks
Page: 436–439 the subject questions about what the subject thought
about the experiment. Then the experimenter explains the real intention of the experiment and asks
the subject to keep the experiment a secret. This
procedure is called:
a. the postexperimental session.
b. the cover story.
c. experimental control.
d. experimental realism.

Essay Questions

1. Why do social psychologists conduct experiments? Choose an experiment (such as the "initiation" study by Aronson & Mills) and use it to illustrate the advantages of the experimental method. What problems would a researcher encounter if he or she tried to study the same phenomenon as it occurs in the real world?

2. Fran Flanders, an advice columnist for a regional newspaper, was curious about why people are attracted to each other. She had a feeling that similarity leads to attraction, but she decided to conduct a scientific investigation to test her hunch. She found several couples who had been dating for a year or more and gave them a questionnaire that measured their attitudes and opinions on a variety of topics. Next, Fran gave the

same questionnaire to several pairs of individuals who knew each other only as casual acquaintances. When she examined the questionnaire responses, lo and behold, she found that the attitudes of the couples who had been in long-term relationships were far more similar than the attitudes of casual acquaintances. "Great," Fran concluded, "I knew it all along! Now I can tell my readers that the key to good relationships is having similar attitudes!"

Do you agree with Fran's conclusion? Why or why not? If you were an experimental social psychologist, what approach would you take to testing Fran's hunch about why people like each other?

3. Why is the random assignment of subjects to groups such an important component of experimental research? What is gained by randomly assigning subjects? What would be lost if subjects were not assigned randomly?

4. Explain the meaning of the terms "control" and "impact" as they pertain to social-psychological experiments. Why is each of these factors important in conducting effective research? What difficulty does the need for both pose for the careful researcher?

5. According to Aronson, what are the three basic ethical problems that social psychologists face in conducting experiments? Would a carefully devised code of ethics, if stringently followed, be able to completely eliminate such problems? If researchers refrained from doing research involving deception, would these ethical issues be settled once and for all? Why or why not?

Readings About the Social Animal

Multiple-Choice Questions

Chapter 1   Research in Social Psychology as a Leap of Faith
Elliot Aronson

Answer: a   1.   What does Aronson mean when he says that science is a "self-corrective enterprise"?
a. even if a certain study is not perfect, other researchers will improve on it.
b. researchers conduct experiments as a way of improving—"correcting"—the human condition.
c. the inherent tendency of all human action is to gradually improve over time, and science, as a human endeavor, exhibits this same quality.
d. a panel of experts reviews each and every research article before it is accepted for publication, and this ensures that no errors in scientific research go undetected before the results are made public.

Answer: b   2. Aronson invokes James' notion of a "leap of faith" to argue that:
a. religious faith is an important topic of social-psychological research because our beliefs affect our attitudes, which, in turn, affect our behavior.
b. researchers should do the best work they can, with the understanding that when other researchers analyze their studies, they will probably improve on it, thus benefiting science as a whole.
c. if you have faith that you can do a particular study, then you will succeed.
d. science alone cannot solve our social problems; we must trust in higher powers that are not open to scientific investigation.

Answer: a   3. Aronson uses the example of Seymour's advice to his younger brother, Buddy, from a short story by Salinger, to suggest that:
a. a researcher should attempt to answer questions that have always interested him.
b. a researcher should always try to study the questions that others have identified as the most important.
c. researchers should always strive to be "provocative rather than right".
d. writing novels is more valuable than conducting scientific research because literature is easier for most people to understand than science, so literature can have a much larger social impact.
e. it is not wise for there to be two scientists in one family, because they will rarely, if ever, agree on anything.

Answer: c 4. Aronson maintains that "one of the by-products of excessive caution is excessive self-consciousness." In the context of conducting research, this statement means that:
- a. scientists should not always be concerned with following proper methodological procedures.
- b. engaging in scientific inquiry, which is by nature a slow, careful enterprise, leads one to develop a cautious and conservative personality.
- c. being too careful and cautious can stifle scientific inquiry by making researchers reluctant to pursue interesting and unusual questions.
- d. if a researcher is not careful, science can degenerate into an undisciplined, "circus-like" enterprise.
- e. many researchers are by nature shy and withdrawn, which means that their findings often go unnoticed because they fail to publicize them.

Chapter 2 Opinions and Social Pressure
Solomon E. Asch

Answer: a 1. The Asch experiment forces subjects to choose between two powerful conflicting forces. They are:
- a. their own sense perceptions and the influence of group opinion.
- b. obedience and rebellion.
- c. the desire to be "contrary" and the need to "fit in".
- d. the contrived reality of the research laboratory and the "real world" contextual influences that operate outside of the experimental setting.

Answer: c   2. In Asch's experiment, what percentage of subjects exercised complete independence—that is, what percentage never agreed with the opinions of the majority?
a. 75%
b. 50%
c. 25%
d. 0%

Answer: d   3. Asch's experiment sought to determine the influence of majority opinion on individual opinion along two dimensions—the size of the majority and its degree of unanimity. Which of the following statements correctly describes what Asch found out about these two key variables?
a. Individual opinion was not influenced by the size of the majority, but it was influenced by having a partner who also went against the majority.
b. Individual opinion was influenced by the size of the majority, but it was not influenced by having a partner who also went against the majority.
c. Individual opinion was not influenced either by the size of the majority or by the presence of a partner who also dissented.
d. Individual opinion was influenced by both the size of the majority and the presence of a partner who also went against the majority.

Answer: d   4. Which of the following was *not* studied by Asch in his experiments on opinion and group pressure?
a. the effect of the size of the majority
b. the degree of unanimity of majority opinion
c. the effect of the "desertion" of a partner to the majority
d. the effect of the similarity of partners' social backgrounds on their willingness to form dissenting alliances against majority opinion

Chapter 3 Behavioral Study of Obedience
Stanley Milgram

Answer: b   1. The major reason why Milgram conducted his experiments on obedience was:
                    a. he received a large research grant from the federal government to investigate how citizens might be made more loyal and obedient.
                    b. to understand how the Nazi regime could have carried out its genocidal plans during WWII.
                    c. to discover whether anti-social persons were more cruel than pro-social persons.
                    d. to analyze the psychological and physiological responses to stress of persons who possess "authoritarian" personality traits.

Answer: b   2. In Milgram's study, the primary dependent variable was
                    a. how profusely the subject sweated, stuttered, and trembled when he continued to administer shocks to the "learner".
                    b. the maximum shock a subject administered before refusing to continue in the experiment.
                    c. the number of times the experimenter had to prod the subject to continue to administer the shocks.
                    d. how painful the subject considered the shocks to be to the learner, as measured on a 14-point scale.

Answer: b   3. Which of the following was an unexpected manifestation of tension that Milgram and his associates observed in some subjects?
   a. drop in their blood pressure
   b. nervous laughter
   c. sadistic comments
   d. Some subjects tore up the money they received for participating in the experiment, which Milgram interpreted as an act of defiance toward the authority of the experimenter.

Answer: d   4. According to this article, several features of the Milgram experiment help to account for the high levels of obedience displayed by the subjects. Which of the following is *not* one of those features?
   a. Subjects believed the experiment would increase scientific knowledge on an important subject.
   b. The subjects felt a sense of obligation and commitment to continue the experiment, even after they began to feel uncomfortable administering high-voltage shocks.
   c. lack of guidelines about the limits of experimental research
   d. The experiment allowed subjects to discuss their actions among themselves, so that they could come to a consensus that it was right to continue to follow the experimenter's orders.

Chapter 4 "From Jerusalem to Jericho": A Study of Situational and Dispositional Variables in Helping Behavior
John M. Darley and C. Daniel Batson

Answer: d 1. The "Good Samaritan" experiment was designed to assess the influence of which of the following types of variables?
a. exogenous and endogenous
b. egoistic and altruistic
c. latent and manifest
d. situational and personality

Answer: b 2. Only one of the two independent variables in the "Good Samaritan" experiment was found to be significantly related to *whether and how much* help was given. This variable was:
a. the content of the talk the subjects were to give.
b. how hurried the subjects were.
c. the type of religiosity exhibited by the subject.
d. the degree to which the victim seemed to be in need of help.

Answer: c 3. Darley and Batson found that type of religiosity affected the *kind* of aid a subject offered to the victim. Specifically, they observed that:
a. "rigid" helping styles were prevalent among subjects who viewed religion as a "quest" for meaning in their personal and social worlds.
b. subjects who held orthodox religious beliefs tended to listen carefully to the victim's claims that he was really all right.
c. subjects who scored high on the "religion as quest" scale were more mindful of the victim's definitions of his own needs.
d. religiously orthodox subjects were cold and callous toward the victim.

Answer: d   4. From the results of the "Good Samaritan" experiment, Darley and Batson conclude that:
   a. seminary students, as a group, are more hypocritical than the general population.
   b. being in a hurry is inversely related to being religious, probably because hurried persons are very involved in worldly, material concerns and do not consider other-worldly, religious issues.
   c. personality variables are strong predictors of whether or not a person offers assistance to someone in need.
   d. situational variables affect whether or not a person offers assistance to someone in need.

Answer: b   5. In discussing their findings, Darley and Batson suggest that the best explanation for why some subjects failed to stop and render assistance is because:
   a. they were too preoccupied memorizing their speeches to even notice the victim.
   b. they experienced a conflict between helping two different persons—the experimenter and the victim.
   c. they were afraid that the victim was really a very dangerous street person who would harm them.
   d. being shy, quiet individuals, as most seminarians are, they did not want to create a scene on the sidewalk, especially if the victim turned out to be drunk or disorderly.

Chapter 5   A Study of Prisoners and Guards in a Simulated Prison
Craig Haney, Curtis Banks, and Philip Zimbardo

Answer: a   1.   The Stanford Prison Experiment was designed to test what Haney, Banks, and Zimbardo call the "dispositional hypothesis". This hypothesis holds that:
a. prison conditions are the result of the personality traits and innate characteristics of the guards and prisoners.
b. prison reform is not possible.
c. prison conditions are the result of a complex interaction of social, economic, and political factors.
d. the psychological profile of prisoners shows that they are significantly less violent than the guards.

Answer: c   2.   In order to test the dispositional hypothesis adequately, Haney, Banks, and Zimbardo had to do which of the following:
a. find a real prison and real prisoners to study.
b. find a sample of persons to play the role of guard who exhibited personality profiles that matched the hypothesized "guard mentality".
c. create the functional equivalent of actual prison conditions in order to gauge the psychological effects of prison on persons who had a "normal" psychological profile.
d. recruit more than 100 subjects, in order to simulate the crowded conditions that exist in real prisons.

Answer: c   3. To determine whether the guards and prisoners were merely role-playing and enacting stereotypes or were experiencing deeper personal involvement in the simulated world of the prison, it was necessary for Haney, Banks, and Zimbardo to:
a. establish clear role demands and rigid guidelines for behavior so that the subjects were compelled to always be "in role".
b. conduct follow-up interviews with the experimental subjects for several years after the prison study was completed to see how participating in the study affected their lives.
c. observe the subjects when they weren't aware of being observed, or when they were in situations with minimal role demands.
d. recheck the psychological profiles gathered for each subject before the experiment began to see if those who were beginning to become too personally involved in the study were prone to such extreme behavior.

Answer: b   4. Haney, Banks, and Zimbardo noted several coping strategies that their prisoners displayed. These strategies tended to follow a patterned sequence where prisoners:
a. were extremely hostile from the beginning, and became increasingly aggressive with each passing day.
b. initially experienced disbelief at loss of privacy and the total control of the institution, then acted rebelliously, then acted passively.
c. rebelled within minutes of incarceration, only to have their group rebellion put down, with the result that individuals began to bargain with the guards for special treatment.
d. immediately singled out the weakest prisoner to serve as the scapegoat.

Chapter 6   Making Sense of the Nonsensical: An Analysis of
             Jonestown
             Neal Osherow

Answer: b   1. Osherow points out that Jim Jones carefully controlled the information that was available to his followers in order to prevent them from developing a questioning attitude regarding the Temple. In addition to controlling the flow of information, Jones also employed which of the following techniques to keep followers from adopting a critical view of life in the Temple?
                 a. killing the messenger of bad news
                 b. attacking the credibility of the sources of critical information
                 c. developing an elaborate coded language, which was known only to the Temple faithful
                 d. conducting rigorous and systematic brainwashing sessions where Temple followers who were beginning to question Jones' teachings would be reprogrammed

Answer: c   2. Despite his obviously inhumane practices and the internal inconsistencies in his preachings, Jones was able to maintain his followers' loyalty. Osherow explains this with all but which of the following:
                 a. People seek to justify their choices by altering their attitudes.
                 b. If people experience pain and humiliation as part of belonging to a group, then they tend to value membership in that group more highly.
                 c. Using power to make people comply is more effective in the long run than setting up a situation where people internalize social controls.
                 d. Slowly but continually increasing the level of demands on a person's time and energy lead them to make greater commitments.

Answer: a   3. Osherow notes that after the Jonestown mass suicide, cults and unusual religious practices came under close media scrutiny. One result of this was that many "untraditional" religious practices were seen as dangerous. According to the article, which of the following questions can serve as a basis for distinguishing between beneficial alternative lifestyles and dangerous cult practices?
a. Does membership in a group close off other life choices?
b. Is the group committed to "revolutionary actions"?
c. Is individual responsibility preached as part of the religious doctrine?
d. Is there a single leader who controls the group?

Answer: d   4. According to Osherow, the author of the article on Jonestown, the mass suicide of nearly a thousand people can best be understood as an act of:
a. prejudice.
b. reactance.
c. aggression.
d. conformity.

Answer: c   5. The "upper echelon" of Jones' followers were typically attracted to membership in the Temple by:
a. their need for clothing, food and shelter.
b. their need for a "family" environment.
c. their interest in a utopian socialist society free from racism.
d. their belief that Jones was the Messiah.

Chapter 7 Effects of Varying the Recommendations in a
Fear-Arousing Communication
James M. Dabbs, Jr. and Howard Leventhal

Answer: d   1. Which of the following variables was *not* investigated in the Dabbs and Leventhal experiment on tetanus inoculation?
a. effectiveness of inoculation
b. painfulness of inoculation
c. level of fear
d. allergic reaction to inoculation

Answer: d   2. The dependent variables used in the Dabbs and Leventhal experiment to assess the effect of fear arousal on persuasion were:
a. subjects' intentions to take shots and their level of fear as measured on a 7-point anxiety scale.
b. subjects' intentions to take shots and their evaluations of the importance of shots in preventing disease.
c. subjects' actual shot-taking behavior and their perceptions of how painful the shots were.
d. subjects' intentions to take shots and their actual shot-taking behavior.

Answer: c   3. Dabbs and Leventhal's main experimental finding was that:
a. the dependent variables were affected by manipulations of belief in the effectiveness of tetanus shots.
b. the dependent variables were affected by manipulations of pain.
c. the dependent variables were affected by manipulations of fear.
d. the dependent variables were unaffected by any of the experimental manipulations.

Answer: d   4. Dabbs and Leventhal point to several factors that they did not systematically control, which could have affected their results. Among these factors are:
a. the order of presentation of the manipulations of fear, effectiveness, and pain.
b. the subjects' direct experience with medical practices and techniques.
c. the subjects' academic field of study—science and pre-med students may have been more knowledgeable about inoculation procedures than students majoring in the humanities or social sciences.
d. the effects of not giving all subjects in the experiment specific instructions on how to get a tetanus shot.

Chapter 8   Attribution Versus Persuasion as a Means for Modifying Behavior
Richard L. Miller, Philip Brickman, and Diana Bolen

Answer: c   1. The hypothesis of Miller et al.'s first experiment, which attempted to modify children's littering behavior, was that:
a. both attribution and persuasion manipulations would lead to initial behavioral change and to stable, persistent behavior modification.
b. attribution manipulation would lead to behavioral change; persuasion manipulation would not.
c. both attribution and persuasion manipulations would lead to initial behavioral change, but only attribution would have a more long-lasting effect on behavior modification.
d. only those children who were lectured on the ecological problems of littering and pollution would exhibit any significant change in their littering behavior.

Answer: c   2. Miller et al. gave subjects a pretest before conducting Study 1 in their research on the relative effects of attribution versus persuasion in producing behavioral change. The importance of conducting this pretest was:
a. to get the children prepared for the increased number of tests, drills, and assignments that the experiment would involve.
b. to introduce the students to the experimenters.
c. to discover existing differences among the classrooms in how much they littered.
d. to discover how knowledgeable the children in each classroom were regarding issues of ecology and pollution.

Answer: d   3. In discussing their results on the relative effectiveness of persuasion and attribution techniques in producing behavioral change, Miller et al. advance which of the following explanations for their findings?
a. Persuasive techniques are superior to attribution techniques because they involve more forceful appeals.
b. Persuasive techniques do not threaten the self-concept, and that is why they are more effective.
c. Attribution techniques are relatively less successful because they are less likely to arouse resistance, counterarguing, or reactance.
d. Attribution techniques are relatively more successful because they suggest something positive about the subjects and bolster their self-concepts.

Answer: d   4. Miller et al. warn against seeing their findings either as the basis for specific educational reforms or as an effective step toward ending social inequalities. They cite several reasons why they hold this less-than-optimistic view. Which of the following is *not* one of those reasons?
   a. Long-standing individual differences are unlikely to be rectified by short-term interventions.
   b. Attribution techniques are incompatible with the traditional educational curriculum and procedures.
   c. Using false attributions, even for good ends, involves a risk to the teacher's sense of credibility.
   d. All children should be given a chance to succeed, but designing programs to aid a particular group gives them an unfair competitive advantage.

Chapter 9   Television Criminology: Network Illusions of Criminal Justice Realities
Craig Haney and John Manzolati

Answer: c   1. Research on television crime drama, including that of Haney and Manzolati, has found that:
   a. television viewing decreases persons' estimates of their own risk of victimization.
   b. heavy television viewing is not associated with increases in persons' fear of crime.
   c. compared to corporate "white-collar" crime, street crime is far more likely to be portrayed on television crime shows.
   d. crime is usually portrayed as the logical outcome of persons' responses to the stresses and strains of social and material deprivation.

Answer: c   2. According to Haney and Manzolati, crime on television tends to be presented as the result of:
    a. the existence of socioeconomic inequalities.
    b. corporate fraud.
    c. personality traits of the criminal.
    d. a too-soft criminal justice system, which actually teaches criminals how to be even worse offenders.

Answer: b   3. Haney and Manzolati argue that the portrayal of police work as swift and certain may lead television viewers to:
    a. not support increases in criminal justice budgets, on the grounds that the police are already doing a very efficient job.
    b. presume that defendants are guilty.
    c. presume that only the most diabolic criminals are never brought to justice.
    d. discount reports of police brutality.

Answer: a   4. While acknowledging research that presents evidence linking viewing television violence with subsequent violent behavior, Haney and Manzolati maintain that viewing television crime drama has another, perhaps more important, effect. This is:
    a. confusing viewers about the causes of, and the solutions to, crime.
    b. helping to bring about the systematic, intentional brainwashing of the public by right-wing, law-and-order advocates who wish to install a police state.
    c. teaching us the importance of safeguarding our Constitutional rights.
    d. showing us that violence in American society can be curbed by reducing economic inequality.

Chapter 10 The Impact of Mass Media Violence on U.S. Homicides
David P. Phillips

Answer: a 1. Phillips chose to study the effects of publicized prizefights on homicide rates because:
   a. violence in prizefights is presented by the media as rewarded, exciting, real, and justified.
   b. prizefights have never been studied before, except in the laboratory.
   c. prizefights are especially popular among people who are highly aggressive, compared to less-aggressive people.
   d. Phillips wanted to see if boxing, as a particularly violent sport, elicited more violent behavior than other sports such as hockey, football, or soccer.

Answer: a 2. Drawing on laboratory research conducted by Berkowitz, Phillips tested the "modeling of aggression" hypothesis. Phillips' data indicated that:
   a. highly publicized fights are followed by larger increases in homicides than less-publicized fights.
   b. "aggressor" modeling exists after a prizefight.
   c. "victim" modeling doesn't exist after a prizefight.
   d. viewers of prizefights engage in "non-modeling" in which they model neither aggressors nor victims.

Answer: a   3. Phillips' study of the effects of media violence has added to laboratory research on media violence in which of the following ways?
a. It supported the link between media violence and aggression found in the laboratory.
b. It has shown that the link between media violence and aggression is nonexistent.
c. It has demonstrated that the presentation of media violence—especially prizefights—must be carefully controlled or everyone who witnesses such events is likely to become a perpetrator of violence.
d. It has demonstrated that although prizefights lead to imitative aggressive behavior, other factors such as "precipitation" and "gambling" cannot be ruled out as rival explanations for the findings.

Answer: a   4. Phillips' study of the correlation between the occurrence of a prizefight and homicides found that after a prizefight:
a. homicides increased significantly, with the greatest number of homicides occurring three days after the prizefight.
b. homicides decreased significantly, demonstrating the catharsis effect.
c. homicides increased significantly, with the greatest number of homicides occurring within the first three hours after the prizefight.
d. homicides increased only if the "underdog" won the fight.

Chapter 11 Contrast Effects and Judgments of Physical Attractiveness: When Beauty Becomes a Social Problem
Douglas T. Kenrick and Sara E. Gutierres

Answer: c
1. In their series of three studies on the "contrast effect" and ratings of physical attractiveness, Kenrick and Gutierres hypothesized that:
   a. exposing judges to extremely unattractive stimuli before they rated a photo of a woman of "average" attractiveness would have no effect on how the judges rated the photo.
   b. exposing judges to extremely attractive stimuli before they rated a photo of a woman of "average" attractiveness would result in the judges rating the photo as more attractive.
   c. exposing judges to extremely attractive stimuli before they rated a photo of a woman of "average" attractiveness would result in the judges rating the photo as less attractive.
   d. exposing judges to extremely unattractive stimuli before they rated a photo of a woman of "average" attractiveness would result in the judges rating the photo as less attractive.

Answer: d   2. The results of the first experiment conducted by Kenrick and Gutierres supported their hypothesis. However, one alternative explanation could not be completely ruled out: The subjects who were watching *Charlie's Angels* may have been more generally negative in their judgments toward women than control subjects, due to differences in personality, background, or some other unknown characteristic. To control for this in Study 2, Kenrick and Gutierres:
a. had all subjects complete a full battery of psychological tests designed to detect differences in personality.
b. assigned subjects to experimental conditions on a "matched sample" basis; that is, they made sure that the subjects in the experimental and the control groups were as much alike as possible.
c. used subjects who were watching a television show other than *Charlie's Angels*.
d. manipulated exposure to media beauty by using a different attractiveness stimuli *and* randomly assigned subjects to experimental conditions.

Answer: c   3. In Study 3 of their series of experiments on the "contrast effect," Kenrick and Gutierres modified their procedures in order to examine the effect of two additional variables on judgments of attractiveness. These two variables were:
a. providing subjects with occupational information on the woman in the photo and the inclusion of female judges.
b. the inclusion of female judges and the inclusion of photos of male targets.
c. exposure to peer evaluations (by having confederates comment on the photo) and the inclusion of female judges.
d. exposure to peer evaluations (by having confederates comment on the photo) and the inclusion of photos of male targets.

Answer: b   4. Taken as a whole, the results of the studies conducted by Kenrick and Gutierres on the "contrast effect" support which of the following statements?
a. Initial judgments of a potential romantic partner's attractiveness may set into motion a "self-fulfilling prophecy".
b. Initial impressions of potential romantic partners will be adversely affected by recent exposure to media images of highly attractive individuals.
c. Male and female judges rated the photos very differently, indicating that only men are influenced by media images and cultural standards of physical beauty.
d. Individuals who encounter a "representative" sample of opposite-sex persons in their everyday life will not develop a bias against average-looking potential partners.

Chapter 12 The Effect of Attitude on the Recall of Personal Histories
Michael Ross, Cathy McFarland, and Garth J.O. Fletcher

Answer: b 1. Ross et al.'s research on how attitudes affect recall attempted to answer which of the following questions?
   a. Would recall of repressed childhood memories be aided by psychological therapy or counseling that was designed to change a person's current attitudes?
   b. Would subjects' recall of their past behaviors be influenced by manipulations of their current attitudes?
   c. Are subjects' current attitudes the result of their need to justify their past behaviors?
   d. Contrary to "common sense," is it easier to recall when long-standing habits were first formed than when more recent habits were formed?

Answer: b 2. The results of the Ross et al. study on the relation between attitudes and recall demonstrated that:
   a. positive messages influenced attitudes more strongly than negative messages did.
   b. negative messages influenced attitudes more strongly than positive messages did.
   c. both positive and negative messages were equally effective in influencing attitudes.
   d. no attitude shifts toward personal hygiene habits were obtained as the result of exposure to persuasive communications.

Answer: b 3. Ross et al., in their discussion of possible interpretations of their findings on the relationship between attitudes and recall, rule out the "self-presentation" interpretation because:
   a. the subjects' responses were anonymous.
   b. the results of the "self-monitoring" variable showed that the effect of attitude on behavior was stronger among low self-monitors, which works against the self-presentation hypothesis.
   c. the results of the "self-monitoring" variable showed that the effect of attitude on behavior was weaker among self-monitors, which works against the self-preservation hypothesis.
   d. there is no difference in recall between familiar supporting arguments and novel opposing arguments.

Answer: a 4. Stated in the most general, but direct, terms, the research results from the Ross et al. study on the link between attitudes and behavior reveal that:
   a. attitudes can influence the recall of past behaviors.
   b. behavior can affect attitudes.
   c. attitudes can direct behavior.
   d. past behavior can affect future behavior.

Chapter 13 Attitude Accessibility as a Moderator of the
Attitude-Perception and Attitude-Behavior Relations:
An Investigation of the 1984 Presidential Election
Russell H. Fazio and Carol J. Williams

Answer: b

1. In their review of research on consistency between attitudes and behavior, Fazio and Williams note that there are two major approaches to studying the attitude-behavior link—the "when" approach and the "how" approach. The major difference between these two approaches is:
   a. in the "when" approach, the focus is on the process by which attitudes guide behavior, whereas in the "how" approach the focus is exclusively on identifying variables that mediate the attitude-behavior relation.
   b. the "when" approach focuses on the question of when attitudes predict subsequent behavior, whereas the "how" approach focuses on the process by which attitudes guide behavior.
   c. the accessibility of attitudes from memory is more important to the "when" approach than to the "how" approach.
   d. the "when" approach has a more cognitive focus, whereas the "how" approach looks at how persons' unconscious motivations govern their behavior.

Answer: d

2. In Fazio and Williams' study of attitude accessibility, they hypothesized that individuals who responded relatively quickly to statements about the 1984 Presidential election candidates would:
   a. be more likely to vote in the election than individuals who responded more slowly.
   b. be more likely to report that they intended to vote for one candidate but would actually vote for the other candidate.
   c. report perceptions of the performance of the two candidates in a later Presidential debate that conflicted with their initial attitudes toward the two candidates—that is, they responded too hastily and later changed their opinion regarding the best candidate.
   d. report perceptions of the performance of the two candidates in a later Presidential debate that were in agreement with their initial attitudes toward the two candidates, and would also actually vote for the candidate whom they had initially favored.

Answer: d   3. Results of the Fazio and Williams' study of the moderating effect of "attitude accessibility" demonstrated that:
a. there is no relation between attitude extremity and latency of response to attitudinal inquiries—that is, there is no relation between how strongly a person feels about someone or something and how quickly they respond to statements about that person or thing.
b. the relation between attitude and behavior is stronger among subjects with low attitude accessibility.
c. individuals with high attitude accessibility tend to be right-wing extremists, as evidenced by the landslide victory of Reagan over Mondale in the 1984 election.
d. attitude accessibility affects the link between attitudes and perceptions and the link between attitudes and behaviors—that is, individuals with relatively accessible attitudes show greater selective perception and greater attitude-behavior consistency.

Answer: c   4. Fazio and Williams discuss the implications of their findings on the functioning of "attitude accessibility" for which of the following real-world contexts?
a. curbing the effects of media violence on heavy viewers of television crime dramas
b. revising Presidential debate formats to make them less favorable to the incumbent
c. designing political or marketing campaigns that target certain population segments as recipients of persuasive communications
d. reforming political campaign practices that use highly impactful—but misleading—messages to sway voters' opinions

Chapter 14 Videotape and the Attribution Process: Reversing Actors' and Observers' Points of View
Michael D. Storms

Answer: b   1. Storms' research on experimental manipulation of visual orientation has its theoretical foundation in the work of Jones and Nisbett (1971) on attribution. In that work, Jones and Nisbett argue that:
a. actors tend to explain their own behavior as resulting from internal, personal causes, whereas observers explain actors' behavior as resulting from external, environmental causes.
b. actors tend to explain their own behavior as resulting from external, environmental causes, whereas observers explain actors' behavior as resulting from internal, personal causes.
c. altering actors' attributions is the key to successful psychological therapy.
d. attributions are unaffected by point of view or perspective.

Answer: c   2. The main hypothesis in Storms' research on the effect of videotape reorientation of actors' and observers' causal attributions involved which of the following specific predictions?
a. Observers who saw themselves on videotape would become relatively more situational in attributions of the actors' behavior.
b. Actors who saw themselves on videotape would become relatively less dispositional in attributions of their own behavior.
c. Actors who saw themselves on videotape would become relatively less situational in attributions of their own behavior.
d. Visual orientation would have no influence on attributions.

Answer: a   3. Storms argues that the relatively greater amount of change from initially dispositional attributions toward situational attributions, compared to the lesser amount of change from initially situational attributions toward dispositional attributions, is probably the result of:
a. a high base rate of importance for personal, dispositional attributions among most persons, that is, a "ceiling effect" for dispositional attributions was found.
b. experimenter "demand characteristics".
c. the tendency of observers who saw a videotape from the actors' point of view to develop a "self-discovery" perspective.
d. the tendency of most people to not "blame the victim".

Answer: d   4. Storms discusses the implications of the effects of videotape reorientation on attributional processes for psychological therapy and human relations training. While he points out the possible beneficial effects of having a patient develop a "self-viewing" perspective, Storms also notes that this could sometimes be "distherapeutic" mainly because:
a. it could make patients think that they didn't need to continue to seek professional help.
b. self-viewing, by increasing persons' situational attributions, could lead patients to blame all of their problems on society rather than on themselves.
c. the costs of therapy are already high, and introducing the use of costly videotape technology would push patient fees even higher, making therapy even more inaccessible to the average citizen.
d. patients may discount the effects of situational forces on their behavior and end up blaming themselves too much, which can actually lead them to get worse, not better.

Chapter 15 Persuasion via Self-Justification: Large Commitments for Small Rewards
Elliot Aronson

Answer: b 1. In his article tracing the development of the theory of cognitive dissonance, Aronson points out that cognitive dissonance theory was formulated as a response to:
a. Freudian theory.
b. reward-reinforcement theory.
c. reactance theory.
d. cognitive consistency theory.

Answer: a 2. Aronson argues that dissonance effects are powerful and long-lasting mainly because the arousal of dissonance:
a. entails "personal involvements" and the need for self-justification.
b. threatens an individual's stable view of the external world.
c. evokes strong, but repressed, early-life traumas.
d. makes persons feel empowered.

Answer: a 3. Assessing the permanence of opinion change that results from the inducing of dissonance is very difficult, according to Aronson, primarily because:
a. ethical constraints force researchers to debrief subjects immediately after an experiment is concluded.
b. subjects, who are very often college students, either graduate or drop out of school, making them unavailable for repeated experimental measurement.
c. the passage of time introduces the subject to other experiences that could effect the original experimental manipulation.
d. research shows that subjects become bored participating in the same experiment over an extended period of time.

Answer: b 4. Aronson maintains that even though dissonance theory has many conceptual similarities to earlier social-psychological theories, it was more influential than those earlier theories mainly because:
   a. dissonance theory introduced a new method to social scientific experimentation—the formulation of testable hypotheses.
   b. dissonance theory's hypotheses directly challenged the predictions of the then-dominant reward-reinforcement theory.
   c. the earlier theorists could not benefit from technological advances in laboratory procedures.
   d. dissonance theory made "non-obvious" predictions, when judged against the earlier theoretical work of Lewin, Lecky, and Heider.

Answer: c 5. Which of the following factors plays a central role in the arousal of dissonance?
   a. lack of commitment to performing a particular behavior
   b. lack of responsibility for the consequences of action
   c. the contradiction of, or challenge to, the self-concept
   d. justification of behavior to powerful authority figures

Chapter 16 Compliance Without Pressure: The Foot-in-the Door Technique
Jonathan L. Freedman and Scott C. Fraser

Answer: d
1. The main prediction in Freedman and Fraser's first field experiment on compliance, in which they were ostensibly concerned with the inventory of household products in subjects' homes, was that the subjects:
   a. in the One-Contact condition would be most likely to comply with a large request.
   b. in the Agree-Only condition would refuse to carry out the first, smaller request.
   c. in the Familiarization condition would refuse to comply with the first, smaller request.
   d. in the Performance condition would be more likely to agree to the larger request than subjects in any other experimental condition.

Answer: a
2. The major reason why Freedman and Fraser found it necessary to conduct a second experimental test of their compliance hypothesis was:
   a. the first experiment didn't adequately answer the questions of why and how agreeing to an initial request increases compliance with a second request.
   b. the first experiment didn't adequately answer the questions of why and how complying with the first, smaller request failed to increase compliance with the second, larger request.
   c. the first experiment involved unethical experimental practices that invalidated the findings.
   d. the second experiment was conducted to take advantage of a new interviewing technique that allowed the same experimenter to contact the subjects on both the first and second requests.

Answer: b   3. In their second experiment, where subjects were asked to install a large sign on their front lawns, Freedman and Fraser found all of the following results *except*:
    a. there were no significant differences among the experimental conditions in the proportion of subjects who complied with the initial request.
    b. in the conditions where the first and second requests were similar in nature, there was significantly more compliance than in the conditions where the first and second requests were different in nature.
    c. merely having been given a first request tended to increase compliance with a second request, regardless of whether subjects agreed to perform the first request.
    d. having different interviewers for the first and second requests had no significant effect on the degree of compliance with the second request.

Chapter 17 Reducing Weight by Reducing Dissonance: The Role of Effort Justification in Inducing Weight Loss
Danny Axsom and Joel Cooper

Answer: a   1. Axsom and Cooper, in their experiment on the effectiveness of different weight-loss therapies, maintain that the therapeutic process is influenced by which of the following concepts?
    a. effort justification
    b. the psychodynamic schema of id, ego, and superego
    c. systematic desensitization
    d. the idea, borrowed from architecture, that "less is more"

Answer: b   2. According to the article on weight reduction by Axsom and Cooper, the factor that underlies the effectiveness of virtually all forms of psychotherapy is:
   a. changing a negative self-concept to a positive self-concept.
   b. expending effort to participate in the therapy.
   c. learning logical, rational decision-making procedures.
   d. learning to accept oneself for the person one is.

Answer: d   3. The results of Axsom and Cooper's weight-reduction experiment showed that by the end of the fifth (and last) session, subjects in the high-effort condition had lost _____ weight than those in the low-effort condition. A year later, subjects in the high-effort condition had lost _____ weight than those in the low-effort condition.
   a. significantly more; significantly more
   b. significantly more; about the same amount of
   c. slightly less; significantly more
   d. slightly more; significantly more

Answer: d   4. In Axsom and Cooper's experiment, which of the following pairs of variables were manipulated?
   a. choice/weight loss
   b. effort/weight loss
   c. length of session/level of effort
   d. effort/choice

Answer: b 5. Axsom and Cooper argue that the continued weight loss experienced by some of their subjects during the six months following the experiment occurred primarily because:
a. the eating plan used in the experiment was highly effective and nutritionally sound.
b. subjects continued to pursue the goal of weight loss, which had been made more attractive by the experimental manipulation of effort justification.
c. the experiment lead to the formation of an "antecedent" that helped subjects follow the successful weight-loss techniques they had learned.
d. the initial loss of weight reduced subjects' anxiety about being overweight in a society that overemphasizes being thin and fit.

Chapter 18 Dishonest Behavior as a Function of Differential Levels of Induced Self-Esteem
Elliot Aronson and David R. Mettee

Answer: a 1. Aronson and Mettee's main hypothesis is that persons who experience lowered self-esteem will be more likely to cheat than persons who experience heightened self-esteem. The major assumption underlying this prediction is that:
a. dishonest behavior is inconsistent with high self-esteem, and people strive for cognitive consistency.
b. persons who are most susceptible to having their self-esteem lowered are already predisposed to engage in cheating behavior.
c. persons with high self-esteem never cheat because they have "more to lose" and little to gain by cheating.
d. low self-esteem creates an attitude of "I have nothing to lose," so that persons with low self-esteem are more likely to risk being caught cheating.

Answer: d   2. The *main* reason that Aronson and Mettee administered the California Personality Inventory (CPI) to their subjects in the card-cheating experiment was:
   a. to measure the subjects' chronic self-esteem.
   b. to determine whether some subjects might be too sensitive to participate in an experiment involving deception.
   c. to determine which subjects displayed personality characteristics that would lead them to engage in cheating or other dishonest behavior.
   d. to provide the experimenters with a "cover" for manipulating subjects' self-esteem by providing bogus test results.

Answer: c   3. By analyzing both the cheating behavior of subjects and their chronic levels of self-esteem as measured by the CPI, Aronson and Mettee found evidence for which of the following?
   a. People with high chronic self-esteem were disproportionately clustered in the "High Self Esteem" (HSE) experimental condition.
   b. In the "No Feedback" condition (NSE), more "low chronics" cheated than "medium chronics."
   c. The greatest proportion of cheaters were "low chronics" in the "Low Self Esteem" (LSE) experimental condition.
   d. The greatest proportion of cheaters were "low chronics" whose self-esteem was not manipulated by the experimenters.

Answer: c 4. In discussing the results of their study on self-esteem and cheating, Aronson and Mettee acknow-ledge that alternative explanations of their findings are possible. In their view, the *major* rival explan-ation is:
a. anger and aggressiveness directed toward the experimenter by subjects in the low self-esteem condition.
b. cognitive consistency theory.
c. compensation—that is, low self-esteem subjects cheated to make sure they won some money, thus "compensating" for not having done well on the bogus personality test.
d. reward-reinforcement theory—"It pays to cheat."

Chapter 19 Using Cognitive Dissonance to Encourage Water Conservation
Chris Dickerson, Ruth Thibodeau, Elliot Aronson & Dayna Miller

Answer: a 1. Of the four conditions tested in Dickerson et al.'s study of water conservation among women taking showers, which was the one designed to arouse the most dissonance (the "hypocrisy" manipulation)?
a. mindful plus commitment
b. mindful only
c. commitment only
d. unmindful and no commitment

Answer: c 2. The results of Dickerson, et al.'s water conservation experiment revealed a statistically significant difference between:
a. the mindful and unmindful groups.
b. the committed and uncommitted groups.
c. the hypocrisy group and the control group.
d. the hypocrisy group and all other groups.

308   Readings About the Social Animal

Answer: d   3. The major dependent measurement recorded of subjects' behavior that was used as the basis for analyzing the results of Dickerson et al.'s water conservation experiment was:
a. the attitudes the subjects held about the value of water conservation.
b. the degree to which subjects agreed with statements such as "I always turn off the water when soaping up."
c. whether or not subjects were willing to sign a petition that advocated water conservation.
d. how long subjects ran the water during their showers.

Answer: b   4. One argument that is an alternative to the dissonance reduction explanation given by Dickerson et al. is that subjects in the "hypocrisy" condition:
a. were more likely to hold liberal political beliefs and thus be more friendly to ideas such as recycling and water conservation.
b. were "primed" to think more about water conservation, thus enhancing those attitudes.
c. actually felt less dissonance in the "hypocrisy" condition and therefore were less likely to conserve water.
d. felt a temporary decline in their self-esteem and were therefore more compliant to the experimenter's requests.

Chapter 20 The Effects of Observing Violence
            Leonard Berkowitz

Answer: b   1. Berkowitz's study of the effects of filmed aggression on behavior was designed to test which of the following theories?
a. the serial killer syndrome
b. catharsis
c. cognitive dissonance
d. compliance

Answer: b   2. Berkowitz's experimental findings suggest that one of the key factors affecting whether viewing filmed violence will lead to aggressive behavior is:
a. if the violence is especially graphic.
b. if the violence is portrayed as justified.
c. if the type of violence in the film is consistent with the viewer's past behavior.
d. if the violence is seen in a large group.

Answer: c   3. Which of the following is *not* a conclusion about aggressive behavior drawn by Berkowitz as a result of his research?
a. People who have been angered and then see filmed violence will act more aggressively than people who have not been angered before seeing filmed violence.
b. Aggressive behavior is most often directed toward specific targets.
c. Films with violent themes and scenes make anyone who sees them act more aggressively and at approximately the same level of aggression.
d. A frustrated person can enjoy fantasy aggression.

Answer: a   4. From his own research and from his analysis of related work by others, Berkowitz maintains that the most important danger in viewing film violence is that:
a. for a short period right after viewing violence, a person is predisposed to act violently.
b. it has long-term effects on memory, which can lead the viewer to act aggressively for a long period after viewing the film.
c. violent films are so impactful that the emotional trauma of viewing them is never eliminated.
d. a "systematic desensitization" to violence occurs, such that the more viewers watch violent films, the more violence those films must contain in order to have the same arousing effects.

Chapter 21 The Facilitation of Aggression by Aggression: Evidence Against the Catharsis Hypothesis
Russell G. Geen, David Stonner, and Gary L. Shope

Answer: b   1. Geen et al. argue that the mixed and inconclusive data on aggression catharsis is probably the result of:
    a. poor operationalization of the concept.
    b. differences in experimental conditions that affected inhibitions against aggression.
    c. differences in types of subjects used in different experiments.
    d. differences in experimenter demand characteristics.

Answer: a   2. In their "attack manipulation," which was designed to create different levels of instigation to aggression, Geen et al.:
    a. had the confederate shock the subjects when he disagreed with their attitudes on 12 controversial issues.
    b. had the confederate shock the subjects when they made mistakes on a code-learning task.
    c. insulted the subjects during an interview conducted prior to the experiment.
    d. intentionally recruited two separate groups of subjects—one that scored high on chronic levels of aggression and one that scored low on the same measure.

Answer: d   3. In the Geen et al. experiment on aggression, subjects administered the most intense shocks in which of the following treatment conditions?
    a. "attack—experimenter shocks" condition
    b. "attack—no shocks" condition
    c. "attack—confederate shocks" condition
    d. "attack—subject shocks" condition

Answer: b 4. Geen et al. acknowledge that there are two plausible explanations for their findings that aggressing leads to committing further acts of aggression. These two explanations involve:
a. a weakening of restraints against violence/ desire to punish.
b. weakening of restraints against violence/ consistency-seeking behavior.
c. weakening of restraints against violence/desire for justice or revenge ("an eye for an eye")
d. physiological catharsis/increased instigation to aggress.

Chapter 22 Peacetime Casualties: The Effects of War on the Violent Behavior of Noncombatants
Dane Archer and Rosemary Gartner

Answer: b 1. Archer and Gartner maintain that State violence is not included in investigations of murder and aggression mainly because:
a. the State is a complex bureaucracy that can easily conceal its actions from public scrutiny.
b. State violence enjoys legitimacy.
c. the media is in collusion with government to suppress all news of State violence.
d. the effects of State violence are relatively minor compared to the vast number of crimes committed by individuals.

Answer: c 2. Archer and Gartner maintain that war, as the most dramatic form of State violence, may result in increases in post-war homicide rates mainly because of which of the following processes?
a. catharsis
b. arrested moral development
c. social learning
d. frustration-aggression

Answer: b   3. Archer and Gartner's analysis of post-war homicide rates reveals that warring nations:
   a. were less likely to experience homicide rate increases than non-combatant nations.
   b. were more likely to experience homicide rate increases than non-combatant nations.
   c. with the highest numbers of wartime casualties were less likely to have homicide rate increases, because the citizens of those countries had already experienced too much death and destruction.
   d. were more likely to experience homicide rate increases than non-combatant nations, but only among minority populations.

Answer: c   4. Even though it is a commonly accepted hypothesis, the "violent veteran" explanation for post-war homicide rate increases is not supported by Archer and Gartner's analysis of the evidence. They based their dismissal of this "myth" on:
   a. their extensive interviews with veterans of three different wars.
   b. the fact that homicide rate increases *during* the wars were as high as *after* wars, so that veterans could not have been responsible for the wartime homicides.
   c. the fact that post-war increases in violence and homicide occurred among demographic groups who did not serve in combat.
   d. the fact that research has shown that military training "wears off" very quickly after combat duty ceases.

Chapter 23 Deindividuation and Anger-Mediated Interracial
           Aggression: Unmasking Regressive Racism
           Ronald W. Rogers and Steven Prentice-Dunn

Answer: c   1. In their study of interracial aggression, Rogers and
                Prentice-Dunn predicted that if the white subjects
                in their experiment were not angered, they would:
                a. experience deindividuation.
                b. attack black victims more severely than white
                   victims.
                c. attack white victims more severely than black
                   victims.
                d. quickly make friends with all of the victims,
                   regardless of race.

Answer: b   2. Which of the following variables was *not* investigated by Rogers and Prentice-Dunn in their study of interracial aggression?
                a. deindividuating vs. individuating cues
                b. low shock intensity vs. high shock intensity
                c. race of victim
                d. insult to the subjects vs. no insult to the
                   subjects

Answer: c   3. In the Rogers and Prentice-Dunn experiment on
                interracial aggression, they found evidence of a
                significant interaction effect between which of the
                following variables?
                a. deindividuation and race
                b. deindividuation and insult
                c. race and insult
                d. shock intensity and race

Answer: d   4. Rogers and Prentice-Dunn's findings on interracial aggression suggest the operation of what they term "regressive racism". This process:
   a. can be fully explained using the "ambivalence-amplification" hypothesis of Katz.
   b. can account for whites' aggressive behavior toward blacks, but cannot explain blacks' aggressive behavior toward whites.
   c. involves the expression of unprejudiced values that are fully internalized.
   d. refers to the tendency for persons of any race to adopt chronologically earlier styles of interracial behavior when they are aroused.

Chapter 24 Predictors of Naturalistic Sexual Aggression
Neil M. Malamuth

Answer: d   1. Malamuth notes that in his research program on sexual aggression, he has employed two types of aggression measures—a laboratory measure and a naturalistic measure—which have opposite advantages and disadvantages. The advantage of the laboratory measure of aggression is that:
   a. it is a self-report measure and, therefore, is immune to errors occurring from social desirability pressures.
   b. it assesses behavior in a setting that is high in ecological validity.
   c. almost all previous research has used it, so it allows for comparisons among studies.
   d. it is an objective measure that does not rely on subjects' self-reports.

Answer: b   2. Which of the following was *not* one of the six predictor variables that Malamuth used in his study of self-reported naturalistic sexual aggression?
   a. sexual responsiveness to rape
   b. exposure to media violence
   c. hostility toward women
   d. antisocial personality characteristics

Answer: d   3. Malamuth's findings on the predictors of naturalistic sexual aggression demonstrate that:
   a. all of the predictor variables he identified were significantly related to naturalistic sexual aggression.
   b. the primary causal factor in naturalistic sexual aggression is psychoticism—that is, having an antisocial personality.
   c. the Additive model of combining predictors was superior to the Interactive model in accounting for the occurrence of naturalistic sexual aggression.
   d. the presence of any one of the predictor variables—by itself—is unlikely to lead to high levels of sexual aggression.

Answer: a 4. In discussing the implications of his findings on the occurrence of naturalistic sexual aggression, Malamuth argues that his results lend support to other research on:
a. how media depictions of violence may change persons' attitudes in such a way that actual aggressive behavior occurs.
b. how increasing prison sentences for rapists may actually lead them to commit more acts of violence, both while they are in prison and once they are released.
c. how research on sexual aggression should continue to search for single, primary factors that predict when sexual aggression will occur.
d. how rapists develop rationales and justifications for their acts.

Chapter 25 The Nonverbal Mediation of Self-Fulfilling Prophecies in Interracial Interaction
Carl O. Word, Mark P. Zanna, and Joel Cooper

Answer: b 1. The general hypothesis of the Word et al. study on interaction between whites and blacks is that:
a. black job applicants will respond to what they perceive as whites' negative attitudes toward them with increased friendliness, in an attempt to change the whites' negative evaluations of them.
b. whites and blacks will engage in a sequence of nonverbal, reciprocal interactions that result in a self-fulfilling prophecy.
c. black job applicants will receive the same amount of "immediate" nonverbal communications from a white interviewer as will white job applicants.
d. all recipients of more "immediate" non-verbal communications—regardless of race—will be judged more harshly than recipients of less "immediate" non-verbal communications.

Answer: b 2. In the Word et al. study on interracial interaction, all of the following were significant results *except*:
a. white interviewers sat closer to white applicants than to black applicants.
b. white interviewers made fewer speech errors talking with black applicants than with white applicants.
c. white interviewers spent less time with black applicants than with white applicants.
d. job applicants in the "nonimmediate" condition were judged to be less adequate for the job than job applicants in the "immediate" condition.

Answer: a 3. According to Word et al., the practical, "real world" implications of their findings on self-fulfilling prophecies in interracial interactions are most applicable to the problem of:
a. black unemployment.
b. race riots.
c. affirmative action.
d. desegregation.

Answer: d 4. Word et al. draw on the findings from a number of related studies to develop a rationale for their experiment on interracial interaction. Which of the following researchers do they mention as being associated with the idea that "blackness" is a stigmatizing trait in American society?
a. Merton
b. Rosenthal
c. Mehrabian
d. Goffman

Chapter 26 Nonverbal Affect Responses to Male and Female Leaders: Implications for Leadership Evaluations
Doré Butler and Florence Geis

Answer: a 1. Butler and Geis argue that when people are asked about the qualifications and competence of women leaders, they generally believe them to be _____ men. They also argue that automatic expectations such as non-verbal responses _____ conform to traditional feminine stereotypes.
a. equal to; do
b. better than; do not
c. poorer than; do not
d. better than; do

Answer: b 2. The major point of Butler and Geis's study of leadership is that women leaders:
a. are actually more effective in achieving consensus in a group than are men leaders.
b. evoke more negative non-verbal responses in group members than do men leaders.
c. spend more time talking, but are less effective in achieving consensus in a group than are men leaders.
d. are not allowed to talk as much as are men leaders which leads them to be less effective in moving the group toward consensus.

Answer: c 3. Which group of confederates were most likely to be judged as warm and sensitive but also as dominating?
a. male leaders
b. male non-leaders
c. female leaders
d. female non-leaders

Answer: a 4. According to the results of Butler and Geis's experiment on sex differences in evaluations of leaders, which of the following people would most likely receive the most negative non-verbal response from members in a discussion group?
a. a female solo leader
b. a female non-leader
c. a male solo leader
d. a male non-leader

Chapter 27 Stereotype Vulnerability and Intellectual Performance
Claude Steele and Joshua Aronson

Answer: c 1. According to Steele and Aronson, why do blacks score lower on tests of verbal ability?
a. They have not received as much instruction in verbal thinking.
b. They have not read as much.
c. They are subjected to a stereotype that suggests blacks have low verbal ability.
d. Tests as well as testing situations are oftentimes biased against blacks.

Answer: d 2. For what reason did Steele and Aronson conduct a second experiment in their study of stereotype vulnerability and intellectual performance?
a. To provide a more difficult measure of intellectual performance, since the test in the first experiment was too long.
b. To include Hispanics and Asian-Americans along with blacks as subjects in the experiment.
c. To see if intellectual performance varied by race as a function of the length of the test.
d. To determine if black subjects were disen-gaging with the experiment and weren't trying to perform well.

Answer: a   3. In Steele and Aronson's experiment on stereotype vulnerability, which of the following groups spent the most time on each test item?
a. black students in the diagnostic condition
b. black students in the nondiagnostic condition
c. white students in the diagnostic condition
d. white students in the nondiagnostic condition

Answer: b   4. Suppose male and female college freshmen are given a difficult math test. Half of each group is told the test is a placement test to determine which section of freshman math they will be assigned to. The other half is told the test is to be used as a reference against which to compare gifted high school students' scores and scores will not be associated with individual students who take the tests. Generalizing from Steele and Aronson's work on stereotype vulnerability, which group would most likely score lowest?
a. men in the "placement" condition
b. women in the "placement" condition
c. men in the "reference group" condition
d. women in the "reference group" condition

Chapter 28 Experiments in Group Conflict
Muzafer Sherif

Answer: b
1. The main reason Sherif and his colleagues studied a carefully selected group of boys in a summer camp was:
   a. to compare boys who went to camp with a matched sample of boys who did not go to camp to see if participating in group activities influenced cooperative social skills.
   b. to study the formation and development of group cohesion and group conflict.
   c. to discover the personality traits that were correlated with social interaction skills and demonstrated leadership abilities.
   d. to discover whether and how leaders differ from followers, by comparing their family backgrounds.

Answer: b
2. The subjects in Sherif's Robber's Cave experiments were:
   a. boys labeled as juvenile delinquents.
   b. normal, healthy, intelligent boys from stable, white, middle-class homes.
   c. normal boys from a variety of racial backgrounds chosen from a program for underprivileged children.
   d. boys from two sixth-grade classes in one of the Norman, Oklahoma, school districts.

Answer: d   3. Sherif found in his experiment at Robber's Cave that which of the following conditions needed to exist before status hierarchies developed among the boys in a particular peer group?
a. They needed to engage in competitive games with each other.
b. They needed to engage in cooperative activities with each other.
c. They needed to be given unequal rewards.
d. None of the above; status hierarchies emerged naturally.

Answer: d   4. Sherif describes that the boys at Robber's Cave were immediately divided into two groups. Quickly, a leadership hierarchy developed within each group. Sherif explains that this hierarchy developed:
a. as a result of competition between the two groups.
b. as a result of cooperation between the two groups.
c. as a result of giving the groups unequal opportunities and rewards.
d. naturally as part of the group formation process.

Answer: d   5. Sherif and his associates eventually restored harmonious relations between the Rattlers and the Eagles by:
a. having the two groups engage in competitive games.
b. bringing the two groups together for common social events such as movie-watching and eating.
c. forcing the two groups to cooperate through threats of expulsion from the camp.
d. creating a common, "superordinate" goal.

Chapter 29 Jigsaw Groups and the Desegregated Classroom: In Pursuit of Common Goals
Elliot Aronson and Diane Bridgeman

Answer: c 1. Aronson and Bridgeman review studies that demonstrate the disappointing results of desegregation in improving group relations, self-esteem and academic performance. They argue that these negative results are mainly due to:
a. the failure of authorities to support integration efforts.
b. inadequate funding for schools.
c. the interaction of lack of "equal-status contact" with the competitive structure of the classroom.
d. lack of discipline in classrooms, so that children are not compelled to cooperate.

Answer: d 2. Aronson and his colleagues developed the technique known as the "jigsaw" classroom primarily to:
a. provide data for a theoretical analysis comparing the effects of cooperation versus competition.
b. to take advantage of the altruistic motivations of students, which are stifled by a competitive classroom environment.
c. to replicate the findings of the famous "Robber's Cave" experiment in another "naturalistic" setting—the classroom.
d. develop a cooperative structure for integrated classrooms that could be readily implemented and evaluated—that is, to develop an "action research" program.

Answer: b 3. Aronson and Bridgeman discuss research on the effect of jigsaw techniques on academic performance. This research, conducted by Lucker et al. (1977), found that:
a. both minority and Anglo students significantly improved their academic performance as a result of the jigsaw technique.
b. minority students performed significantly better in jigsaw classes than in traditional classes.
c. unlike most other students, high-ability students suffered from the jigsaw technique, as evidenced by the decline in their reading scores after the jigsaw technique was implemented.
d. all students—Anglo and minority alike—in jigsaw classrooms showed increases in self-esteem and increases in "liking" school.

Answer: a 4. In comparing the jigsaw technique to other techniques designed to develop interdependent classroom learning, Aronson and Bridgeman note that the major difference between the jigsaw technique and other approaches such as "TGT" and "STAD" is:
a. jigsaw attempts to minimize competition; TGT and STAD promote and use competition *across* groups, while encouraging *within-group* cooperation.
b. jigsaw can be effective only where the entire traditional classroom structure of competition is eliminated, whereas TGT and STAD promote and utilize competition.
c. jigsaw is based on established social-psychological principles, whereas other interdependent learning programs do not have a solid, scientific foundation.
d. jigsaw improves both academic performance and racial/ethnic relations, whereas other interdependent learning programs only improve academic performance.

Chapter 30 Subtle and Blatant Prejudice in Western Europe
Thomas Pettigrew and R.W. Meertens

Answer: c   1. The major distinction between blatant prejudice and subtle prejudice is that subtle prejudice is:
  a. more harmful to those against whom it is directed.
  b. illegal as well as immoral.
  c. indirect or covert.
  d. found only in Western nations.

Answer: a   2. Which of the following is a characteristic of blatant, rather than subtle, prejudice?
  a. outward coldness or hostility publicly expressed toward members of a minority group
  b. no expression of either negative or positive emotions toward minority group members
  c. defense of traditional values
  d. the exaggeration of cultural differences

Answer: d   3. In comparison to "Bigots" and "Equalitarians," the "Subtles" in Pettigrew and Meertens' study were more apt to favor which of the following immigration policies?
  a. sending back all outgroup members not contributing to the economy
  b. sending back all outgroup members not born in the country
  c. not deporting any outgroup members
  d. deporting outgroup members who have committed crimes

Answer: b   4. Generally speaking, political _____ score higher on the Subtle Prejudice Scale, and _____ people score higher on the Blatant Prejudice Scale.
  a. conservatives, younger
  b. conservatives; older
  c. liberals; younger
  d. liberals; older

Chapter 31 "Playing Hard to Get": Understanding an Elusive Phenomenon
Elaine Walster (Hatfield), G. William Walster, Jane Piliavin, and Lynn Schmidt

Answer: a
1. In their review of research on the "hard to get" phenomenon, Walster et al. cite several theories that could explain why playing "hard to get" increases one's desirability. Which of the following theories was included in their review?
   a. dissonance theory
   b. modeling theory
   c. reactance theory
   d. balance theory

Answer: b
2. As Walster et al. describe in considerable detail, they attempted five experimental tests of their hypothesis before designing an experiment that confirmed their prediction. The major reason why Experiment VI succeeded when the previous five had failed was:
   a. the experimenters stopped using students as subjects, because students did not have much experience with the "hard to get" phenomenon.
   b. after reinterviewing their subjects and listening carefully to their comments, the experimenters discovered that there were both advantages and disadvantages in attempting to date "hard to get" and "easy to get" women, so they refined their procedures.
   c. they realized that is was only necessary to manipulate one variable—how "hard to get" a woman was for the subject; whereas earlier they had also tried to manipulate how "hard to get" the woman was for other men.
   d. they had been pursuing the wrong research strategy by insisting on measuring the "selectivity" of "hard to get" women.

Answer: b   3. The main finding of the Walster et al. experiments on the "hard to get" phenomenon is:
   a. selectively "hard to get" women will be the least liked.
   b. selectively "hard to get" women will be liked more than uniformly "hard to get" women.
   c. selectively "hard to get" women will be liked less than uniformly "easy to get" women.
   d. selectively "hard to get" women will only be asked out for one date.

Chapter 32 The Search for a Romantic Partner: The Effects of Self-Esteem and Physical Attractiveness on Romantic Behavior
Sara B. Kiesler and Roberta L. Baral

Answer: c   1. The main hypothesis in the Kiesler and Baral experiment on the relationship between self-esteem and attractiveness was:
   a. the less attractive a subject was, the lower his self-esteem would be.
   b. subjects would always prefer attractive partners over less-attractive partners.
   c. moderately attractive subjects with low self-esteem would tend to select moderately attractive partners over highly attractive partners.
   d. there is no relation between subjects' self-esteem and choosing an attractive partner; what matters is whether the subjects are highly attractive.

Answer: d 2. Checks on the self-esteem manipulation, which asked subjects to rate their "present emotional feelings" and their performance on an intelligence test, revealed that:
a. subjects in the low self-esteem condition tended to feel better than subjects in the high self-esteem condition.
b. subjects in the low self-esteem condition tended to rate their test performance higher than subjects in the high self-esteem condition.
c. overall, the self-esteem manipulation was not effective.
e. overall, the self-esteem manipulation was effective.

Answer: c 3. Kiesler and Baral interpret their findings on the relationship between self-esteem and choice of romantic partner in which of the following ways?
a. High self-esteem persons are less "practical" and "realistic" in their choice of romantic partner, which is consistent with their scores on the California Personality Inventory (CPI).
b. People with high self-esteem feel threatened if someone doesn't like them and, thus, have a greater need for affection and reassurance than people with low self-esteem.
c. Changes in perception of the self affect perceptions of the chances of success in choosing romantic partners.
d. Their results are valid regardless of subjects' assessments of the likelihood of rejection by highly-attractive romantic partners.

Chapter 33 Social Perception and Interpersonal Behavior: On the Self-Fulfilling Nature of Social Stereotypes
Mark Snyder, Elizabeth Decker Tanke, and Ellen Berscheid

Answer: a 1. The central hypothesis of Snyder et al.'s experiment on social stereotypes can be most accurately stated as:
a. stereotypes help to create a self-fulfilling prophecy.
b. the stereotype that physically attractive people are really more likeable, friendly, and confident than unattractive people is erroneous.
c. we tend to "fill in the gaps" in our knowledge about someone by selecting information that tends to disconfirm our stereotypes.
d. even if we treat people in a hostile fashion, they will tend to try to counteract our negative behavior by acting in a very friendly way, thus disconfirming our stereotypes about them.

Answer: d 2. Snyder et al. not only had male "perceivers" rate their partners' personality characteristics, they also had "observers" judge the women's conversational interaction with the male subjects. This was done to:
a. provide a check on the manipulation of the target women's attractiveness.
b. make sure that the male "perceivers" did not make mistakes in their ratings.
c. see whether male "perceivers" made their initial assessments of the female partners' personality based on stereotyped beliefs about physically attractive women.
d. see whether the "perceivers" initial impressions of their partners initiated a sequence of behaviors in which the female partners acted in ways that confirmed the "perceivers" stereotypes.

Answer: b   3. Which of the following is an accurate summation of the central finding in the Snyder et al. study of the relationship between stereotypes and social interaction?
   a. Male "perceivers" did not assess their female partners on the basis of stereotypes linking physical attractiveness and positive personality traits.
   b. Male "perceivers'" impressions of their female partners created a self-fulfilling prophecy, whereby the female partners came to behave in ways that were consistent with the "perceivers'" impressions of them.
   c. Male "perceivers" assessed their female partners on the basis of gender stereotypes linking physical attractiveness to femininity.
   d. "Observers" did not detect any differences in social interactions between women assigned to the attractive-target condition and women assigned to the unattractive-target condition.

Answer: a   4. In their discussion of the implications of their study of social perception, Snyder et al. maintain that most research and theory in social perception has focused on how people process information and has neglected:
   a. how people help to *create* the information they process.
   b. the *predictive* power of personality traits.
   c. the link between *physical* attractiveness and personality traits.
   d. the importance of beliefs about the *self* in determining people's behavior.

Chapter 34 Some Evidence for Heightened Sexual Attraction Under Conditions of High Anxiety
Donald G. Dutton and Arthur P. Aron

Answer: d   1. Dutton and Aron's series of three experiments on sexual attraction and emotional arousal was designed to test which of the following hypotheses?
a. An attractive woman will be seen as more attractive by men who encounter her as they are experiencing a calm, relaxed physiological and emotional state.
b. An attractive woman will be seen as more attractive when she is perceived to be in distress and needs help.
c. An attractive man will show a preference for a less-attractive partner when he is in a state of physiological and emotional arousal.
d. An attractive woman will be seen as more attractive by men who encounter her when they are experiencing strong physiological and emotional arousal.

332 Readings About the Social Animal

Answer: b   2. Dutton and Aron discuss two major problems with their first experiment that led them to refine their procedure in Experiment 2. Which of the following was *one* of those two problems?
   a. Experimental subjects may have been less likely to contact the female interviewer for a date because they were more likely to be local residents who knew about the experiments.
   b. A difference in subject populations—that is, people who crossed the suspension bridge may have been different from those who crossed the control bridge.
   c. The suspension bridge tended to attract tourists, many of whom were foreign visitors who were unable to communicate properly with the female interviewer properly.
   d. The fact that the male and female interviewers in Experiment 1 obtained an identical pattern of results suggested to Dutton and Aron that something was wrong with their procedures in the first experiment.

Answer: b   3. Dutton and Aron found it necessary to conduct a third experiment, this time in a laboratory setting, mainly because of their inability to control for:
   a. poor weather conditions, which caused the field experiment to be delayed several times.
   b. the possibility that the female interviewer may have acted differently toward the two groups of subjects by exhibiting different forms of nonverbal behavior.
   c. the amount of time that the interviewer spent with subjects in each condition.
   d. the attractiveness of experimental subjects, who could not be screened for "good looks" in the field setting, as they could in a laboratory setting.

Answer: a   4. In discussing the theoretical implications of their findings on the emotion-sexual attraction link, Dutton and Aron argue that their results best support which of the following theories?
a. cognitive labeling of emotion theory
b. actor-observer theory
c. the self-fulfilling prophecy
d. deindividuation theory

Chapter 35 Keeping Track of Needs and Inputs of Friends and Strangers
Margaret Clark, Judson Mills, and David Corcoran

Answer: d   1. According to Clark, Mills and Corcoran, if Barbara and Susan are very good friends who respond to each other based on the other's needs, their relationship would best be described as:
a. implicit friends.
b. explicit friends.
c. an exchange relationship.
d. a communal relationship.

Answer: c   2. In Clark et al.'s experiment, pairs of friends were believed to represent _____ relationships and strangers were believed to represent _____ relationships.
a. need; communal
b. exchange; input
c. communal; exchange
d. exchange; communal

Answer: a   3. Which of the following best summarizes the predictions made by Clark et al. regarding communal and exchange relationships?
   a. Friends are more likely to pay attention to each others' needs, whereas strangers are more likely to pay attention to each others' contributions.
   b. Both friends and strangers are more likely to pay attention to their own needs than to their partners' needs.
   c. Both friends and strangers are more likely to pay attention to their own contributions than to their partners' contributions.
   d. Friends are more likely to pay attention to each others' contributions whereas strangers are more likely to pay attention to each others' needs.

Answer: b   4. The results of Clark et al.'s experiment on exchange and communal relationships found that friends looked at the lights more often than strangers did in the _____ condition, and strangers looked at the lights more often than friends did in the _____ condition.
   a. inputs; needs
   b. needs; inputs
   c. communal; exchange
   d. exchange; communal

Suggested Videos and Films

Chapter 1: What is Social Psychology?

Invitation to Social Psychology (1975, 25 min., color). Methods and topics in social psychology are discussed, including aggression, helping behavior, attraction, attitudes, and obedience. Narrated by Stanley Milgram. MTI Teleprograms Inc., 3710 Commercial Avenue, Northbrook, IL 60062 (800-323-6301)

Methodology: The Psychologist and the Experiment (1975, 31 min., color). Introduces research methods and experimental design, through the example of Schachter's studies on fear and affiliation. (Also relevant to Chapter 9.) CRM-McGraw-Hill, P.O. Box 641, Del Mar, CA 92014-9990 (619-453-5000).

Social Psychology (1990, 30 min.). This film examines several research studies on stereotyping and prejudice, attributions, and the influence of social roles. Zimbardo's prison experiment and in-group/out-group experiments are analyzed. Insight Media, 121 W. 85th St., New York, N.Y., 10024.

Chapter 2: Conformity

Conformity and Independence (1975, 26 min., color). Classic studies of conformity by Asch, Sherif, and Milgram are analyzed, along with Moscovici's research on minority influence. MTI Teleprograms Inc., 3710 Commercial Avenue, Northbrook, IL 60062 (800-323-6301)

Four More Days (1971, 32 min., color). This film depicts the classic "Stanford prison study" conducted by Phillip Zimbardo and his colleagues. Film Library, New York University, 26 Washington Place, New York, NY 10002.

Group Dynamics: Groupthink (1973, updated 1989, 22 min., color). A presentation of Irving Janis's work on "groupthink," within the context of a board meeting at a pharmaceutical company. The major symptoms of groupthink are discussed, along with important historical events (e.g., the Bay of Pigs) that illustrate this phenomenon. CRM-McGraw-Hill, P.O. Box 641, Del Mar, CA 92014-9990 (619-453-5000).

Obedience (1963, 45 min., b&w). A presentation of Milgram's study of obedience. A classic. Film Library, New York University, 26 Washington Place, New York, NY 10002.

Moral Development (1973, 28 min.). This film recreates the procedure of Milgram's classic obedience study and examines the reaction of various subjects. Responses are analyzed within the context of Kohlberg's theory of moral development as characteristic of preconventional, conventional, or principled reasoning. CRM-McGraw-Hill Films, 674 Via de la Valle, P.O. Box 641, Del Mar, CA 92014.

When Will People Help? The Social Psychology of Bystander Intervention (1976, 25 min., color). Daryl Bem narrates this film which reenacts Latane and Darley's pioneering research on the bystander intervention. Harcourt Brace Jovanovich, 757, Third Avenue, New York, NY 10017.

Mob Psychology and Crowd Control: Disaster at Hillsborough (1994, 52 min., color). On April 15, 1989, the worst disaster in the history of English soccer took place when fans swarmed into bleachers, pushing others up against a wire fence, crushing 95 people to death. This program looks at the police investigation to determine what happened. Films for the Humanities and Sciences, P.O. Box 2053, Princeton, NJ 08543-2053 (800-257-5126).

Conformity, Obedience and Dissent (1990, 30 min.). This film examines why people conform, obey, and dissent in social situations by using examples based on Milgram's obedience study, studies of leadership styles, and the groupthink phenomenon. Insight Media, 121 W. 85th St., New York, NY 10024.

Chapter 3: Mass Communication, Propaganda and Persuasion

Effective Persuasion (1968, 11 min., b&w). Persuasion techniques are illustrated in excerpts of speeches by Martin Luther King, Adlai Stevenson, John F. Kennedy, and Winston Churchill. McGraw-Hill Book Company, 1221 Avenue of the Americas, New York, NY 10020 (800-421-0833).

Killing Us Softly: Advertising's Image of Women (1980, 45 min., color). A powerful demonstration of how advertising fosters gender stereotypes. (Also relevant to Chapter 7.) Cambridge Documentary Films, P.O. Box 385, Cambridge, MA 02139 (617-354-3677).

Still Killing Us Softly: Advertising's Images of Women 30 min.). A second film, based on lectures of Dr. Jean Kilbourne, that describes, through the use of ads from magazines, newspapers, album covers, and billboards, how the advertising industry portrays women and men, focusing on consumers' fears and desires. Cambridge Documentary Films, Inc., P.O. Box 385, Cambridge, MA 02139 (617-354-3677).

The Psychology of Mass Persuasion Discusses the psychology of mass persuasions with a focus on (1) the psychological phenomenon of attitudes, (2) advertising's role in politics, and (3) how advertising and propaganda compare and contrast. HRM Video, 175 Tomkins Ave. No. V212, Pleasantville, NY 10570-0839 (800-431-2050).

Think Twice: The Persuasion Game (1978, 19 min., color). A look at how emotional appeals are used as a means of increasing the persuasive impact of a message. Iowa Films, Media Library, University of Iowa, Iowa City, IA 52242 (319-353-5885).

Chapter 4: Social Cognition

Attribution of Motives (1975, 22 min., color) The nature of our causal attributions is explored. University Films of Canada, 7 Hayden Street, Suite 305, Toronto, Ontario, Canada M4Y 2P2.

Impression Formation and Interpersonal Attraction (1975, 27 min., color). A presentation of attraction research, including work on first impressions, need complementarity, and implicit personality theories. (Also relevant to Chapter 8.) University Films of Canada, 7 Hayden Street, Suite 305, Toronto, Ontario, Canada M4Y 2P2.

Predicting Our World (1975, 28 min., color). Topics such as the need for control, risk taking, learned helplessness, and the "just world" phenomenon are explained and illustrated. University Films of Canada, 7 Hayden Street, Suite 305, Toronto, Ontario, Canada M4Y 2P2.

Productivity and the Self-Fulfilling Prophecy: The Pygmalion Effect (1975, 28 min., color. Presents several scenarios that illustrate the confirmation bias—how one's expectations can affect another person's behavior. (Also relevant to chapters 5 and 7.) CRM-McGraw-Hill, P.O. Box 641, Del Mar, CA 92014-9990 (619-453-5000).

Sports Psychology: The Winning Edge in Sports (1987, 60 min.). Sports psychologist Andrew Jacobs and nationally-known athletes discuss issues that affect team performance such as concentration, motivation, stress, and burnout. RMI Media Productions, Inc., 2807 W. 47th Street, Shawnee Mission, KS 66205; Distinctive Home Video Productions, 391 El Portal Rd., San Mateo, CA 94402 (415-344-7756).

Chapter 5: Self-justification

Attitudes about Attitudes (1975, 27 min., color). Topics include cognitive dissonance theory, predicting behavior from attitudes, and the 3-component model of attitudes. University Films of Canada, 7 Hayden Street, Suite 305, Toronto, Ontario, Canada M4Y 2P2.

Productivity and the Self-Fulfilling Prophecy: The Pygmalion Effect (1975, 28 min., color. Presents several scenarios that illustrate how one's expectations can affect another person's behavior. (Also relevant to chapters 4 and 7.) CRM-McGraw-Hill, P.O. Box 641, Del Mar, CA 92014-9990 (619-453-5000).

Social Animal (1963, 29 min.). This film introduces the general subject matter of social psychology, but focuses on attitude change and cognitive dissonance theory. The classic Festinger and Carlsmith (1959) experiment concerning subject's attempts to justify their behavior is discussed. Western Illinois University, Macomb, IL 61455.

The Holy Ghost People (1968, 53 min.). A TV documentary that chronicles the behavior of members of a fundamentalist religious congregation in Appalachia. During a revival meeting, people donate large sums of money, speak in tongues, and handle poisonous snakes. Although social psychological theories are not discussed, the film can be used as a good discussion starter, especially in concert with a discussion of the Jonestown or Waco disasters. CRM-McGraw-Hill Films, 674 Via de la Valle, P.O. Box 641, Del Mar, CA 92014.

Chapter 6: Aggression

Human Aggression. (1976, 22 min., color). Discusses the frustration-aggression hypothesis, social learning theory, and group factors that influence aggressive behavior. Examines aggression in the context of youth gangs and police training. MTI Teleprograms Inc., 3710 Commercial Avenue, Northbrook, IL 60062 (800-323-6301)

Konrad Lorenz's Discussion with Richard Evans: Aggression. (1975, 31 min., color). Ethologist Lorenz discusses and addresses criticisms of his theory of aggression. Aims Instructional Media Services, 626 Justin Avenue, Glendale, CA 91101 (800-367-2467)

Emotional Development: Aggression (1975, 19 min., color). A look at how aggression is learned and how it can be changed, from the perspective of social learning theory. CRM-McGraw-Hill, P.O. Box 641, Del Mar, CA 92014-9990 (619-453-5000).

Pornography: The Double Message (1985, 28 min.). This film examines research studies that suggest images of rape, domination, and bondage lead to insensitivity and unsympathetic attitudes toward victims of rape. Contains explicit material. Filmaker's Library, Inc., 124 E. 40th, New York, NY 10016 (212-808-4980).

Violence and Sex on TV (1994, 28 min., color). Specially adapted Phil Donahue program that explores the effect of on-screen violence on young people. Discusses whether viewing violence alters their view of reality, and whether the government should restrict content. Films for the Humanities & Sciences, P.O. Box 2053, Princeton, NJ 08543-2053 (800-257-5126).

Chapter 7: Prejudice

Guilty by Reason of Race (1972, 53 min., color). This powerful documentary chronicles the events surrounding the internment of Japanese-Americans in the U.S. during World War II. Footage includes interviews with those interned as well as those who made the decision to create the camps. Iowa Films, Media Library, University of Iowa, Iowa City, IA 52242 (319-353-5885).

Killing Us Softly: Advertising's Image of Women (1980, 45 min., color). A powerful demonstration of how advertising fosters gender stereotypes. Cambridge Documentary Films, P.O. Box 385, Cambridge, MA 02139 (617-354-3677).

Prejudice: Causes, Consequences, and Cures (1972, 23 min., color). A look at the nature of prejudice based on race, gender, and economic factors. CRM-McGraw-Hill, Box 641, Del Mar, CA 92014-9990 (619-453-5000).

Prejudice: Perceiving and Believing (1977, 28 min., color). This film examines stereotypes regarding gender, race, religion, and ethnicity. Narrated by Edward Asner. MTI Teleprograms Inc., 3710 Commercial Avenue, Northbrook, IL 60062 (800-323-6301)

Prejudice: The Eye of the Storm   25 min.). A documentary about the division of a third-grade classroom into blue-eyed and brown-eyed students assigned to inferior and superior roles. Explores how behavior changes dramatically depending on treatment and how frustrations and anger are the result of unequal rewards. Winner of the Peabody Award. Insight Media, 121 W. 85th St., New York, NY 10024; Iowa Films, University of Iowa, Iowa City, IA 52242 (319-353-5885).

Beyond Black and White (1974, 29 min.). A black child psychiatrist discusses black needs and white needs as human needs. Produced at the University of Michigan, the film features Dr. James Comer. Film Video Library, University of Michigan, 919 S. University Ave. Rm 207, Ann Arbor, MI 48109-1185 (313-764-5360).

Bill Cosby on Prejudice (1971, 24 min., color). Presents Bill Cosby, the comedian, as a super-bigot who presents himself as a man who sees others as inferior based on their minority status: Blacks, Italians, Scots, Midwesterners, women, and others. Cosby categorizes individuals by group based on common stereotypes, e.g., lazy, aggressive, irreligious, etc., and emphasizes the inherent contradictions and paradoxes when making stereotyped attributions and judgments. Indiana University, Bloomington, IN 47405-5901.

Chapter 8: Liking, Loving, and Interpersonal Sensitivity

Impression Formation and Interpersonal Attraction (1975, 27 min., color). A presentation of attraction research, including work on first impressions, need complementarity, and implicit personality theories. (Also relevant to Chapter 4.) University Films of Canada, 7 Hayden Street, Suite 305, Toronto, Ontario, Canada M4Y 2P2.

Introduction to Group Process: Member Behaviors in a Group (1982, 21 min.). This three-part tape examines the behavior that takes place in groups. The first segment identifies processes that occur in groups and looks at typical behavior in a newly formed group. The second part of the tape identifies these behaviors, and the final segment shows a constructive group. Health Sciences Consortium, Distribution Department, 201 Silver Cedar Ct., Chapel Hill, NC 27514-1517 (919-942-8731).

Your Erroneous Zones (1980, 97 min.). Based on Dr. Dyer's best-selling book, Dr. Dyer helps identify and expose your erroneous zones—the unhealthy behavior patterns that block you from all kinds of freedoms and experiences. Video Publishing House, 4 Woodfield Lake Ste 505, 930 N. National Pkwy., Shaumburg, IL 60175 (800-824-8889); Films, Inc., 5547 N. Ravenswood Ave., Chicago, IL 60640-1199 (312-878-2600).

Chapter 9: Social Psychology as a Science

Social Psychology: What, Why and How? (1975, 27 min., color). Covers experiments in the laboratory and in field settings, archival studies, and the relationship between theory and data. University Films of Canada, 7 Hayden Street, Suite 305, Toronto, Ontario, Canada M4Y 2P2.

Inferential Statistics: Hypothesis Testing—Rats, Robots, and Roller Skates (1976, 28 min., color). A humorous look at the basic elements of research methods, including hypothesis-testing, control groups, and the importance of random assignment. John Wiley & Sons Inc., 605 Third Avenue, New York, NY 10016 (212-867-9800).

Methodology: The Psychologist and the Experiment (1975, 31 min., color). Introduces research methods and experimental design, through the example of Schachter's studies on fear and affiliation. (Also relevant to Chapter 1.) CRM-McGraw-Hill, P.O. Box 641, Del Mar, CA 92014-9990 (619-453-5000).